BUSINESS CYCLES

During our lifetime we experience any number of business cycle crises which undermine our confidence. We also experience the 'happy days' when our faith in the future becomes almost limitless, and when we forget that the tide will turn again. But do business cycles exist? What creates them? Is it mass psychology, or phenomena in the management of business? Are the banks to blame or should we be looking to the media, the unions, the entrepreneurs or the politicians?

Lars Tvede's story moves back in time to the Scottish gambler and financial genius, John Law, and then on to the distracted Adam Smith, the stockbroker Ricardo, the investment banker Thornton, the extrovert Schumpeter, the speculator Jay Gould and many others. Gradually we reach the computer jugglers of the modern day who, with giant networks of equations, try to solve the same questions that have attracted the attention of classical economists throughout the centuries.

Throughout this volume, business cycle theories are used to explain actual events. We are told how theoretical thinking has reflected the economist's own experiences of hyper-inflations, depressions, speculation orgies, liquidity squeezes and – most recently – the Internet crash. The reader can follow the narrative to discover how economists often thought that problems had been solved until new data changed the economic picture once again.

Lars Tvede holds a Master of Science Degree in Engineering and a Bachelor of Economics. He spent 11 years in investment banking and hedge fund management before moving into the high-tech and telecommunication industries in the early 1990s, where he co-founded several technology companies. He now lives in Zug, Switzerland, where he is engaged in global fund management. Other books by Lars Tvede include *The Psychology of Finance* and *Marketing Strategies in the New Economy*.

BUSINESS CYCLES

From John Law to the Internet Crash

Lars Tvede

Second edition

London and New York

First edition published 1997 by License under the Harwood Academic Publishers imprint, part of the Gordon and Breach Publishing group.

Second (revised and updated) edition published 2001
by Routledge
11 New Fetter Lane, London EC4P 4EE

Simultaneously published in the USA and Canada
by Routledge
29 West 35th Street, New York, NY 10001

Routledge is an imprint of the Taylor & Francis Group

Typeset by Expo Holdings, Malaysia
Printed and bound in Great Britain by MPG Books Ltd, Bodmin

British Library Cataloguing in Publication Data
A catalogue record for this book is available from the British Library

ISBN: 0–415–27050–2

CONTENTS

PREFACE

Canton Zug is the smallest of the Swiss cantons, but even with its tiny size it has everything you would associate with Switzerland. Wooden farmhouses are scattered all over its hillsides, and the sounds of hundreds of cowbells are never far away. During summer most houses are decorated with flowers in all colours of the rainbow.

The Canton is located at the edge of the Alps. It has great views of the peaks of Mount Rigi and Mount Pilatus to the South, and if you go into the hills you may be able to spot the famous peaks of Jungfrau and Eiger to the West. Rivers from the mountains lead down to the local lake, Zugerzee. On the eastern side of the lake lies the old town of Zug. Founded in the 11th century, it has old wooden houses, narrow streets, romantic churches, remains of the defensive wall and towers, and a tiny harbour for the boats on the lake.

Four seasons

The place changes a lot over the year. During the long, warm summer it bustles with life. The many small outdoor cafés are full of happy people, and there are festivals, open markets, concerts and sometimes great fireworks over the lake. The first sign that the summer is about to end is always the same: thunderstorms. You will first see silent lightning far away – not just a few flashes, but hundreds. Then it will roll closer and closer. As it approaches the silence will be replaced by a vague rumbling, and then, as it reaches Zug itself, by aggressive explosions as each flash of lightning hits the lake or the hill-sides. Then the wind, then rain, and then it is all over. After the autumn follows a period of dull and foggy weather. One day it will clear up and as you look up at the snow-covered mountain peaks you know that winter has come.

It was on one of those clear and frosty winter days at the start of 1998 that I walked down Bahnhofstrasse to have lunch with Jorgen Chidekel, an old friend of mine. We like to meet in a restaurant in the central square to talk about things; 'things' meaning mainly the state of the world economy and the prospects for the financial markets. Jorgen is a hedge fund manager, and he lives and breathes these markets. We ordered our meal before I asked as usual:

"So how are things?"

"Still very unsettled. This is a giant crash unfolding", he said.

"I haven't followed it so closely lately, can you give me an update?"

"Sure. Let's start with Russia. The Russian stock market is falling like a rock. Although they have a population of 150 million they now have a smaller economy than Switzerland".

"Smaller than Switzerland?"

"That is right. The valuation of Russia's entire stock market is about equal to a few American Internet companies. And the Asia-Pacific region is of course a mess. There are places where it looks like they were trying to build a new Manhattan. Now they are standing completely empty. It is the familiar old business cycles at work again".

We went further into the details of the crash and theories of business cycles as we had our lunch, and after the coffee we left together. As we were saying goodbye outside the restaurant I asked him what he would recommend doing. "It's a crash, you know. A big one", he said. It was freezing cold and his breath froze in the air in little puffs as he spoke. Finally he broke into a big smile as he finished "But the weather's lovely". And then we grinned at each other and left.

As I watched him head towards his office I imagined how all those little puffs of frozen speech would be floating along Bahnhofstrasse with their frozen message "It's a crash, you know. A big one", and how one of them might perhaps shortly turn the corner into Rigistrasse and mingle with all the other puffs issuing from all the other worried businesspeople. Or perhaps they would carry all the way down to the lakeside, drifting past the boats, "It's a crash, you know … But the weather's lovely".

When I came home that evening I kept my coat on and went into the garden where I sat in a garden chair under a tree. It was pitch-dark and snowing slightly. I had always enjoyed the quiet winter nights where tiny snowflakes fell gently around me, sometimes, as on this night, from a seemingly clear sky. Far away I could see the lights from the ski-sport hotel high up at the top of Mount Pilatus, and below me were the navigation lights of a tour ship which appeared to glide majestically over the lake. It was magical.

My thoughts returned to the lunch when we had spoken of business cycles. Were we individuals only like surfers who were swept away more or less helplessly on these gigantic economic waves? How many really understood what was going on? When there was a slump, many believed that we would never recover, while when there was a boom some thought it would last forever. The problem of business cycles was a complex phenomenon, and each time economists thought they had understood it, new features arose, which entirely altered the picture. It was fascinating.

I thought about when this phenomenon had really become important in people's daily lives. With the crash of 1929? No, long before that. At the time of Adam Smith? No further back still. I decided that it was probably with the introduction of paper money into the European market economy that the phenomenon really had become important. It was a man named John Law that had introduced paper money into Europe. This had stimulated the development of a very large credit market. The credit market had been of enormous significance in creating the phenomenon of the business cycle. So that was perhaps where this phenomenon became really important to millions for the first time.

I thought about John Law. Had he really been aware what it was that he was setting in motion? Probably not. How could he? I tried to visualise him. What had he looked like in the old engravings that I had seen? He was certainly tall. A picture began to take shape in my mind's eye – the profile of a tall, slim man. Since it was the time of the Sun King, his shoes would appear rather feminine with lots of decoration. I closed my eyes and leant back in my garden chair – now the picture became sharper – John Law. I saw in my mind's eye a confident, proud young man standing in the morning sunlight, one hand on his back. It must have been in a park because there were trees in the background. Some distance away, looking at him, stood a little knot of men dressed in the same, funny Renaissance style of clothing. But John Law remained to one side, lost in deep concentration. I could see his head very clearly now, and noticed that small beads of sweat were running down his face. He seemed quite unaware of them and his gaze remained fixed on a certain point. What he was looking at so fixedly was another man. He stared intensely.

And then I saw that John Law had something in his hand…

The Discovery of Business Cycles

"The universe is full of magical things patiently waiting for our wits to grow sharper."

Eden Phillpotts

1
Paper Money

"John Law, I have always felt, is in a class by himself."

Joseph Schumpeter

A gun. He was standing there with a gun in his hand. In a few seconds, when he got the sign, he would try to shoot Mr. Wilson. And Mr. Wilson would of course try to shoot him. But why had he accepted the duel? Why risk death at this young age — and for something so stupid? He could have just excused himself, bowed out; he could have walked away from the problem. Or he could have run, simply disappeared from London for a while, until everything was forgiven and forgotten. But John Law wasn't that kind of person. Just as he always reached out when he saw an opportunity, he also confronted the problems he met. And now, when the problem was that Mr. Wilson had challenged him to a duel, Law was ready to fight his battle[1].

John Law was well-spoken and well-dressed. Although scarred by smallpox, his face looked intelligent — to the girls in his hometown of Edinburgh, he had been known as "beau Law". From the age of 14 to 17 he had been taught banking at his father's counting house, and during these years he had demonstrated an extraordinary talent for mathematics.

THE GAMING HOUSES OF LONDON

When the father died in 1688, he had left his 17-year-old son the revenues from his banking and goldsmith activities. John Law had seemed to have every opportunity before him in Edinburgh, but he had wanted more out of life than what the little town could offer. Much more in fact.

So he had decided to leave Scotland[2] to go to London. Once settled in London, he had soon begun frequenting the gaming-houses to put his talent for the study of numbers into use. And it had worked. After some time he had gained a considerable amount of money. Soon this handsome young Scotchman had become well known and admired, not the least among the ladies. Life had really been fun!

But slowly and insensibly, John Law turned into an irrecoverable gambler. Gradually he started to play with larger and larger amounts until one day he met his Nemesis: he lost so much in a game, that he was forced to mortgage his estate to pay the accounts. Then, in the same year, he had been so stupid as to accept a duel against Mr. Wilson — all because of a slight flirtation with his girlfriend. John Law was now 26 years old, and maybe he was going to die.

ON THE RUN

The duel was short and rough. Law lifted his hand, aimed, and shot Mr. Wilson dead on the spot. But before the day was over, the police came to arrest him, and soon after his apprehension he was charged with murder — and subsequently sentenced to death. Fortunately the sentence was commuted to a fine, as the verdict was changed from murder to manslaughter. Upset about this, Mr. Wilson's brother lodged an appeal, and while the case was pending, Law was detained in prison. But before the appeal was tested, John Law managed to escape — there are no records on how. An advertisement calling for his apprehension that appeared in the Gazette, described him in this way:

> "Captain John Law, a Scotchman, aged twenty-six; a very tall, black, lean man; well shaped, above six feet high, with large pock-holes in his face; big nosed, and speaking broad and loud."

As this description fitted very badly with reality there was speculation that this had actually been drawn up to facilitate his escape. Whether true or not, the fact was that somehow he managed to escape from England across the Channel to the Continent.

Figure 1.1: John Law of Lauriston.
If you look in the French telephone directories, you'll find his family's descendants under the name "Lauriston".

A NEW KIND OF MONEY

John Law traveled around in Europe for three years. Typically, he would spend the mornings studying finance, trade, and the monetary and banking affairs of the countries he visited; the nights were spent at local gaming houses. When he visited Amsterdam he also speculated on the stock exchange. It was probably in the year 1700, when he was 29 years old, that he sailed back over the Channel and returned to Edinburgh. There, he started promoting an idea, that he had developed through his travels in Europe and which he believed in deeply: *If a country was to prosper, it needed paper money*[3]. Paper money, he thought, would facilitate trade much more than the traditional gold or silver currency. And to base the economy on money made of paper was quite possible, because, as he wrote:

> "Money is not the value for which goods are exchanged, but the value by which they are exchanged".

In 1705 he published a pamphlet entitled "Money and Trade Considered with a Proposal for Supplying the Nation with money". Scotland was in a recession at the time that he wrote the manuscript, and he believed that he understood what the problem was. It was about money.

The pamphlet introduced an expression that hadn't been used before: "demand for money". Law attempted to demonstrate to the readers that the supply of money was too low and the interest rates on money too high. The solution would be to increase the supply of money. An expansion of the money supply would lead to lower interest rates, he claimed, and it would not lead to inflation as long as the country didn't use its full capacity.

He also suggested the establishment of a "Landbank" in Scotland[4]. This bank should issue notes up to an amount that should never exceed the value of the land belonging to the state. Buyers of the notes should receive interest and have the option to convert their notes into land at a specific time. This new scheme would have two advantages:

- It would relieve the nation of the burden of buying more and more precious metal to supply coins that matched the growth of the economy.

- It would make it easier for the country to manage the amount of money in circulation so as to match the fluctuating needs of the country.

The proposal was very well written and generated a lot of excitement. But it was also controversial. Critics ridiculed it, and referred to it as the "Sand-bank", suggesting that it would "wreck the vessel of the state". Others supported the idea, however, and eventually it was seriously debated in Parliament. But that was as far as it went; a majority of the members turned it down, claiming that the establishment of any "paper credit" would be an improper expedient for the nation. Disappointed with this, and with the fact that he was unable to obtain a pardon for his manslaughter at the courts in England, he returned to the Continent. There he resumed his former occupation: the games. As years went by, he became well-known for his skills in gambling houses throughout the capitals of Europe. He became very rich.

John Law went on like this for 14 years, playing in Flanders, Holland, Germany, Hungary, Italy and France. In many places he was thought to be a bad influence on young people, and he was in fact expelled for that reason from Venice and Genoa. But he also made influential friends in high places. Among these was the French Duke of Orleans, Philippe d'Orleans, who later turned out to be of particular importance.

The paper money idea kept nagging in the back of John Law's head. You needed paper credit to get Europe to prosper; of that he was sure. It was probably in 1708 that he suggested a Landbank scheme to the comptroller at the French court. The proposition was turned down, perhaps, as some sources claimed, because "Law was not Catholic." After this he tried in Italy, and was turned down again.

A MINOR PROBLEM

But history is odd; sometimes it is the strangest coincidences that decide the faith of nations. When the extravagant "Sun King", Louis XIV, died in 1715, the French throne was left to an heir only 7 years old. Here Law's friend Philippe d'Orleans entered the scene: being uncle to the young king, he took control of the government. Unlike Law, the Duke had very little understanding of banking and high-finance, but unlike any other head of state in Europe, he seriously considered Law's ideas.

It was not an easy job that the Duke had taken upon himself. The finances of France were in a shambles after the disastrous regime of the spendthrift Louis XIV. These were the key figures of the state:

Annual revenue:	145 mio. livres
Annual expenses before interest payments:	142 mio. livres
National debt:	3,000 mio. livres

If we assume that the state had to pay in average 4% per annum in interest on its debt, then this amounted to 120 mio. livres. But the actual surplus available for interest payments was only 145 – 142 = 3 mio. livres. So the country was in deep despair, and as Duc de Saint-Simon later wrote in his memoirs:

> "Nobody could any longer pay, because nobody was paid …"

So what could the Duke do? The five standard options of ancient Europe seemed to be the following:

- Declare national bankruptcy
- Raise taxes dramatically
- "Clip" the coins (call in all coins and exchange them with new ones containing less precious metal)
- Sell privileges of monopoly for, for instance, all the trade within a given commodity or colonial area
- Confiscate possessions of corrupt state employees

The Duke chose a combination of clipping and confiscating. He called in all coins to the Mint and gave in return new coins with only 80% of the precious metal in the old coins. At the same time, trading with the old coins was banned. But this was a very unpopular move, and moreover, the total contribution to the state finances was only approximately 70 million livres.

The Duke also promised any citizen 20% of the fines and confiscations if he could give information leading to conviction of corrupt state employees. This initiative was received with delight by the long-suppressed people and soon the courts were working at high speed. The government confiscated 180 mio. livres, out of which — it turned out — the Duke used about 100 mio. to give special grants to new employees — perhaps replacing those he lost.

The total account now looked like this:

Revenue from clipping:	70 million livres
Revenue from confiscations:	80 million livres
= Total revenue:	150 million livres

By using two of his options, the Duke had recovered the equivalent of only 6% of the national debt or little more than one year's interest payments. And he was unable to do much more by his own initiative; he was neither very competent nor very energetic. John Law was both, and Philippe d'Orleans knew it. In 1716, the year after the Duke had taken the reins of the country, the Duke met with Law to discuss the options. John Law, who was now 44 years old and extremely wealthy, repeated what he had said so many times before: to prosper, you needed paper money, and this paper money should be hard currency: no depreciations; no clipping. He proposed that they set up a bank to administer the royal revenues, which should issue notes entirely backed by either metal or land, in other words a modified Landbank. And the Duke said yes!

INTO THE UNKNOWN

On May 5, 1716, the bank was founded under the name "Law & Company"[5]. It had an assured activity from the outset, as it was declared that all taxes should be paid in notes issued by Law & Co. — France was now introducing paper money!

The capital of Law & Company was 6 million livres. If you wanted to purchase its shares, you had to pay 25% with coins and the rest with "*billets d'etat*". This was a smart move. *Billets d'etat* were the bonds which Louis XIV had issued to finance his vast excesses. These bonds were now regarded as junk bonds[6] and were trading at 21.5 while they had originally been sold at 100. The scenario can be expressed this way[7]:

1. SEEN FROM THE GOVERNMENT'S POINT OF VIEW

Outstanding *billets d'etat* (nominal value):	3,000 million livres
Interest rate:	4%
Annual interest payments:	120 million livres

2. SEEN FROM THE INVESTOR'S POINT OF VIEW

Outstanding *billets d'etat* (market value):	645 million livres
Effective interest rate (120*100/645) =:	18%
Annual interest receivals:	120 million livres

The reason that the effective interest rate was so high (and the market price of the bonds so low) was, of course, that people were afraid of a national bankruptcy. But there was a potential way out: if the government could somehow buy back its own junk bonds at the current, low market price, then it could in effect reduce its debt from 3,000 mio. (the price it had sold them for) to 645 mio. (the current market price). And it could do it without really hurting anyone! If by doing so, it could restore confidence, the state would in principle be able to reduce its interest payments to, say, 4% of 645 million livres by issuing new bonds. The new interest rate burden would be only around 25 million livres/annum.

UNTYING THE KNOT

The problem was how to coax 3,000 million livres worth of junk bonds back to the state without raising their market price. If people really thought Philippe d'Orleans could get out of his squeeze, then they would surely bid the bonds up, and his scheme would defeat itself. It was a small part of this problem that John Law solved by inviting people to pay for shares in Law & Company exclusively with government bonds.

At this stage, Law's "debt-for-equity swap"[8] was very small in proportion to the remaining national debt of 2,850 million livres. The issue of the Law & Company bank-shares brought back only *billets d'etat* worth 75% of six million, totalling 4.5 million livres — nothing compared to the 3,000 million.

But Law had his next move ready. He did three things:

- He made his notes payable "at sight"[9]. This meant, that you could walk into Law & Company any day you pleased, present your Law & Company notes and get the full amount back in coins.
- He made his notes payable in original coin. If the government resorted to clipping coins (as so often before), John Law would still pay back the original amount of metal.
- He declared publicly that any banker who issued notes without backing it with sufficient security "deserved death".

The result: the new paper money was accepted as hard currency and was from the outset traded at 101 — that is with a premium of 1 when compared to coins of the same nominal value. Within a short time, this presence of a reliable means of exchange began to stimulate trading: business got better, and demand for notes rose by the day. Soon Law & Company was able to open new affiliates in Lyons, Rochelle, Tours, Amiens and Orleans. One year later, in 1717, the price (in coins) on Law's paper money had risen to 115.

This was when John Law made his third strategic move, which was even more brilliant than the two first. He proposed that the government of France should make a new debt-for-equity swap on a scale which could eventually absorb all remaining *billets d'etat*. The Duke should agree to the establishment of a company which was granted monopoly for trading with two colonial areas, which France had claimed for itself in 1684: the Mississippi River and the State of Louisiana. When the equity was to be sold to the public, people should pay with *billets d'etat*, and the national debt would disappear. The Duke was excited, and preparations for this new "Mississippi scheme" began.

Meanwhile, the Duke turned his interest to Law's Bank. By now it was no longer to be regarded as an experiment; it was an established success. He decided to bolster it further with a number of new privileges, including the sole right to refine gold and silver. And then he agreed to what he had not been willing to do from the start: he renamed it "Banque Royale". The bank was now clearly under his control, and he could do with it whatever he pleased. What he did was based on four observations:

- People had gained confidence in paper money.
- Paper money was a cheap way for the government to borrow.

- As paper money traded at a premium, it was apparently in short supply.
- Paper money seemed to bring prosperity.

So why not print more paper money? If people bought the bank notes for coins, he could spend that coin. So he instructed the bank to print 1,000 million livres worth of notes — more than 16 times as much as it had done before. As the chancellor, D'Aguessau, disagreed with this, he was immediately replaced by the more loyal D'Argenson.

ON WITH THE MISSISSIPPI SCHEME

Meanwhile, John Law was about to launch his Mississippi scheme. At the beginning of 1719, the privileges of the new Mississippi company were expanded so they now included:

- Exclusive trading rights for the Mississippi River, the state of Louisiana, China, East India and South America.
- A nine-year monopoly on minting the royal coinage.
- The right to act as the national tax collector for nine years.
- A monopoly for trading tobacco.

In addition to this, the Mississippi Company was given all possessions of the Senegal Company, the China Company and not least the French East India Company. With the latter under control the new giant was expected to challenge the almighty British East India Co.

Given all these privileges it was not difficult to think that the company should make enormous profits. It was named "Compagnie des Indes" and a new public issue of 25 million livres worth of shares was announced — an issue that would raise the total equity to 125 million livres. John Law declared that he expected the shares to be honored by a total dividend of 50 million livres — equal to a 40% annual return on the investment. But the offer was really much better than that. The shares were bought neither with coins nor with notes. You could pay with the Sun King's junk bonds. The calculation was as follows if you wanted to buy for example 0.5 million livres worth of shares:

Nominal share price:	0.5 million livres
Expected annual dividend:	0.2 million livres

Figure 1.2: Stock traders, pick-pockets, investors and soldiers in Rue Quincampoix in 1720. Often soldiers had to be sent to clear the road in the evening.

Bought with 0.5 million livres nominal *billets d'etat* at rate 0.2:	0.1 million livres

Real yield on investment (0.2*100/0.1) = 200%! So you could apparently expect a real return of about 200% per annum! 200%!!!

Applications to buy the stock started pouring in immediately and it was soon obvious that the issue was highly oversubscribed. As the staff needed several weeks to produce a list of the new subscribers, John Law was unable during this time to tell the names of the shareholders. This waiting period had a dramatic psychological effect. A crowd of people started gathering in front of Rue de Quincampoix from early morning to late evening to hear the result. Soon this crowd numbered thousands and filled the whole street. And it was not a usual crowd. It included dukes, counts and marquises; all eager to make a killing. When the list of the shareholders was finally produced, it was clear that the issue had been oversubscribed at least six times. In the free market, prices of the stocks soared to 5,000 livres or 10 times the subscription price. Law and the Duke of Orleans decided to take advantage of this excitement and make a new issue of 1,500 million livres, 12 times as large as the two first.

THE GREAT BOOM

That issue really ought to have worried the investors. Consider this: they paid with junk bonds which the seller — the state — would simply borrow. No new capital — only the interest — was injected into the company. But the profits per share were now diluted 13 times as the capital was increased correspondingly.

But the public didn't worry. The giant issue was over-subscribed three times. And then something very strange happened: Although only four years had passed since France had been in the deepest despair, the entire country now started to virtually boil over in joy and happiness. Prices on any luxury item began rising and the production of rich laces, silks, broad-cloth and velvets increased many-fold. Artisans' wages rose four-fold, unemployment fell, and new houses were built everywhere. As everybody watched prices rise, everybody rushed to buy, to invest and to hoard before prices went even higher.

In Paris, the pot was boiling more than anywhere else. It was estimated that the population of the capital increased during this period by 305,000 inhabitants. Often the streets were so crowded with new carriages that nobody was able to move. And the city imported art, furniture and ornaments from all over the world as never before; not only for the aristocracy, but now also for the middle class. People who had bought stocks on margin suddenly found that a few thousand livres could grow to more than a million. Soon a new word was added to the French vocabulary: "millionaires".

The greatest benefit was, however, for the aristocracy. Many a bourgeois family, which during the preceding depression had been severely squeezed, were now saved by speculation in the Compagnie des Indes stock. One of these was the Duke of Bourbon, who made so much money in his stock transactions that he could rebuild his residence in Chantilly in a style of incredible magnificence. His speculation also enabled him to import 150 selected racing horses from England and to buy up an enormous amount of land.

Many other members of the bourgeoisie made it big, but probably the greatest winner of all was Richard Cantillon, an Irishman working as a banker in Paris. Cantillon bought a huge pile of stocks before the price really took off and eventually profited by the equivalent of almost 20% of the annual French tax revenue.

OCCASIONAL TREMORS

Stock-trading is rarely a one-way street; even the wildest bull market has its set-backs. And so indeed had the Compagnie des Indes. On more than one occasion it fell sharply during a few days, enough to wipe out many a margin-trader. During such an occasion, M. de Chirac, a physician, went to see a lady who was feeling ill. Chirac wasn't feeling too well himself: he had bought Indian stocks which had been falling drastically for several days. So when he took the lady's pulse, his mind was in the garden behind Hotel du Soissons. Musingly, he said:

"It falls! It falls! Good God! It falls continually!"

Panicky, the lady stumbled to reach the bell while she cried:

"Oh, M. de Chirac, I am dying! I am dying! It falls! It falls! It falls!"

Astonished, Chirac asked the lady what she was referring to.

"My pulse! My pulse! …", she answered, "… I must be dying!"

Fortunately M. de Chirac was able to calm the lady by explaining that he had been referring to the India stock price, not to her pulse.

But the shares could also rise, and at times violently so. Once, a speculator taken ill sent his servant to sell 250 shares because he had heard that they were trading at 8,000 livres per share. When the waiter came to the market, he saw that it was in fact even better, and sold at no less than 10,000. When he came back, he gave his master the expected revenue of 4 million. Then he went to his room, packed his things as well as the remaining 0.5 million — and left the country as fast as he could …

LAW GETS RATHER POPULAR

As the bull market continued, something strange happened outside John Law's house in Rue de Quincampoix: the entire street was transformed into a stock exchange filled with speculators scalping the price movements of Compagnie des Indes. Stock-jobbers and brokers rented any house they could get in the street at prices 12–16 times over the usual, and even bars and restaurants were transformed into trading houses. Together with the speculators and the money came the thieves and swindlers. It was not unusual that a troop of soldiers had to be sent to clear the Rue de Quincampoix at night.

Eventually the noise and the crowd became too much for John Law, who found a new residence in the spacious Place Vendome. But he couldn't move away from the people, because in their eyes he was the epicenter from which all activity generated. To the French people, he was greater than any king had ever been; the greatest financial genius, the man who had single-handedly created the new prosperity of a nation. The aristocracy bribed Law's servants with large amounts to get an audience with him. Whenever he drove in his carriage, a royal troop of horses had to ride before to clear the street of admirers. And the speculators and the stock-brokers had to know every move he made. As Saint-Simon noted in his memoirs:

> "Law besieged by applicants and aspirants, saw his door forced, his windows entered from his garden, while some of them came tumbling from the chimney of his office."

And the Duchess of Orleans:

> "Law is so run after that he has no rest, day or night. A duchess kissed his hands before everyone, and if a Duchess kisses his hands, what parts of him would ordinary ladies kiss?"

So, like bees moving with their queen, the crowd moved with John Law. Soon booths and tents were erected all over the square in front of his home, and the square was transformed into a hectic marketplace; a marketplace where not only stocks and bonds were traded, but where any kind of business took place. And the noise was even worse than it had ever been in Rue de Quincampoix.

The Duke received complaints about this new mess; not the least from the chancellor, whose court was situated on the same square. Because of the noise it had become impossible for him to hear the advocates. John Law agreed to look for a new solution and bought Hotel du Soissons, which had a large garden to the back. At the same time a verdict was published that forbade stock-trading in any other place than in that garden. The crowd moved once again, and more than 500 tents and pavillions were erected behind the hotel. At this time anyone and everyone in Paris seemed to be speculating in the India stock, which was in an accelerating bull-market. The story goes that the sober Abbé Terrason and his equally sober and intellectual friend M. de la Motte had congratulated each other that neither of them took part in the public madness. A few days later, however, la Motte fell into temptation and went to buy some India stock. But as he was entering Hotel de Soissons, who did he meet coming out from the building? The Abbé, of course, who had just bought at the market. For a long time after that episode, both of them avoided the subject of speculation during their frequent philosophical discussions.

Meanwhile the Duke was printing still more notes through Banque Royale. Why shouldn't he? — Wasn't it evident that the money-printing had made the country prosper? And if so, why not print more? Money was simply like oil to the economic machinery, wasn't it? The more oil, the better the machinery worked!

But then, one day in early 1720, something quite strange happened. A man appeared in front of Banque Royale with two carriages containing an enormous pile of these notes. And he was angry. Very angry …

Before paper money

Money is any item simultaneously serving as a unit of account, a medium of exchange, a store of value, and a standard of deferred payment. Many items have fulfilled this function throughout history, including beans of cacao trees, seashells, cowries, cows, beer, salt, copper bracelets, horses, chicken, amber, cylinders cut from coral, dried fish, furs, tobacco, grain, sugar, cocoa, playing cards, nails, rice, slaves, etc., etc. The Greeks used silver as their currency, and the Romans introduced gold coins after conquering the Etruscans.

Paper money was first introduced into China about AD 910 but abandoned again after a few hundred years because it created inflation.

2
Cash Payment

> *"Down he went over the sharp rocks, and the water with him.* He *was clashed to pieces in his bark; but the waters, maddened and turned to a foam by the rough descent, only boiled and bubbled for a time and then flowed again as smoothly as ever. Just so it was with Law and the French people. He was the boatman and they were the waters."*
>
> Charles Mackay

Prince de Conti believed he had a good reason to be angry. He wanted to buy some fresh India shares, but Law had prevented him. That arrogant Scottish bastard! So here was the prince in front of the bank, with his two carriages filled with notes. He entered the door.

> "Voila, monsieurs! Your notes, which are "payable at sight". Now, do you see them? Well then, hand over the coins!"

The bank handed it over, filling his two carriages with coins.

When the Duke heard about the event, he was shocked and simply ordered de Conti to refund two-thirds of the metal. It so happened that the public didn't like de Conti and so blamed him for this unreasonable act. But nevertheless, the event had an important effect: a small seed of doubt had been sown in people's minds. What if a lot of other people wanted to change their notes? What if everybody wanted to change their notes — would there be enough gold to do it? What if *I* want to change my notes?!

During the next few months some of the more astute speculators started to take their profits. Richard Cantillon, the now 23-year-old Irish-born banker, sold out his entire portfolio, netting a gain of around 20 million livres. Then he quit his banking carreer and left France to travel in Europe and later London (where he wrote one of the world's first books about economics, which we shall return to later). Two others, Bourdon and La Richardiere, started quietly to present their notes in Banque Royale and change them to coins in small quantities at a time. They also started buying up silver and jewelry, which — together with the coins — they secretly sent to Holland and England. Vermallet, a successful stock-trader, also sold out and packed 1 million livres worth of gold and silver coins in his carriage. He covered it with hay and cow-dung, disguised himself in peasant's clothes and drove to Belgium. While many people left the country, those who stayed started to hoard metal coins as distrust in notes mounted. Coins were either hidden under people's mattresses or exported: The French money supply was beginning to fall.

Figure 2.1: Philippe d'Orleans.
It was under his rule that France introduced its first paper money, and experienced a fantastic boom, then a disastrous depression. The experiences of Banque Royale gave the word "banque" such a bad sound in France, that most French banks even today are called anything else, like "caisse", "crédit", "société", or "comptoir".

What the Duke did in this situation was completely contrary to what he should have done. Firstly, he revalued notes by 5% vis-à-vis coins. Obviously the point was to regain psychological initiative, but as it had no effect on the capital flight, he revalued by a further 5% — again with no effect. In February 1720 he prohibited the use of coins altogether. No person in France was allowed to have in his possession more than 500 livres worth in coins, under risk of fines and confiscation. It was also forbidden to buy silver, precious stones and jewelry. Anybody who gave information leading to confiscation of such tangible values would receive half the value — paid in notes, of course. And then, lastly, the Duke printed 1,500 million livres worth of notes between February 1st and the end of May, increasing the total paper money supply to 2,600 million livres. The point of all this was obviously to force people to use notes again, but it didn't work. The economy began to break down. What was to become of France in the future? Who was to blame?

John Law. John Law was to blame. Wasn't it him who cooked up this paper money idea in the first place? And what about his Mississippi scheme? Was India stock in reality worth any more than Banque Royale notes? Were they? Better sell the stuff! The stock-price collapsed, and with it, thousands of investors went broke. When people lost their money, they couldn't pay other people. The chain-reaction was merciless, and something had to be done to convince the shareholders that Compagnie des Indes was getting in gear. The remedy was simple: the poorest wretches and criminals in Paris were conscripted to be sent to New Orleans to dig for gold for the company. More than 6,000 "pouvres" joined the scheme, and processions of these people thronged through the streets of Paris, ready to be sent to the port, from where they could sail to America. At first people liked the project: six thousand is a lot of workers. If they could find gold, it would surely get the company going. And if you made new coins out of that gold, this might even get France up and running again? For a short while, Compagnie des Indes rallied at the stock market[1].

NO GOLD IN NEW ORLEANS?

But if you looked very closely at the poor people's faces as they passed, you might discover some weeks later something odd: most of them were back again. Two out of three sold their new clothes and tools and returned to their homes before reaching the boats. Better poor in Paris than digging gold in New Orleans. The stock began to fall again.

Now the Duke was getting desperate. It seemed that every move he made to regain confidence had an adverse effect. The more he did to make people abolish the use of coins, the more they seemed to want them. He decided to merge Banque Royale with Compagnie des Indes, hoping one would bolster the other. It didn't work. In the beginning of May, he finally called in an emergency council attended by John Law and all the ministers. First point on the agenda: 2,600 livres worth of notes were circulating, each officially redeemable in gold and silver coins. The actual amount of coins was less than half of that and many of them were hidden under people's mattresses (a habit for which Frenchmen were notorious centuries after). The council chose to devaluate the notes by half, effective from the 21st of May. But this was simply too much for the French people. With unrest mounting and the threat of a revolt, the edict was cancelled just one week later — the 27th of May. That was also the day when Banque Royale suspended payments in metal and John Law was dismissed from the ministry.

The same night, however, the Duke sent for Law, who entered the royal palace through a secret door. The Duke did everything he could to console Law and expressed how unfair it seemed that he should become the subject of such hatred from the public. Two days later he invited him to the Opera, where everyone could see them together. But this was nearly fatal for Law. As his carriage arrived at his house afterwards, a mob attacked it with stones. Only the fact that the coachman quickly passed the gates, which the servants slammed after them, saved Law from being lynched. Horrified by this, the Duke sent a detachment of Swiss guards to be stationed at Law's house night and day. But even so, Law did not feel safe. After a short while he moved to the Royal Palace, where he could enjoy the same protection as the Duke.

The Duke was now in full retreat. To help clean up the mess, he decided to call in D'Aguessau, the chancellor whom he had dismissed two years earlier. To persuade him to come to the rescue, he sent Law in a post-chaise to meet him. D'Aguessau agreed and returned with Law, and shortly after, on the 1st of June, the edict against free possession of coins was abolished. At the same time, 25 million livres worth of new notes, backed by the revenues of the city of Paris, were issued. And on the 10th of June, Banque Royale was reopened, prepared to change notes into metal again. But not into the usual metal: part of the payment was now in copper!

HEAVY METAL

During the following months, there was a permanent crowd in front of the bank as everyone wanted to change their notes to piles of copper which they sweatingly dragged away. On several occasions the crowd was so great that someone was squeezed to death. On the 9th of July, soldiers closed the gates to ease the pressure, and the people outside it started throwing stones. A soldier fired back, killing one person and wounding another. Eight days later, 15 were killed under the pressure. Furiously, the crowd put three of the dead on stretchers and marched to the gardens of Palais Royale. Here, they found John Law's carriage and broke it to pieces.

The Council's next emergency step was to bolster the Compagnie des Indes further by extending its trading privileges so that it had a monopoly on all maritime trade out of France. But this meant that thousands of independent merchants would lose their business, and petition after petition was presented to the Parliament to complain. The Parliament refused to approve the matter. The Duke became so furious that he sent the Parliament and all its members into exile in the remote Pontoise. In order not to appear defeated, the members of Parliament decided to engage in demonstrative extravagance. Every night they held a great ball for the ladies, and each day they resorted to card games and other diversions.

On the 15th of August, a new edict was imposed on the poor Frenchmen: all notes for sums between 1,000 and 10,000 livres could not pass unless used to buy annuities, to place money in bank accounts or to pay installments on Compagnie des Indes shares. In October, many of the privileges were taken away from the Compagnie des Indes and all notes deprived of value. Stock holders were obliged to deposit their shares with the Company, and those who had agreed to buy new shares were forced to purchase them at almost 30 times the current market rate. As many tried to avoid this horrendous punishment by leaving the country, orders were sent to all borderposts to detain anybody trying to get out until it was clarified whether they had ordered purchases of Compagnie des Indes shares. Those who got out anyway were sentenced to death in absentia.

John Law now lived a life in terror. The most-hated man in France, he could only leave his royal refuge either incognito or with a powerful escort. He requested permission to move to one of his country estates, a dispensation the Duke was more than happy to grant. A few days later, he received from the Duke a kind letter in which he was given permission to leave France when he pleased. The Duke also offered him whatever amount of money he might want, an offer which he respectfully declined. Then at the age of 49, five years after the adventure had begun, he left for Venice taking with him only a large diamond. John Law hoped for some time that he would be called back to help reestablish a sound credit system, but as the Duke died in 1723, he lost all hope. The rest of his life he supported himself through gambling. Several times he had to pawn his diamond, but each time he won enough to be able to recover it. Finally, in 1729, he died in Venice, 58 years of age and very poor.

How the French money supply declined in 1720

The effective money supply in France declined for three main reasons:

- Capital flight. *People took gold and silver coins out of the country.*
- Decrease in the turn-over (velocity) of money. *People hoarded coins because they didn't trust paper money and perhaps later because of restrictions regarding how many coins each individual could keep. These restrictions have probably encouraged people to keep as many coins as possible.*
- Reduction in bank credit. *The edict imposing that all notes for sums between 1,000 and 10,000 livres could only be used to buy bonds, Compagnie des Indes shares and place money in bank accounts reduced the effective money supply.*

A modern economist would probably have suggested to abandon the gold standard, encourage increased lending, lower the interest rates, increase public spending, lower the taxes, and let Compagnie des Indes print more money to buy bonds.

3
The First Economists

"The age of chivalry is gone. That of sophisters, economists and calculators has succeeded; and the glory of Europe is extinguished forever."

Edmund Burke

The year the Duke of Orleans died and John Law gave up all hope of being invited back to France, was also the year Margaret Smith expected her first child. She lived in Kirkcaldy, a small town some 15 kilometers from Law's hometown Edinburgh. She was alone; her husband had died just a few months before the baby was born. The baby turned out to be a boy, and on the 5th of June 1723 he was given the name Adam[1].

Adam's childhood was peaceful, disturbed only by an incident in which, at the age of 2, he was kidnapped by a gang of gypsies and quickly recovered. As the boy grew up, Margaret Smith noticed that he showed a keen interest in the society around him. Although Kirkcaldy was a small place with only 1,500 inhabitants, there was quite a lot to look at. The town had extensive commerce, and ships from many places berthed close to the houses. Adam loved to sit on cliffs by the sea, overlooking the ships coming in and out.

YEARS OF TRANSITION

Those were years when England and Scotland were in economic transition. Just as in France, the English Government had been embarrassed by the growth of a huge, public debt. The device to solve this problem had been quite like that in France. A firm named "The South Sea Company"[2] had taken over the obligation of payments of the national debt and had in

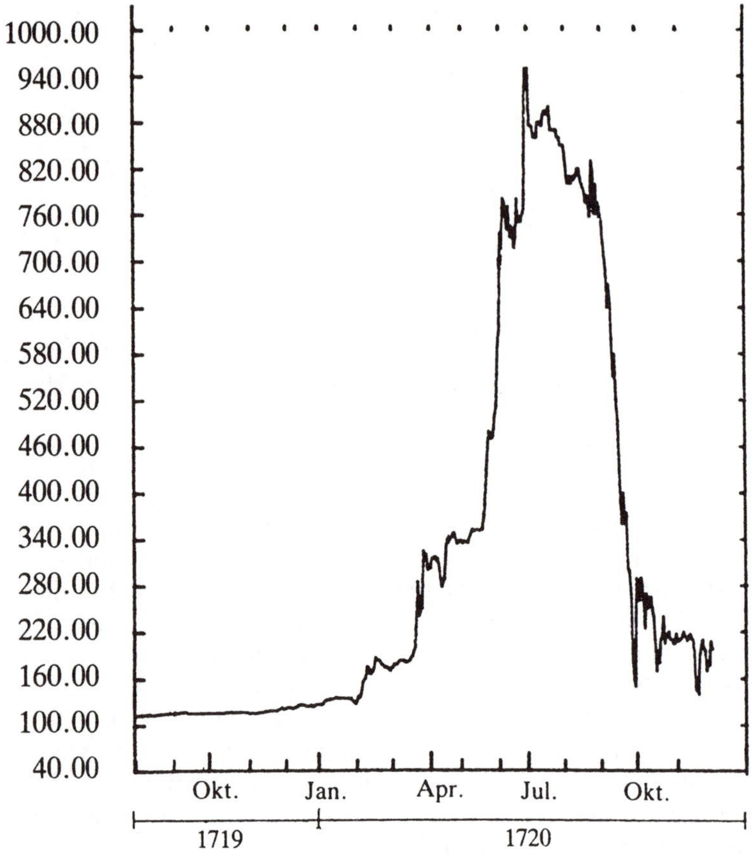

Figure 3.1: The South Sea Company.
The "South Sea Bubble" had taken-off before Compagnie des Indes collapsed in France. Sources from those years indicate that it was partly money going out of the French adventure, that blew up the English bubble. The South Sea Company was based on a debt-for-equity swap, as Compagnie des Indes.

return acquired the monopoly on trade with South America. A number of share issues had been gobbled up by an eager public and the price of these shares had been bid up to prices 10 times the nominal value, even though there was little evidence that any South Sea trading was going to materialize (as we shall see later, 90 years were to pass before it actually did). In June, 1720, the stock had peaked, and during the next three months it fell by no less than 85%, under conditions resembling the meltdown in France.

At that time, England had a fairly well-established (if not well-understood) system of paper credit[3]. Means of payment included not only gold and silver coins, but also notes issued by the Bank of England or other banks as well as promissory notes and inland bills. In addition to the coins, notes and inland bills, interest-bearing papers such as Exchequer bills and East India bonds were also in circulation — albeit with a lower turnover. The Master of the Mint was no less than Isaac Newton, who had been appointed to the job in 1696[4]. When still young, Newton had noticed that not only governments could use the idea of "clipping" coins — many citizens did it, too. Some would put a pile of coins in a sack, shake it thoroughly, and then collect the dust[5]. Others would, more rudely, cut off a slice around the edge before they passed them on. To prevent this, Newton had suggested that coins should be given a milled edge, so that it would be easy to detect if they had been clipped.

At this time the industrial revolution was already in its infancy, and conditions were getting ripe for an economic boom. First of all, the British navy was quickly conquering new markets where British products could be sold. Secondly, an "agricultural revolution" had already started in the countryside, as farms were becoming larger and more productive. This process released manpower: more and more young people travelled to the cities to look for jobs, to study or to set up new business ventures. Most would travel to London, which at the time had somewhere between 500,000 and 750,000 inhabitants. Others chose the next largest town, Bristol, with 43,000 inhabitants. And still others moved to Norwich (36,000 inhabitants), Liverpool (22,000), Manchester (20,000), Salford (20,000), Birmingham (20,000) and other centers of commerce.

LOCAL HERO

Back in Kirkcaldy, Adam had finished his basic school education at the age of 17, and then he decided to move too. Adam Smith said goodbye to his mother Margaret, saddled his horse, and rode more than 500 kilometers of dirtroads to Oxford, where he was to study. While the 17-year-old John Law had been an aspiring "man of the world" when in 1688 he had headed for the London gaming houses, this can hardly be said about Adam Smith. In fact, he was probably one of the most absent-minded students ever to have entered the doors of Oxford University. When preparing tea, people would not be surprised to see him put his buttered bread into the pot and then complain over the taste of the tea. When he had a romantic attachment to a girl, he could be at a party without discovering her presence. And often, people would see him speaking to himself. But when Adam Smith seemed to forget everything around him, it was because he was focusing his mind completely on something else. He could concentrate.

He also had a great capacity for expressing himself. He could spend an evening at a social gathering dwelling in his own thoughts, but once anybody caught his attention by a direct question or a provocative statement, he would start talking as if he were giving a lecture on the subject. He could pursue the question on and on and become completely lost in its details, until people regretted that they ever involved him in the debate.

He found the lectures in Oxford rather uninteresting and most of what he actually learnt came out of his own, independent reading. He completed his Oxford education and returned home in 1750, where he was appointed to the Chair of Logic at Glasgow University and in 1752 to the Chair of Moral Philosophy. During these years, trade was gradually developing along the Clyde River, and this contributed to the development of new local industries. Adam Smith followed the developments in business with great interest, and was quite happy with his job at the university.

Figure 3.2: Glasgow as it looked when Adam Smith was teaching at its university.

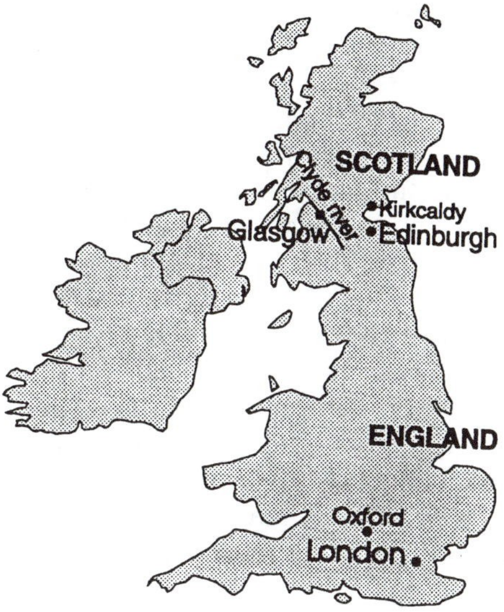

Figure 3.3: Map of England and Scotland when Adam Smith moved to Oxford.
Smith was born in Kirkcaldy, studied in London, and taught in Glasgow. John Law was born in Edinburgh and Thornton and Ricardo in London.

SYMPATHY AND SELF INTEREST

One of Adam Smith's ambitions was to develop a theory of ethics derived from man's natural instincts and feelings rather than from artificial doctrines. He believed that every man had a basic desire to be accepted by others, to receive their "sympathy." To obtain this sympathy, man (in his own self-interest) would try to behave in a manner which people would respect and admire. Inside him a sense of ethics would develop, a conscience, which would filter his thoughts before turning them into actions, omitting those that would not command the sympathy of others. So ethics was a question not of utility, not of benevolence or moral doctrine, but of self-interest.

Adam Smith saw the economic progress of society in the same light. He came to the conclusion that the driving force in the economy was the self interest of every individual, and that any attempt to suppress the individual would consequently suppress the economy as a whole. In 1755, he wrote a paper in which he expressed this view:

> "Little else is required to carry a state to the highest degree of opulence from the lowest degree of barbarism, but peace, low taxes, and tolerable administration of justice; all the rest being brought about by the natural course of things. All governments which thwart this natural course, which force things into another channel, or which endeavour to arrest the progress of society at a particular point, are unnatural, and to support themselves are obliged to be oppressive and tyrannical."

In 1759 he published his first book, "Theory of Moral Sentiments", which became very popular in Scotland. It also ensured him a job as personal tutor to the Duke of Buccleuch, who agreed to pay him 300 pounds a year (twice the university salary) plus expenses, if Smith would join him on a two-and-a-half-year study tour in Europe. Obviously he agreed, and one day in 1764, Adam Smith found himself on a sailing boat heading for the French side of the Channel.

MEETING QUESNAY

France had long since overcome the crises of the Duke, John Law and the Mississippi scheme, and was now competing with Britain for colonial dominance. It was now also a country with a growing intellectual élite. During his stay, Smith met with many of these, including Quesnay, who was 29 years older than Smith. Quesnay had many powerful friends and was, in fact, personal physician to Louis XV, the child king whom Philippe d'Orleans had replaced during the days of John Law.

A part of Quesnay's inspiration came from Cantillon, the Irish banker who had made millions on the Mississippi adventure and subsequently left for England. Cantillon had died in 1734, extremely rich, when his house in London was burned down by his cook. Among the 37-year-old millionaire's possessions that his descendants found was a manuscript for a book which they later published. This book, "Essai sur la nature du commerce en general," contained an analysis of many economic phenomena. Seen in retrospect, by far the most important among these were his theories of money supply, velocity of money and capital markets. Cantillon had understood how the effective money supply was influenced not only by how much money was floating around, but also by its velocity; by how fast money shifted hands:

> "To some degree, an acceleration, or a higher velocity of money circulation, will have a similar effect as an increase in the supply of money."

This worked both ways. If, as he had witnessed during the Mississippi panic, people started hoarding money, perhaps hiding it under their mattresses, the effect was equivalent to a fall in the money supply. Money had to change hands; otherwise it could not grease the market machinery and depression would ensue.

Although Quesnay was inspired by Cantillon, he also contributed with path-breaking thoughts of his own, and indeed he managed to set a footprint so strong, that the economist Joseph Schumpeter 200 years later would describe him as one of the four most important economists ever[6]. One of his major contributions was his so-called "*tableau economique*," a table showing how a given amount of money released into society turned into a flow. It would not flow forever, however, as each receiver of money on average would save a portion before spending the rest. In this way he demonstrated that the impact of the release of new liquidity into society was larger than the nominal amount released. So the physiocrats understood that capital was essentially a series of advances, and that income would flow and would, in a sense, multiply in that process.

Everybody regarded Quesnay as the informal leader of the popular "physiocrat" movement, which had invented a popular slogan:

> "Laissez faire, laissez passer"

The physiocrats were a growing movement opposing the French mercantilist tradition of state intervention and nationalist protectionism. The physiocrats believed in the abolition of monopolies, trade barriers and privileges and advocated individualism and the concept of "natural law"; that the laws of society should reflect laws that were somehow given in the order of nature. The name of the movement meant just that, in fact: it meant "Rule of Nature". The physiocrats also thought that the individual was a better judge of his own best interest than the state could ever be. And they preached the full respect of private property.

Adam Smith listened, was skeptical, but also interested. Apparently he was not very busy, because in his first year in France, he began, as he later expressed it, "to write a book in order to pass away the time." Smith stayed in France until 1766, when he returned to Scotland with the first part of the manuscript for this book. Little did he know that these pieces

Figure 3.4: Adam Smith.
Like the French physiocrats, Smith believed the economy would correct itself if left alone. His work became the foundation of English Classical Economics, which can be traced from Ricardo through Mill and Marshall to Pigou.

of paper in his luggage would eventually become part of a book which economists would praise as:

> "… in its ultimate results probably the most important book that has ever been written" (T.H. Buckle in 1872)

or

> "… the most successful not only of all books about economics but, with the possible exception of Darwin's "Origin of Species", of all scientific books that have appeared to this day." (J. Schumpeter in 1954)

But he did know that he wanted to work very thoroughly with the manuscript. That same year, when he was 43 years of age, he bought a house by the beach in Kirkcaldy where he planned to continue the work.

TAKE-OFF

During the 1750s, more and more businessmen in England were beginning to use primitive machines, many of which were based on waterpower and some on fossil energy. Most often, small industries could be found scattered around on the hillsides, where streaming water could drive the machines. In Smith's hometown, you could find collieries and salt-pans, and a nailery. One of his close friends, James Oswald, had another nailery outside the town, but still within walking distance from Smith's home. Here, scrap iron was imported from the Continent, while coal could be found almost at the factory's doorstep. Later Smith would refer to his experiences from these small factories when explaining the keys to industrial progress.

Three years after Smith's return, two important technological inventions appeared in his country. One was the "Waterframe," a new spinning machine designed by Arkwright, which improved productivity in the cotton industry dramatically. But even more significant was the first steam engine, which was patented by one of Adam Smith's close friends, James Watt. These and other inventions were the origin of heavy industries in areas with coal supplies.

The machines had two dramatic effects. One was that more could be produced per input of capital. The other was that it was necessary to plan further in advance: to build a new industrial factory plant was very different from ordering the goods at a number of small family workshops. The profit potential had become larger, but so had the uncertainty; the risk that the market might change before equipment could be put to use. Nobody could know for sure how this development would influence the workings of the economy, but it surely it had to mean something!?

Table 3.1: Innovations leading to the Industrial Revolution

Year	Innovation	Industry
1709	Coke-smelting process	Iron and steel
1733	Flying-shuttle	Textiles
1761	Manchester-Worsley Canal	Water transport
1764	Spinning Jenny	Textiles
1769	Steam engine	All industries
1769	Waterframe for spinning	Textiles
1776	Four-course rotation of crops	Agriculture
1776	Steam blast for smelting iron	Iron and steel
1779	The spinning "mule"	Textiles
1784	Reverberatory furnace with "puddling process"	Iron and steel
1785	Power loom	Textiles

Source: "The Kondratieff Waves", Nathan H. Mager, New York, 1987.

THE MASTERPIECE

While the local capitalists were busy setting up factories with the new machines, Adam Smith used up a lot of feather pens from 1766 to 1773 as he concentrated entirely on his manuscript. When it was finally finished, it had become huge. Spanning five books, "The Wealth of Nations" gave its readers an overall description of the mechanics of the capitalist economy, which was far more comprehensive than the theories in Cantillon's book. In the first book Smith set out to describe what he saw as the major reason why the economic output of some countries grew: division of labor. Division of labor explained the dramatic rise in productivity and the "invention of all those machines". Rather than assuming some theoretical, "rational" man, Adam Smith would typically illustrate his points through real examples (and on the spot: once while explaining a theory of division of labor in a tannery, he got so absorbed with his subject that he fell in the tanning pit).

In "The Wealth of Nations", he illustrated his theory about division of labor by describing, not a tannery, but a pin factory, which he had once visited. Here, 10 workers produced a total of 48,000 pins a day.

> "But if they had all worked separately and independently, and without any of them having been educated to this peculiar business, they certainly could not each of them have made twenty, perhaps not one pin in a day …"

As division of labor was the prime source of wealth of a nation, he advocated free trade to facilitate the international division of labor (this was one point where he was in disagreement with the physiocrats).

"The Wealth of Nations" continued to analyze, among other subjects, price mechanisms, where prices were described as fluctuating around a "natural" or "equilibrium" price. Other chapters dealt with wages, profits, time-risks undertaken by entrepreneurs, interests, rent, capital and taxation. As regards the role of the state, he recommended this to be minimized:

> "I have never known much good done by those who affected to trade for the public good."

The public sector should never interfere with the market, he thought, but should concentrate on protection of its citizens, on general justice and on certain specific tasks such as education, transportation and regulation of paper credit.

THE INVISIBLE HAND

The most important part of Smith's work however, was not his partial analyses (of which most was correct); but the fact that he deduced a crucial underlying principle: freedom was economically efficient. The capitalist economy would work best, he concluded, if you let every individual be the judge of his own interest, and if you relied on the forces of self-interest:

> "He intends only his own gain, and he is in this, as in many other cases, led by an invisible hand to promote an end which is no part of his intention."

And:

> "The desire of bettering our condition comes from us in the womb, and never leaves us till we go to the grave".

Over and over, he repeated this message in various contexts:

> "It is not from the benevolence of the butcher, the brewer, or the baker, that we expect our dinner, but from their regard to their own interest. We address ourselves, not to their humanity, but to their self-love, and never talk to them of our own necessities but of their advantages."

That Smith stated this principle so emphatically did not mean that he envisaged a free market economy as a utopian paradise. He thought that employers would always try to squeeze labor wages, merchants try to eliminate competition, producers conspire to raise prices, workers be bored, and some would always remain poor. But overall the system would grow rapidly and *an "invisible hand" — the market forces — would swiftly correct any deviations from this path of growth.*

Smith's work soon became very influential. More and more often, members of parliament would refer to it during their speeches[7], and in 1782, one of Smith's admirers, Lord Shelburne, was elected Prime Minister. Shelburne sought Smith's advice on a number of issues and once wrote:

> "I owe to a journey I made with Mr. Smith from Edinburgh to London the difference between light and darkness through the best part of my life."

When Smith was in London, he often stayed with Shelburne, and through him and other members of parliament, he maintained an increasing influence on the debate of the day, in spite of his occasionally strange behavior. When given a piece of paper to sign, Smith, absorbed in his own thoughts, might carefully copy another man's signature already there — instead of writing his own. People chose to forgive.

A BRIGHT YOUNG BANKER

One of those in parliament who admired Smith was a remarkable man named Henry Thornton[8]. Thornton had been elected to the House of Commons at the age of 22. Born in 1760, he had joined his father's counting house (as John Law had done 93 years before) when 18 years old. Young Thornton was surprised to see how his father conducted his business, trading in every commodity that moved, wheat, tobacco or whatever. The son was not impressed with this, and as any ambitious youngster, he was also quite dissatisfied with his salary. At 24, he left in order to work in a bank called "Down & Free". He did an excellent job there and was soon invited to be a partner in what was subsequently called "Down, Thornton & Free".

But banking in England was not always easy. It was fairly common, for example, that banks tried to set up organized runs against each other[9]. Another serious problem for the credit system was bad communication. If the population in any local region for some reason started to smell economic danger, they would bring their bills to their local "country bank" for payment in coins. If the bank was afraid of running short of metal, it would send for more from its correspondent bank in London. And if sufficient amounts of coins did not arrive in time, panic would break out, and people would start a run on other local banks. As dispatches were sent for more metal in London, the London banks would start feeling the pain, and panic could spread in the capital and even beyond the borders.

Such a process could start due to the simple reason of bad roads. Most of the English country roads were made of clay, which turned into thick mud whenever it rained. After the snow had melted in springtime, they were often in such bad shape that their surfaces had to be leveled by ploughs drawn by up to 10 horses. In most places the roads were full of holes due to the common practice of transporting coal and other hard-

Figure 3.5: Henry Thornton.
"The father of central banking" was born in 1760, at the beginning of the industrial revolution. Thornton was known among his contemporaries not only as a successful banker, but also as public advisor, and for giving away, as a rule, six-sevenths of his annual income to charity.

ware strapped to the sides of pack-horses. And the stage-coaches were clumsy, with no springs and heavy wheels.

Sending for dispatches was also expensive. Between 1700 and 1750, the British Parliament had passed 400 road acts[10] allowing erection of gates and collection of toll on the highways. And these were the times when famous gentlemen-thieves such as Dick Turpin, Claude Duval, Jonathan Wild and Jack Shephard would hide in the woods, ready to attack any passing traveler, not the least, of course, a carriage full of metal coins from some London correspondent bank!

COMMERCIAL DISTRESS

As a banker, Thornton had noticed that whenever you had enjoyed a few years of relative prosperity, a panic was apparently unavoidable. He knew that it had happened again and again. When he looked back through his century, he could see that England had had economic crises in the following years: 1702, 1705, 1711–12, 1715–16, 1718–21, 1726– 27, 1729, 1734, 1739–41, 1744–45, 1747, 1752–55, 1762, 1765–69, 1773–74, 1778–81, 1784 and 1788–89[11]. Each of these 18 times the economy had pulled itself out on its own, and most of the time had reached a higher plateau on the revival. But each time, it had only been a few years before a new crisis ensued, and everything came tumbling down again.

In the years after the crisis in 1788–1789, business had been booming, however, and a phenomenal number of new country banks had been created and the emission of new notes of bills had expanded. But in 1792, trade and manufacture started to level. In November the stock market experienced a sharp break and the currency started to slide. In February France declared war against England, and in March there were runs on a number of country banks which sent couriers to London for coins — but this time the London banks were just as squeezed themselves. So was Thornton's bank, which had grown to be one of London's largest. Thornton later wrote:

> "In the year 1793, a season of great commercial distress, we experienced greater difficulties than most other banks in consequence of the sudden reduction of very large sums which we had held at interest for some very considerable banks."[12]

The crisis was solved when the Bank of England decided to issue 5 million pounds worth of new bills to stimulate the economy. During the preceding crisis of 1783, the bank had stopped a capital flight through reduction of money supply — by limiting the amount of paper credit, thus forcing money rates up. Now, it proved that it could halt an *internal* crisis by doing just the opposite. Apparently they were beginning to learn.

LAISSEZ FAIRE — OU NON?

Money supply swelled after the new issue, and Thornton's bank survived. But it was probably this crisis which drew his mind to the theory of credit. Why did these financial crises occur? What could be done to stop them? Should one leave it to Professor Smith's invisible hand or should one — like the Bank of England had just done — intervene? Thornton had little literature to turn to (a list of the books in his library written after his death mentions only six titles about economics, one of which was "The Wealth of Nations"). He had to base his reason on common sense and experience. But while Thornton was thinking about the problem of instability, the economy continued to challenge. Just two years after the last crisis, a new one started, this time even more severe. As a result of the panic, the gold reserves of the Bank of England suddenly fell from 5 million pounds to 1.25 million, and on the last day of the year, the Bank decided to introduce rationing of payments in metal. The effects of this were disastrous. During the next month, panic spread even further and an increasing number of merchants and banks closed. On February 26th, 1797, the Bank of England threw in the towel and suspended payments altogether. This, of course, was a great defeat.

IF PHILIPPE D'ORLEANS HAD KNOWN THIS …

The following day, the House of Commons set down a committee to investigate the causes of the problem, and one day later the House of Lords instigated a similar committee. The first of these two committees called in 19 witnesses, the latter 16. Both called in Henry Thornton, who seems to have been the only representative of the private London bankers in the hearings.

His evidence was amazing[13]. As he spoke, you could sense that Thornton had a remarkable understanding of the nature of banking. He clearly spelled out the responsibilities of the Bank of England and gave a detailed introduction to the instruments that ought to be in the central bankers' toolbox. In retrospect we know at least part of the reason for the accuracy of his statements: during evenings and weekends he had embarked on a book about the nature of that very subject. This book, which is still regarded as one of the great classics in the history of economics, was published in 1802 under the title:

"Paper Credit of Great Britain."

It was one of those rare books that soared above contemporary works yet was at first underrated because it never emphasized the novelty of its arguments. Many of the principles explained in it are still regarded as essential in credit (or monetary) theory, and today Thornton is often described as the "father of central banking" — a title which John Law would have aspired to, had Philippe d'Orleans not made his scheme go berserk.

One of the great achievements in "Paper Credit" was Thornton's realization that in many respects, *you could treat all the different means of credit as one total.* Today any economist will routinely speak of "money supply" defined as some aggregate. "M2", for instance, consists of "notes and coinage, checking accounts of private persons and companies, and other accounts, including small-time saving deposits." But before Thornton, the analytical practice was to focus on each source of liquidity at a time. Thornton thus created a powerful tool to observe interactions between the volume of money (liquidity), velocity of money (which we remember from Cantillon) and interest rates. Here are some of his observations:

- A high interest rate will prevent capital flight or even attract liquidity to the country.
- A high interest rate will persuade people to part with their cash by putting it on bank accounts. By maintaining a high rate, the central bank can thus lower velocity, suck up money and consequently dampen activity. Low rates, in contrast, will increase money supply and stimulate activity.
- The public expectation of future inflation will influence present interest rates. If people fear future inflation, present rates will be correspondingly higher.

- An unintended contraction of credit can lead to an economic depression. On the other hand, too large expansion of credit (through increased lending) can lead to overheating the economy.
- An increase in the money supply will lead to increased inflation if the economy is fully employed. If it is underemployed, it might lead only to increased growth.

A CREDIT TRAP

Thornton explained that if you increased money supply by, say, lowering interest rates below expected profit rates, this would lead to a higher level of borrowing and, subsequently, of business activity (Thornton mentioned the early phases of John Law's scheme in France as an example). But then he added a very important observation: Given increased activity, society would be able to absorb more money. Every increase in money supply would afterwards seem justified, as long as ensuing growth in activity could follow suit — until you reached full employment. This was crucial as *it could lead the central banker to expand the money supply much too far without seeing the danger before it was too late*. The system was in other words unstable — *more credit seemed (deceptively) to justify more credit, and less credit seemed to justify less*. The concept of such inherent instability was of course very different from Adam Smith's invisible hand concept and indicated that the economy might have the ability to lead itself off the track (because of positive feed-back) as well as back on the track (negative feed-back). There was not one invisible hand, but two!

SAY'S LAW

Meanwhile, Adam Smith's book was also spreading beyond England's borders. One of those who had read it was Jean Babtiste Say, a French businessman who had picked it up in 1788. Say had invested in new technology and ran a French cotton spinning industry. Being very busy, he had little time to write himself, but eventually, in 1803, he published his own, "Traite d'économie Politique". This book was in many ways a condensation and clarification of what Smith had written 26 years before.

Indeed it displayed a clearer structure and more consistent argumentation than had Smith in "The Wealth of Nations". But it also contained a number of additions, one of which brought him fame: the "Law of Markets". The problem was this: To Adam Smith, saving would not have much effect in disturbing the progress of the economy. But many had questioned this view. What if people were in fact saving up their money so that nobody would buy the output from increased production? Did the presence of the ever-growing credit system change the rules? Say's answer to this was simply that *supply creates its own demand*:

> "… a product is no sooner created, than it, from that instant, affords a market for other products to the full extent of its own value. Thus, from the mere instance of the creation of one product immediately opens a vent for other products."

The reasoning was simple: if you produce something and manage to sell it, then you have earned some money which you can spend. Because of this, sustained shortage of purchasing power could never be a long-term problem to a society — unless caused by a similarly low production. If consumption temporarily fell behind production, then interest rates would fall, and this would encourage companies to invest and things would get back in gear. This was a very important conclusion because it seemed to render invalid all explanations of crises based on sheer "overproduction". But the theory left the problem of explaining that crises in fact occurred all the time unaddressed.

THE GREAT BULLION DEBATE

In 1809, South America was finally opening up to British merchants and a wave of optimism ensued (the event that the South Sea Company could have used 90 years earlier). This led to a large increase in the British money supply, and shortly after, the currency started to slide relative to gold, giving Great Britain an inflation problem. Then, in August, September and October 1809, three articles criticizing the policy of the Bank of England appeared in "The Chronicle"; and soon after a related article was published in "Edinburgh Review" under the headline: "The High Price of Bullion, a Proof of the Depreciation of Bank Notes." The author was an acquaintance of Thornton, a 37-year-old London stock-broker and financier. His name was David Ricardo[14].

What they were mainly remembered for

Some of the strongest, lasting successes of the economists mentioned in this chapter were:

- *Francois Quesnay: His "tableau economique" and the concept of "laissez faire".*
- *Richard Cantillon: Understanding of the effects of "velocity of money".*
- *Adam Smith: The importance of the pursuing of self-interest. The damaging effects of protectionism in all its forms.*
- *Henry Thornton: The concept of aggregate money supply. The courses and effects of fluctuations in aggregate money supply. The potential beneficial effects of active central bank intervention.*
- *Jean Babtiste Say: The fact that supply can create its own demand.*
- *David Ricardo: The importance of calculating marginal effects in economic theory.*

Ricardo's article was an academic debut. He had received a very basic education in school and had joined his father's stock brokerage business when only 14 years old. Since then, he had established his own brokerage business where he primarily traded government securities. His motto was:

"Cut losses, let profits run."

Following these rules (and presumably a number of others), he had become extremely wealthy. Until he reached the age of 27, it had not occurred to him that he should ever spend time on economic theory. Why should he? — economic reality worked just fine with him! But in 1799, while he was at a holiday resort, he had come across "The Wealth of Nations" — and become fascinated. "Someday ...", he had thought, "... I just might consider throwing in my own hat." In 1808 he had met a struggling journalist, James Mill, who had the same interest in general economics as Ricardo[14]. Unlike Ricardo, Mill had a formal university training, which he had received at Edinburgh University (where Smith had taught). Ricardo and Mill began taking long walks together where they discussed politics and economy — and where Mill began to suggest that Ricardo should contribute to science. And this was what happened when Ricardo published these articles.

Ricardo's article in the "Edinburgh Review" contained 17 specific references to Thornton and 13 to Adam Smith. His conclusion was that the cause of the depreciation of the currency was the over-issuing of notes, and not — as Thornton had claimed — excessive imports due to bad harvest and war expenditures. His recommendation was that England should return immediately to the gold standard, which had been abandoned in 1797. When in 1810 the "Bullion Committee" was established to clarify the roots of the problem, Thornton, who was a member of the committee, yielded to Ricardo's conclusion. It is a curious fact that the publication of the committee's report was to lead very nearly to Thornton's own bankruptcy: a panic followed its publication and Thornton had to slip a word to one of his friends that "Down, Thornton & Free" could use a few time-deposits fast. Fortunately he had many faithful friends, and enough money was deposited to save the bank. Ricardo, in turn, had been squeezed by inflation and stood to benefit from a return to the gold standard.

In 1816 the debate resumed, and Ricardo published "Proposals for an Economical and Secure Currency," in which he again suggested that England return to the gold standard; not by using gold coins, but by requiring the Bank of England to change paper money to gold on demand — just like Law & Company had done from the outset. This would be a self-stabilizing system, he thought, for the following reasons:

- If the Bank of England issued too much paper, it would have to import gold to back it …
- … a process which in itself would reduce the money supply and diminish the Bank of England's potential for issuing new bills.

Thornton disagreed. He did not think a monetary system could be self-stabilizing, and therefore the Bank of England should — and could — make the necessary adjustments to the money supply. And he believed that fluctuations in money supply would not only affect prices, but also economic activity. In 1820 a plan much similar to what Ricardo had proposed was tried. It led to a drastic fall in prices, a disastrous recession and shortly after, a new abandonment of the gold standard. Exactly 100 years after the failure of John Law's scheme, the economy still seemed extremely unstable, and it was now clear that paper money wasn't the only cause of economic instability.

Who were right and wrong in the "Great Bullion Debate"?

During the "Great Bullion Debate" Ricardo and Thornton disagreed in particular on the following 3 subjects:

Ricardo's opinion	Thornton's opinion
Changes in the money supply influence only the general level of prices	*Changes in money supply can also influence economic activity*
Changes in the money supply have no influence on interest rates	*Changes in money supply have an influence on interest rates*
Only an increased money supply can cause depreciation in the exchange rate	*Exchange rates can also be influenced by real factors such as harvest and government transfers abroad*

Thornton *was right on these issues, but because* Ricardo *became very famous for his other contributions to economic theory, his faulty theories about money supply had a considerable influence for at least a century.*

Meanwhile, the Bank of England *argued that it was only meeting the legitimate needs of trade. However they missed an important point: During periods of prosperity businesses are eager to borrow, and during recessions they are afraid and try to reduce their debts. So by passively giving business what it wants the central bank does nothing to limit the commercial fluctuations.*

The Bullion Committee's *analysis was essentially right, but their recommendation was problematic, because a return to the old paper/gold parity implicated a period of deflation. This made it difficult to pay back loans and encouraged business to postpone investments. The result was a severe crisis.*

Finally, almost everybody ignored the big problems associated with a gold standard. Firstly it involved a requirement to import very big amounts of gold as the economy developed. Secondly it created a temptation for people to convert their paper money to gold during a crisis. Once they did that there were very few means for the central bank to counter the monetary contraction because they were running short of their required resource, which was gold. So a gold standard might prevent inflation, but it did not prevent depressions.

4
From Crash to Crash

"Anyone who trades in markets where prices are continuously changing knows that participants are very much influenced by market developments. Rising prices often attract buyers and vice versa."

George Soros

Ricardo's friend James Mill maintained his interest in economics throughout his life. Together with Ricardo and a number of other distinguished men, he founded the "Political Economy Club", about which the economist Jevons later wrote:

> "Whether its continued existence be due to the excellence of its monthly dinners — in respect of which the club does not seem to study economy — or to the economical debates which follow each dinner, I will not attempt to decide."[1]

Much of James Mill's work was devoted to promoting Ricardo's ideas, but he also dealt with economic theories and questions of his own. One of these was "the grand practical problem to find means to limit the number of births" — a problem which he saw as a major threat given limited food supply. Mill should know from first-hand observation: Ricardo had been the third of 17 children and Mill himself was the father of nine.

A BRIGHT KID

One of these nine children was John Stuart, who was born in 1806[2]. John very early showed signs of exceptional intelligence and James soon started to educate him. When John reached the age of 3, he was taught

Greek and arithmetic. When he reached 8, he learned Latin, and soon after geometry, algebra, chemistry and physics. At 12, John was taught logic, and the year after he was introduced to political economy. One of the ways in which James taught him economics was by taking walks (like with Ricardo) in which he gave his son lectures on different aspects of Ricardian economy. Every morning, John had to deliver a complete, written report about what the father had said the day before. These reports were afterwards used as a draft for "Elements of Political Economy", which was published in 1819. This was quite a remarkable effort, considering that John was only 13 years old at the time.

Four years after the publication of the book, James considered his son's education finished, and the 17-year-old John Stuart Mill joined the East India Company. This gave him an extremely useful insight into private business and public affairs, and it did not prevent him from writing and studying during his free time. When he reached 20, he had published seven major articles about economics, politics and law, and edited a book about philosophy. Judging from his works it seems that philosophy was his major interest, but yet in sheer numbers of pages written, economy ended up being his largest subject.

John Stuart Mill viewed economics as a science rather than an art. He simplified and stylized reality and built his reasoning on hypothesis. He believed that "induction" — drawing final conclusions from observed facts — was not realistic in economics, as you were unable to isolate with certainty specific facts from the messy whole. You had to develop theories first, and then study reality to see if it at least *seemed* to support your model. For that reason you should never forget to study the actual behavior of people.

SOURCES OF INHERENT INSTABILITY

His best contribution to economic theory was written during his 23rd and 24th years (but not published until many years later). The title was "Essays on Some Unsettled Questions of Political Economy". One of the essays was an analysis of Say's Law. The notion that supply creates its own demand would hold in a simple barter economy, he claimed, but not necessarily if money was used as a medium, *because people could save up the proceeds from their sales, so that supply didn't necessarily create equal demand* — at least for a while. The critical factor, which could trigger such imbalances, was swings in general confidence.

During the following years he published a number of other articles about economics. In 1826, he wrote "Paper Currency and Commercial Distress", in which he introduced the concept of "competitive investment". His idea covered the problem in which a market, through for instance a technological invention, suddenly expanded. In such a case, every businessman might very well have a fair judgement about the new market size and what his "fair share" of it should "statistically" be. But as those who reach a new market first can make the most money, many will rush to try to get an unproportional share of the cake:

> "Everyone calculating upon being before all his competitors provides himself with as large a stock as he thinks that the market will take off; not reflecting that others, like himself, are adding to the supply, not calculating upon the fall of price which must take place as soon as this increasing quantity is brought to the market. This deficiency is soon changed into an excess."

In this way, *a temporary excess of demand of a specific item could soon after lead to the opposite: a temporary excess of supply*. In the same article, he introduced a distinction between "professional traders" and "speculators", the first basing their behavior on long-term economic analysis, the latter on short-term price trends:

> "The few who watch prospectively the signs of future supply and demand, anticipating a great rise of price, make considerable purchases. These purchases produce a considerable immediate rise; and this in turn tempts many, who look no further than to the immediate turn of the market, to purchase in expectation of a still greater advance."

This meant that *the speculator's "trend-extrapolation" was another positive feed-back process* — and one which could easily explain why booms could get completely off track, as in the Mississippi scheme and the South Sea Company.

In 1845, Mill began writing a major work about economy. This book, "Principles of Political Economy" became something of a record in speed writing. He completed the work, with 971 pages (in fact it was 5 books), stuffed with detailed and, in many cases, novel analysis, in just 18 months. In this work, which became an international classic, he related velocity of money — Cantillon's old concept — with the general upswing and speculation. The upswing was possible, he claimed, even if money supply did not increase, if only velocity did. The driving force in such a boom would again be confidence. His book was hardly finished before the next crash appeared.

THE CRASH OF 1847

The year 1847 was interesting for many economists and businessmen. It was interesting for John Stuart Mill because his new book was published in that year. It was also interesting for Lord Overstone, England's most successful banker. Overstone viewed financial crises as a phenomenon that could be analyzed independently, and he spoke and wrote about the subject from time to time. One day he had a conversation with Walther Bagehot, the chief editor of the Economist, and Bagehot quoted him later on for describing the different phases of the boom-bust cycle as follows: "Quiescence, improvement, confidence, prosperity, excitement, overtrading, convulsion, pressure, stagnation, ending again in quiescence."

Overstone had for some time been concerned about the ability of the bank of England to halt a severe banking crisis and panic. As a skilled banker he followed these markets very closely and tried to figure out when the economy was moving into a danger zone. During the fall of 1845 he had begun to sense that such a situation was evolving, so he sat down to write about it to his good friend G.W. Norman. It was not that Overstone thought that a crash was imminent, but the early warning signs were definitely there: "We have no crash at present…", he wrote, "…only a slight premonitory movement in the ground under our feet." He was right: the crash came in 1847.

The trigger was installment payments for railroad shares. It was common at the time to sell shares in such a way that buyers only had to make initial installments to start with and then perhaps hope that they could sell the shares again at a profit before the next installments were due. A series of these new installments, totaling approx. 6.5 million pounds, were due in January 1847. And people had difficulties paying them. The full-blown crisis broke out during the summer, and 22 British companies defaulted during August, followed by 47 in September and 82 in October. It didn't take long before the crisis spread beyond the British borders to Holland, Belgium, New York and Germany.

The year 1847 was also interesting for a young gentleman named Karl Heinrich Marx. Karl Marx was born in a little Prussian town called Trier on 5 May, 1818. He had since grown up in a traditional middle class environment and later on managed to get accepted into the prestigious Berlin University. His specialty at the university became philosophy, and after leaving Berlin University he took a doctor's degree at Jena University. In 1842, when he was 24 years of age, he got a job as an editor at Reinische Zeitung. This had all been very fine until, just five months later, the newspaper got banned by the government. After this rather disappointing beginning of his career he moved to Paris where he worked as journalist for several magazines — until he got expelled from France two years later. So here was a young man who had studied philosophy at what was generally considered the finest university in the world. And then, when he wanted to write about his ideas, the society wouldn't allow him! He became angry.

Karl Marx became a radical critic of religion, Negroes, Jews (although he himself was a Jew), and of capitalists and capitalist society. He got soon involved in the organization of the Communist League — a radical movement that wanted workers to take control over business and the state. Karl Marx aimed to show that a capitalist economy was unfair and seriously flawed, and that it consequently would be replaced by a socialist/communist system. The workers should consequently get mobilized as soon as possible and then, when the time was ripe: strike and take control. The question was of course exactly when a good moment for the take-over would occur.

The crash of 1847 was an important inspiration for him, because it had triggered some exciting events. There had been several communist uprisings across Europe, and although they had all been crushed they did indicate something to him: It had clearly been an economic crisis that had triggered the attempted revolutions, and it would probably be new crises that would trigger the next attempt. He took an ambitious approach: he would not only show that one system (capitalism) was flawed and the other (communism) was better, but he would also provide a road map for how the transition would take place. His conclusion was that it would be one of the frequent economic crises in the capitalist system that would trigger the workers' uprising and the revolution. So he decided to analyze why there were regular economic crises in market economies.

While he thought about the issue the kettle started to overheat again. The 1850s brought new waves of speculation in railway stocks, as well as in wheat (England), land (USA) and heavy industries (Continental Europe). In 1857, The New York branch of Ohio Life Assurance Trust Company suspended its payments[4]. Soon a chain-reaction started and many of the railway stocks that so many people had invested in began a free fall on the stock exchanges.

This triggered an incredible burst of energy from Karl Marx. It was happening again – he had to get the theory out! Within six months he wrote the first drafts of what would eventually become his classic suite of books, Das Capital ("Capital"), about capitalist economy. Here he described what he himself called "in every respect the most important law of modern political economy". The process that he described may be summarized as follows:

- Booms are often created by technical innovations.
- The effect of technical innovations is that capitalists employ more capital (machines, etc.) and fewer people (workers) in the production process.
- It is the people who create the value, and since the ratio of people to capital is falling, the ratio of profits will fall as well.

He concluded "The rate of profits falls not because the worker is exploited less, but because altogether less labor is employed in relation to the capital employed". He carried on to state that decreased profit rates would lead to increased indebtedness until the final collapse would come and the communists take over.

Karl Marx's theories of capitalist crises were rather confused, if not meaningless, but he is still remembered as a contributor to the business cycle theory not because of what he concluded or predicted, but because of how he approached the problem. He was one of the first authors to attempt to provide a systematic theory of how crises. and depressions could develop in a capitalist economy.

Walter Bagehot on business cycles and money

John Stuart Mill and Karl Marx were not the only authors to theorize about the reasons for recurring crises. One of the most famous financial journalist of all time was Walther Bagehot. Bagehot's father-in-law, James Wilson, had founded the famous magazine "The Economist" and Bagehot was employed as a financial editor there after finishing an education as lawyer. He published in 1873 "Lombart Street: A Description of the Money Market", where he described the roles and effects of banking. He agreed with Juglar that there were inherent processes in the economy that created expansions and contractions, but he focused on money as the primary culprit. His conclusion was therefore that an economy with money would fluctuate more than a pure barter economy.

GOLDEN OPPORTUNITY

In 1864, a new crisis started in France and spread to England and Italy two years later. This time, the objects of speculation were wool, shipping and various kinds of new enterprises.

But this was nothing compared to the nightmare that was waiting around the corner, the most devastating, international depression of the century. The financial crash that preceded it started in 1873, which was the year when John Stuart Mill died.

It is difficult to pin down which events were the real precursors of the crash of 1873, but if we start in 1869, we will be sure not to miss any part of this amazing story. At that time, there was a lively market at the New York Stock Exchange Gold Room. People said that dealers traded gold in this room, but as gold was essentially the international currency (most of the European countries were now on the gold standard), what was really traded was dollars: if you bought gold, you paid with dollars. If the price of gold (as measured in dollars) went up, it really meant that the international price of dollars went down.

Two of the most active traders in the Gold Room were Jay Gould and Jim Fisk[5]. Jim Fisk was fat, happy and charming, and an able salesman. But he was often like a bull in a china shop. Jay was an astute, cynical speculator who had been trained at Eire Lake Railroad, where he had met Jim Fisk. Gould had made a lot of money on booming railroad stocks which he still owned. Now he decided to try an incredible plan which could add even further to his wealth: he would buy up gold to depress the exchange rate of the dollar. But not just a little gold. He would buy a terrible lot of gold. As the dollar fell, this would increase America's exports (giving more business to the railways) and it would also stimulate American inflation — reducing the debt burden on his railways.

At that time, there was some 115 million dollars worth of gold in America, of which 100 millions were locked up in the vaults of the Treasury. As the margin requirements were extremely slack, Gould could buy 10 million dollars worth of gold on future contracts by putting up only 50,000 dollars of his own, as long as people believed in his general credit-worthiness. But before he started, he had to take some precautions — just in case President Grant should decide to sell some of the Treasury's gold and thus force its price down. His solution was to cultivate a friendship with Grant's former brother-in-law, Abel Gorbin, who should introduce him to the President. This eventually happened on Fisk's steamboat where Gould tried to find out what Grant's reaction to a rise in the gold price would be. The meeting didn't turn out to Gould's full satisfaction, however, as Grant apparently had no clear idea about how he would react to a gold-craze.

On September 16, Gould asked Gorbin if he could send the President a letter explaining why it would be wrong to sell gold until the grain crops had been moved. After the letter was finished, they sent a messenger with the train to Pittsburg. As the messenger arrived just after midnight, he hired horses and rode all night to Washington, where he finally found President Grant playing croquet on his lawn. The messenger handed over the letter and asked if there was a reply. "No, nothing," the President answered, whereafter the messenger returned to Pittsburg to send a telegraph with the short message:

"Delivered all right"

But something went wrong under the transmission: the telegram, which was received by Gould and Gorbin, said something quite different. It said:

"Delivered. All right"

Seeing this, Gould decided to start moving. After having promised Gorbin a free trading line of 1.5 million dollars, he started buying up gold. He bought in the free market at a price around 135 dollars, and gradually the price started to edge upwards. On September 22, a day when Fisk was leading the charge of the trading room, the price closed at 141.5. That evening, Gould visited Gorbin, who had some very disturbing news: he had just received a letter from Grant, who expressed his dissatisfaction with the fall of the dollar, implying that he might start selling gold from the Treasury.

Through the assistance of Gorbin, Gould met with the President again, and this time at a public party, where everybody could see them together. Gould tried to convince the President that a rise in the dollar price would do great damage to exports and should at least be postponed until large, pending export orders had been cleared. After this brief meeting, he began trying to convince everybody else that the President had promised to back him all the way. Then he took a deep breath and resumed buying.

THE GREATEST RAID …

He entrusted most of the business to the broker Henry Smith, who recruited a number of others, who again recruited others to make a total of probably 50 or 60. Together they bought up gold until they had sucked up almost all the metal on the market. And when there was no more gold left, he kept buying through forward contracts until he had 40 million dollars worth of gold contracts in addition to his 15 million worth of cash gold. During this process, the price rose to 146 dollars — which meant that singlehandedly, he had managed to force down the dollar by almost 8%.

But then something odd had happened. For some reason, the price had stuck at 146, as if somebody else was selling large amounts at that specific price, or as if somebody knew that the Treasury would start selling. Through the use of forward contracts, Gould had now bought more gold than existed on the free market. Paradoxically this was potentially a very strong position, because when the sellers had to deliver and could not get the stuff, where would they have to buy it? From Gould, of course, who would be able to dictate the price. But why, then, did it stop at 146? Was it because Grant would sell?

Fortunately, the President was coming to visit Gorbin soon, and Gorbin convinced Grant that he should sit on his hands. Encouraged by this, Gould told his old friend Fisk that he could be part of this fantastic raid — one of the greatest in history — and one that was backed by everybody from the President to the doorkeepers in Congress. Gould told Fisk that he could be in charge of the gold purchases and of spreading rumors to the colleagues in the Gold Room. Fisk jumped in and started buying on his own account through forward contracts on "phantom gold" — gold that was actually not there. The sellers were selling short for future delivery, hoping that the Treasury would release some gold, which they could snap up at a lower price. Gould told Fisk that Grant wanted to see gold at 1,000 dollars, a rumor which Fisk quickly passed on to the traders.

This was the time when (as John Stuart Mill would have predicted) the public joined in. Soon you saw dentists, merchants and even farmers from all over the country buying up gold in anticipation of further price increases. The power of this new wave of buy-orders came as a shock to the professional shortsellers, who started covering their contracts by buying at any price as the 146-dollar barrier was broken. But Gould was no longer buying. He knew time would eventually run out, and had in fact started to sell. Fisk knew nothing about this and kept buying on his own account what was, in fact, Gould's gold.

Then it happened. Grant sent Gorbin a letter warning him that the Treasury would start selling. Gorbin immediately insisted that Gould should close his account and pay out his profit. Gould agreed to this if Gorbin would keep silent about the letter. He knew that he was on the verge of disaster. He still had his cash stock plus 35 million worth of forward contracts — to sell it would be like moving an elephant through a public restaurant without anybody noticing. And he probably only had a few days or even a few hours the next morning to do it.

His first decision was to leave Fisk behind. One elephant might just be able to sneak out unnoticed. There was no way that two could do it. So the next morning, he encouraged Fisk to keep buying, while he speeded up his own secret sales. Amazingly, the gold kept rising as the public kept buying. Steadily and at an enormous trading volume, it edged up dollar by dollar. Meanwhile Gould sold and sold until there was nothing left to sell. But he kept on selling, building up an increasing short-position in the forward contracts. A reporter from the New York Herald saw the drama and described it in this way:

> "The revengeful war whoops of the furious Indians, the terrific yells issuing from a lunatic asylum, would not equal in intensity the cries of speculators in the Gold Room."

As the public kept buying, gold kept advancing and the atmosphere was loaded. Would it eventually top 1,000 dollars? Was Grant in it or not? Would the Treasury sell? Then, at 12:07, when the price had just reached 165, the announcement arrived: the Treasury would sell.

It has been estimated that Gould made 1.5 million dollars within the next 14 minutes. During these 14 minutes, the price of gold fell from 165 to 133 dollars, and all the paper profits of the bulls were wiped out. The bears had been saved from their squeeze, and Gould had succeeded with his scheme. As a consequence Gould became the most detested man in Wall Street, and as Fisk said of him: There was "nothing left but a heap of clothes and a pair of eyes."

THE END OF THE BOOM

Gould had kept his interests in railway stock. At this time, the public interest in railway stocks was as high as ever. But the fact was that overcapacity was developing as too many rushed to gain market share (John Stuart Mill's "competitive investment"). After 1868 the annual construction of new railway mileage had soared, and now pressure could be felt. Gould controlled the Eire Lake Railroad which competed with Vanderbilt's New York Central Line, and Vanderbilt had just lowered his price from 125 to 100 dollars per carload[6]. Gould decided to try to regain his market share by lowering *his* price to 75 dollars. Vanderbilt then moved to 50 dollars. Gould moved to 25 dollars. And then Vanderbilt moved to 1 dollar — far below his production costs. After that, Vanderbilt got all the business. In fact, he got much more business than there had ever been before, as Gould started to buy up steers in Buffalo to ship them through the New York Central Line.

This price-war was symptomatic of the situation. Prosperity had lasted too long and people had invested in too many businesses that could not pay back the interest. During 1872, 89 railroads defaulted on their bonds, including Gould's Eire Lake Railroad. Out of 364 listed railroads, 260 were unable to pay any dividends. By the end of the year, more and more of the railroad stocks started sliding at the stock exchange and the atmosphere grew more cautious. In Europe, the situation was very similar. After years of booming investment in building sites, commodities and railway stocks, things were getting shaky and confidence beginning to slide.

TOTAL COLLAPSE

Sometimes, panic starts in the most unexpected places. This time, it began in Austria, where a wave of fear suddenly came just after the opening of the Vienna World Exhibition on May 1st 1873. Many Austrian banks were up to their ears in railroad shares and were dragged down as marginal speculators failed. Soon the panic spread to Germany, and from there on to Belgium, Italy, Switzerland and Holland. On September 8, 1873, it reached Wall Street. On that day, the New York Warehouse and Security Co. defaulted. And then nobody could stop it:

September 13: Kenyon, Cox Bank defaulted
September 17: Pandemonium defaulted
September 18: Jay Cooke and Co. defaulted

The 19th of September started calmly, but during the afternoon, most of the railway stocks suddenly started to fall. It was suspected that this was engineered singlehandedly by Jay Gould, who was thought to have unloaded all his railroad shares beforehand. The fall immediately turned into all-out panic in which everybody desperately struggled to find a buyer for their shares. The next morning, the doors of the stock exchange never opened, and the president rushed for an emergency meeting with

Figure 4.1: Jay Gould.
Gould became one of the most hated traders in the history of the American stock exchange.

Figure 4.2: Jim Fisk.
Fisk apparently left the gold adventure with a huge debt, but all the gold he had bought had been in other people's names. Afterwards, he simply refused to honor his obligations. John Stuart Mill recognized that economic theory had to leave room for characters like Gould and Fisk, and for various sources of inherent instability.

his treasury secretary and several officials and businessmen, including Commodore Vanderbilt. The problem had only one solution, and unlike the British Bullion Committee 76 years earlier, these people only needed a few hours to choose that solution:

"Increase the money supply!"

The Treasury released 13 million dollars for purchasing government bonds, and 10 days later the exchange was reopened.

But the fact that the exchange reopened did not mean that the crisis was over. The panic was the beginning of a depression of a magnitude which America had never seen before. Unemployment in New York rose to 30%, then to 40%, and then 50%. The construction of new railway mileage dropped from 5,870 miles in 1872 to 4,097 in '73, and further to 2,117 in '74. In 1875, it reached the bottom with 1,711 new miles added[6]. John Stuart Mill had been right: confidence mattered, and so did speculation. A boom could take place even if stimulated by neither an increase in the money printing nor any external stimulus. It could take place if people reduced their savings, if velocity of money increased, or because of competitive investment. And a burst could appear simply as a reaction to a boom. One hundred and fifty-four years after the collapse of Law's scheme, it began to look more and more as if instability was an inherent property of the capitalist economy. Maybe there was an invisible hand to restore the balance after waves of collective greed and fear, but it was sorely needed: people were only human.

MR. JEVONS AND THE SUN

Perhaps it is only fair to add that economists could be distinctly human too. William Stanley Jevons was a good example.

Jevons was born in Liverpool in 1835 and had gone to the University College in London. However, his father had lost his business in the crash of 1847, and Jevons had consequently been forced to leave the studies and work instead, and it took him no less than 12 years to earn enough money to go back and complete the studies.

Jevons provided during his career a number of great contributions to the body of economic thought. In 1871, just two years before the great crash, he published his book "The Theory of Political Economy", where he provided a valuable description of marginal analysis and provided the first description of "rational man" — an assumed person in economic constructs that would only make rational decisions. He explained how rational consumers would try to maximize their utility and would stop spending money on a given item when they thought that the marginal utility would be higher if they spent the next money on something else.

And then there was the issue with the sun. Jevons knew from first hand experience how painful economic depressions could be and he was probably inspired by the crash of 1875 when he started writing a series of articles (published between 1875 and 1882) about business cycles. One of his sources of inspiration was Mill's Principles of Political Economy. Jevons noted Mill's emphasis on public mood swings, but he thought that his assumptions were highly inadequate for explaining the recurring booms and depressions, which he found were relatively regular. Which process would explain why people get greedy and scared at regular intervals? Mill had not solved that problem at all. So Jevons had looked everywhere for some external factor in the economy that could stimulate these big fluctuations. He thought and he speculated while pouring over mountains of statistics. The first basic conclusion that he reached was that agriculture (the harvest) constituted a very important part of the economy, so it was possible that the explanation came from something that happened on the farms. But what could it be? Diseases in the crops?

The explanation that he finally proposed was that it was fluctuation in the intensity of the sunshine — created by the regularly occurring "sunspots" (large fireballs on the surface of the sun that appear at regular intervals). His first article — coinciding with the great crash of 1875 — provided an attempt to show that there had been an 11.1-year cycle in the British grain harvest from 1254 to 1400, and that this corresponded very well with the cycle in sunspot activity, which astronomers at the time claimed was 11.1 years. Increased sunspot activity would create increased sunshine, which stimulated plant growth and thus led to a better-than-average harvest. Case solved!

Well, perhaps not quite. The astronomers would soon after revise their sunspot cycle length to 10.45 years, and this meant that Jevons' model got embarrassingly out of synch. So he looked at the harvest statistics again and concluded (surprise, surprise) that the actual cycle length had in fact been 10.45 years, and not, as he previously had stated, 11.1 years. So not to worry: the theory was OK.

The problems did not stop there, however. New British crop reports did not fit into his model, and he was now forced to make another adjustment. His new claim was that sunspots led to crop fluctuations in other countries, and that these fluctuations had an indirect impact on British trade and manufacturing. This meant that there was no strict, direct causality between the sun-spots and the business cycles in Britain, but a strong indirect one. This indirect effect was created both because of the change in the price and quantity and production of agricultural products, but also (now that the theory was known) by the merchants' expectations about sunspots: they would discount sunspot fluctuations in their planning decisions. The mere *expectation* of sunspots could thereby create economic cycles even if, for whatever reason, the sunspots failed to appear at the expected time. This was of course a brilliant and truly innovative way to explain inconsistencies between what a theory predicted and what the data showed. Few bought it, though. There were not many of his contemporaries who truly believed that sunspots were a primary explanation of business fluctuations — or that they even were relevant (and no sane scientist believes it now).

What remains of Jevons' sunspot theory (and of many of Karl Marx's theories) is not the faulty conclusions, but the analytical approaches. Modern economists often use the term "sunspots" today, and what they refer to is not bursts of fire on the sun, but situations where phenomena that by themselves do not effect the economy, can alter common beliefs and thus indirectly affect the economy. Jevons' approach survived.

How the central bank could "increase the money supply"

Central banks had discovered 3 important ways to create money:

- *The first was to* buy equities *(and pay with money). This had a direct effect (the injection of money) and an indirect effect (bond prices went up so that interest rates went down, which encouraged more private borrowing).*
- *The second was to* lower the discount rates *(the interest rates that the central bank offered to the private banks). This encouraged banks to borrow from the central bank so that they could increase their private lending.*
- *The third was to* reduce the reserve ratio requirements *for the private banks. Lower reserve requirements enabled the private banks to increase their lending.*

5
Five Pioneers

> *"Men often stumble over the truth, but most manage to pick themselves up and hurry off as if nothing had happened."*
>
> Winston Churchill

Charles Babbage was born in 1891, 18 years after the great railroad crash, in London[1]. In 1810 he entered Trinity College in Cambridge to study chemistry and mathematics. His favorite subject of the two was mathematics, and he soon realized that his understanding of this science was better than that of his tutors. Together with some friends he founded the "Analytical Society", which would, among other things, promote new developments in the study of mathematics.

Babbage found mathematics to be truly fascinating, but it also involved some routine work. One example was the tedious calculation of logarithm tables. There was only one way to do it: two men would calculate an entire table by hand, independently of each other. Then one would read up his figures, and the other check against his. One day at the University, Babbage was sitting with such a logarithm table in the Analytical Society room, when another member came to ask him what he was doing. Babbage looked up and answered that he was thinking of whether it was possible to make a machine that could do such calculations automatically.

COCKWHEELS, STEAM AND PUNCH-CARDS

That moment became decisive for the rest of his career. As soon as the idea had entered his mind, he began working on the project. Shortly after, he constructed a simple, mechanical device, which could facilitate the calculation of their tables. But while he had been working on this little machine, his mind had been wandering. Maybe, mankind could go much further? Maybe you could construct machines that could solve all kinds of mathematical questions, and thereby accelerate the development of human understanding? Maybe, mankind could even some day build machines that could *think*?

On 14 June 1822 he presented a paper entitled

> "Observations on the application of Machinery to the Computation of Mathematical Tables"

The paper described an advanced mathematical machine, which would be driven by a steam engine and a system of falling weights. The idea gathered considerable interest, and the following year the project commenced as the largest government-financed project in Great Britain. Babbage expected that he could have the machine finished within two to three years. That estimate turned out to be very wrong, however, because whenever his team of instrument makers had finished a part, Babbage had improved the design, and all the cockwheels had to be dismantled and the whole thing reconstructed. After 10 years like that, the project finally shipwrecked altogether, as his chief toolmaker quit.

Babbage's reaction to this defeat was remarkable. During the 10 years he had seen more and more clearly that computers would eventually be built, and that they would become crucial for science. In 1822 he had published a book entitled

> "On the Economy of Machinery and Manufacturers"

which is today considered a pioneering work in operations research. There was no doubt in his mind of the potentials of his idea, and instead of giving up, he now raised his ambitions even further and started designing a much more sophisticated machine, but this time only on paper. The new design was for a gigantic machine. Driven by six steam machines, it would be a programmable computer, that could receive instructions via punch-cards. It would be able to solve any arithmetic or logical calculation, and at the incredible speed of one calculation per second!

A FRENCH PHYSICIAN

When Charles Babbage embarked on this new project, Clement Juglar was only 24 years old, and still studying medicine at the University. Juglar was born in Paris on October 15, 1819, the son of a doctor from Basses-Alpes and a mother from Normandie[2]. Three years later he graduated as a doctor, but he could never concentrate entirely on this occupation; his interests were directed more towards questions of social and economic orientation, and especially the process of change in the economic environment. When he was 29, he began working with social studies, and two years later, he published a number of articles in the "Journal des Economists" about the fluctuations in the number of births, marriages, and deaths in France. The articles also investigated fluctuations in prosperity in France, and this was what later became his absorbing interest.

The year 1862 became an important one for both Charles Babbage and Clement Juglar. In that year, Babbage's first, simple calculation machine was displayed at London's Science Museum, where he spent much of his time telling the audience about his "computer", which was finished on the drawing-board, but still not built. In the same year Clement Juglar, who was then 43 years of age, published what became his conclusions regarding the courses of economic fluctuations:

> "Les Crises commerciales et leur retour périodique en France, en Angleterre et aux Etats Unis"

Although few took notice of this book at the beginning (maybe because of its title?), it was a revolution.

WHAT THE CLASSICAL ECONOMISTS MISSED

Clement Juglar had discovered something that the classical economists had missed[3]. The classical economists had found many traces of inherent instability, but also inherent factors which contributed to stability. They considered monetary factors such as money supply, interest rate and velocity of money, and real factors including random disturbances, investment, saving, (under)consumption and (over)production. And as practioners of business, they also remembered to include some surrealistic factors such as public confidence, folly and panic. But remarkably, none of these giants had attempted to hammer out a coherent, unifying theory to explain the business cycles. Why was that?

Because, amazingly, they hadn't discovered them. When you read their books and articles, you could find many references to "crises", but although Petty had used the term "cycle" in his "Treatise of Taxes and

Contributions" from 1662, none had realized that *this could be a phenomenon that could take place even if nothing happened to initiate it.* They had all considered booms and crises as caused by specific phenomena — by external shocks or mistakes. In some cases, as we saw with Mill, they had found phenomena which could lead from one excess to the opposite. But none of them had treated these phenomena as phases of a fundamental, wavelike movement inherent in a capitalist economy. And because they didn't see it that way, none of them had focused very much at the possibility of mapping and calculating the dynamics of a system.

Clement Juglar's new book was entirely different from the earlier literature written about crises. Juglar realized before anyone else, that the frequent crises were not simply a number of independent accidents, but a repeated, periodic manifestation of inherent instability in the economic organism. Having perceived this, he moved on to classify the different phases in this cyclic movement. He wrote of the "upgrade", the "explosion" and the "liquidation" phase. To classify these, he collected and analyzed statistical time series covering the longest possible time-spans. Studying these long time-periods, he believed he was able to identify an average duration of the cycle of nine to ten years. Clement Juglar expressed an understanding that the instability was inherent, when he wrote:

> "The only cause of depression is prosperity"

Depression did not happen, he thought, because something had gone wrong. *Depression came because something had gone too well.* This notion was in complete contrast to the dominant "mistake" view of the day; that crises occurred because of irresponsible issuance of paper money, the presence of monopolies, abuse of customs privileges, trade barriers, failures of harvests etc. No, crises came because of prosperity!

Juglar made two improved editions of his book and kept studying the business cycle problem throughout his life. He never contributed much more than his first book (and its later editions), but this was quite enough for one man.

It is often so in science, that important facts and concepts are described many times without the authors really understanding the significance of what they saw. Only when somebody realizes the full meaning of the events can we really say that it has been "discovered". Before Juglar's book, many had described elements of economic instability, but they had not understood the concept of cycles. After Clement Juglar, scientists would rarely say that they studied "crises". They would study "business cycles". As Schumpeter later would express it:

> "It was he who discovered the continent; several writers had discovered islands near it before"[4]

Even shortly before he died at the age of 86, you could still find Clement Juglar bent over his piles of statistics, curious to the end. Charles Babbage was also enthusiastic to his last days. After his exhibition in 1862, he returned to his project, and visitors in his last years found him still eager to show off his workroom. Like Juglar, he understood the full significance of his work, and to the end he believed that mankind would some day build his computer, and that it would eventually change the way economic science worked. What neither of the two thinkers could know, however, was that the machine Babbage had envisioned would become necessary if you should really understand of the phenomenon Juglar had discovered. Neither could they know that such machines would eventually reveal secrets about these cycles that were almost beyond belief.

Clement Juglar's main achievements

- *Juglar was the first to use time series such as interest rates, prices and central bank balances systematically and thoroughly to analyze a well-defined economic problem. This approach became standard for business cycle research and economics in general.*
- *He described the morphology of business cycles (their phases) in a way that was frequently used later.*
- *He was the first to understand clearly that depressions were adaptations to the situations created by the preceding prosperity.*

THE PLEASURE MACHINE

Charles Babbage's machines would be of little use to the economists if there were no relevant equations to feed them with. Someone had to start a process toward development of a coherent mathematical representation of economic behavior.

Enter Leon Walras. Walras was born in Normandy, France in 1834. His father was an economist, and Leon learned many things from him, including the basic principle that economics is about maximizing utility. After his school years he tried to enter Ecole Polytechnique, but failed twice before making it into Ecole des Mines instead.

Failing twice to enter a university is not a great start of an academic career, and it didn't look much better when he dropped out of Ecole des Mines. After leaving the school Walras began living a bohemian life in literature and journalism, teaching himself more economics along the way. At one point he wrote a romantic novel, at another he worked as a clerk at a railway, then as a journalist and then as a lecturer. And then he wrote two books about philosophy. In 1870 he applied for a teaching job at the first chair of Political Economy at the University of Lausanne. The line-up of candidates can't have been very impressive, because the board voted narrowly to allow this somewhat dubious character for the post.

THE ECONOMIC MACHINERY

Lausanne is located on hillsides facing Lake Geneva and with a breath-taking view to the Swiss and French Alps. Walras must have liked either the place or the job (or both), because he stayed in the same place and job for 22 years, and for the first time in his life he became successful. In 1874 he wrote an article about mathematical solutions to economic problems. "Principe d'une théorie mathématique de l'échange". He mailed an offprint of the article to Jevons, who wrote back asking if Walras was aware of some articles that Jevons himself had published on the subject. Walras responded that he had not been aware of these articles and that he would be happy to mention them in his writings so that the French-speaking audience could get to know them. Walras continued to develop his network of fellow economists which he corresponded with frequently. In 1889 he published the first version of his "Elements of Pure Economics", which he kept improving in new editions over a number of years. The book started with a description of pure and applied economics — a sort of state-of-the-art resumé. Then he continued to state that economics must be described in mathematical terms, where marginal analysis could be applied. This was followed by sections that provided detailed descriptions of how mathematical principles could be used to describe and analyze one economic problem after the other. His main approach was to describe a general equilibrium, a scenario where the activities of all market participants ("agents") add up to create a stable situation. Gradually, page by page, he guided the reader towards a complete model. Firstly he introduced a very simple scenario with just two agents exchanging goods in a barter economy. Then he added multi-party exchanges, then multi-product exchanges, then production and the markets for productive services, then saving, then capital formation, then money and finally credit. The whole construction was based on various simplifying assumptions, including that there was perfect competition, perfect mobility, and perfect price flexibility. He would under each scenario show how an equilibrium situation could be developed, although he did mention that several alternative equilibria were a possibility.

Walras' mathematical approach to economics reminded somewhat of the way that a physicist would model the behavior of a machine. This was no coincidence; Walras was enormously influenced by Newton and by the French mathematician Pierre-Simon de Laplace. He was also very inspired by a book of static mechanics by Louis Poinsot — in fact so much so that he kept the book by his bedside for several decades.

A machine will always work with a specific well-defined purpose, like making a wheel spin, or the spindle of a weaving machine move. The same applied for an economic machinery: it had to work towards well-defined goals. One of Walras' contemporary authors contributed to the definitions of these goals. His name was Francis Ysidro Edgeworth. Edgeworth was born in Ireland but didn't go to school — he was taught at home. He managed subsequently to enter university and became later on a lecturer at Trinity College in London. Edgeworth was not very highly regarded. There were two reasons for that. Firstly, he had a highly peculiar style of writing, filled with Greek quotes and references to classical literature (his publications were in fact so difficult to read that even other professional economists could have severe difficulties digesting them and understanding what they actually meant). Secondly, he tended to be so humble that the readers often didn't recognize him for the truly original thoughts that he sometimes introduced.

Edgeworth had noted that the people participating in the economic machinery were often supposed to be "rational men" trying to maximize individual "utility". Now, the problem was how to define this utility, and how to break it into its smallest possible units. In 1881 he proposed to define it in terms of "atoms of pleasure". These would not be easy to measure, though:

> "Atoms of pleasure are not easy to distinguish and discern; more continuous than sand, more discrete than liquid; as if it were nuclei of just-perceivable, embedded in circum-ambient semiconsciousness."

The purpose of the Walras' economic machine was, you may say, to maximize the production of atoms of pleasure.

Walras' successor

Walras was a pioneer — a person that inspired other people — so when he retired in 1892 it was important for the university to find a successor that would be able to follow in his footsteps and continue to inspire and lead the new movement. The university chose an Italian gentleman, Wilfredo Pareto, for this task. Pareto had been born in Paris but spent most of his life in Italy, where he graduated as an engineer. He chose a career in the railway industry, where he worked as engineer and later on as director of two companies. It was not until 1890, when he was 42 years of age, that he began studying economics before taking up Walras' previous chair in Lausanne in 1893. Pareto worked there for seven years before he inherited a fortune and decided to retire. However, he stayed in Switzerland and kept writing about economics until his death in 1923.

Pareto's great advantage was that he was an engineer by education and that he had a long technical work experience behind him. He had therefore a formidable knowledge of mathematics, which he applied constantly throughout his works. His disadvantage was that he, like Edgeworth, was a terrible writer, with a writing style that resembled that of a very intelligent man that is very drunk. He would often state a lot of half theories at the same time on the same page, then move on to something else only to finish the thoughts much later in the text.

Pareto's name is used very frequently in modern times when economists refer to "Pareto optimum" or "Pareto equilibrium" as the state of an economic system where it produces the largest possible number of Edgewood's atoms of pleasure. The methodogies that he and Walras developed would be used again and again as the first business cycle theories would be developed.

The First Business Cycle Theories

"Let every student of nature take this as his rule, that whatever the mind seizes upon with particular satisfaction is to be held in suspicion."

Francis Bacon

6
The Archaeologists

> *"For well over a century, business cycles have run an unceasing round. They have persisted through vast economic and social changes; they have withstood countless experiments in industry, agriculture, banking, industrial relations, and public policy; they have confounded forecasters without number, belied repeated prophecies of a "new era of prosperity" and outlived repeated forebodings of "chronic depression."*
>
> Arthur F. Burns

It was in the year 1876, 14 years after the publication of Juglar's book, and five years after Charles Babbage's death that Ricardo's and Mill's old "Political Economy Club" held a centenary celebration of "the Foundation of Economic Science"[1]. Chairing this meeting was Mr. Gladstone, with Mr. Lowe on one side and the French Minister of Finance Mr. Leon Say on the other. After the usual extravagant dinner, Mr. Lowe stood up to give the first presentation. The message in his speech was that he did not feel that the future of political economy would have that much to offer:

> "… at present, so far as my own humble opinion goes, I am not sanguine as to any very large or any very startling development in political economy."

He thought that improvements from sociology might contribute a bit to furthering political economy, but not much. The developments in this science had culminated:

> "The controversies which we now have in political economy, although they offer a capital exercise for the local faculties, are not of the

> same thrilling importance as those of earlier days; the great work has been done".

So was indeed the spirit of English Economic Science at the time. Since the culmination of Classical Economics, many small steps forward had been taken, but few that seemed big. Apparently, all the important theories had already been developed. If the speaker knew about the early thoughts of such pioneers as Babbage and Juglar, it hadn't made much of an impression on him.

A MATHEMATICIAN AT CAMBRIDGE

In the year of that speech Alfred Marshall was 34 years of age and working as a teacher of Moral Sciences at Cambridge University. Marshall was a mathematician by education and had originally gone to Cambridge to teach just that. He was interested in many other things, however, and not the least in how to find a cure for poverty. But as he began to propose his own solutions to this problem, he was ridiculed by his colleagues and friends. "He had no business discussing this subject …", they said, "… unless he had some basic training in business or political economy." So reluctantly he decided to study some of the basic books about economy. At first he read John Stuart Mill's "Principles", and afterwards a number of other books, including Ricardo. The way he studied these books was peculiar: he sought to identify all the logical postulates in them and then expressed these in mathematical equations. Soon he was hooked; unable to leave a subject which at first he had only intended to touch upon briefly. This was a beginning of a career, the results of which would later put the words in Mr. Lowe's speech to shame.

In 1879, Marshall started to write his own book, which was published 11 years later with the title "Principles of Economics". Although he used his mathematics as a shorthand language to condense and to clarify, he subsequently translated everything into common English. "Principles of Economics" gained fame mainly for its introduction of new marginalities concepts, but it also contained a theory about the business cycle. This theory was primarily based on the effects of price-fluctuations:

> "For when prices are likely to rise, people rush to borrow money and buy goods and thus help prices to rise; business is inflated and is

> managed recklessly and wastefully; those working on borrowed capital pay back less real capital than they borrowed, and enrich themselves at the expense of the community. When afterwards credit is shaken and prices begin to fall, everyone wants to get rid of commodities and get hold of money which is rapidly rising in value; this makes credit fall all the faster, and the further fall makes credit shrink even more; and thus for a long time prices fall because prices have been falling."

As he claimed that prices can "fall because prices have been falling", it is clear that he was aware of the presence of positive feed-back processes. In his "Money, Credit and Commerce", he described a similar process on the stock exchange, which took place when prices were beginning to fall:

> "Some speculators have to sell goods in order to pay their debts; and by so doing they check the rise of prices. This check makes all other speculators anxious, and they rush in to sell."

One reason that Marshall laid so much emphasis on the price element could be that price changes were the only variable which could be firmly related to business cycles; statistics were not very good in those days, and the business cycle research was in need of more hard facts.

NEW PIECES OF THE PUZZLE

Marshall was one of the first economists to provide theories about business cycles, or "trade cycles" as they were often called at the time. Some of the other pioneers were Arthur Pigou, Dennis Robertson and Ralph Hawtrey.

PIGOU: CYCLES DRIVEN BY PSYCHOLOGY

Few people ended up admiring Marshall as much as Arthur Cecil Pigou. Pigou was born in The Isle of Wight in 1877, the son of a retired army officer. He managed to obtain a scholarship at a prestigious public school, and after that at Cambridge University, which he entered in 1896 (age 19). He was a talented student, and the University offered him consequently a teaching post after his graduation. Pigou became a good teacher — rather brilliant, in fact — and he was highly productive (he published no fewer than three books during his first five years in the job). His main source of inspiration was Marshall, who held a chair in Economics at the same University, and he would often say to his students that "it is all in Marshall". Marshall was getting old, though, and announced his retirement in 1908. This was Pigou's chance: he knew that he was still rather young and unproven, but perhaps he could take over the chair?

His dreams were fulfilled: at the age of 30 he had taken over the prestigious job from the grand master! He continued to write, and while his first three books in all honesty weren't terribly exciting, many of those that followed were. One of his best contributions was "Industrial Fluctuations", which was published in 1929. In this book he linked business cycles to shocks caused by real factors, as well as to psychological and autonomous economic factors. He argued that errors of optimism create subsequent errors of pessimism and he pointed out that bankruptcies rarely destroy capital (capital equipment is merely taken over by new players when a company goes down), but that they create *fear*, and that this was the important effect. Capital changes hands, but the willingness to invest in new capital was reduced when people saw capital change hands through bankruptcies.

He did not believe fully in the notion that an invisible hand would restore a balance in a distressed economy. An example of the problem was that changes in price levels often took place during the different phases of the business cycles. The consequence of those changes could be that conditions no longer were the way that it had been expected when businessmen had originally entered into contracts. Price changes created windfall gains for some and losses for others, and this would again create further changes in expectations. An alternative problem occurred if prices were kept too rigid because businessmen had an interest in maintaining things the way they were planned to be. This rigidity could prevent markets from clearing (preventing trade from taking place in a smooth manner).

Pigou tried to estimate quantitatively the significant factors causing business cycles and their amplitudes. Here is how much he thought that each factor contributed to the overall cycle:

- Crop variations: one-half
- Wage rigidity: one-eighth
- Price rigidity: one-sixteenth

He proposed various measures that could restore balance in the markets when needed. One of his suggestions was that governments could provide more and better economic information in order to prevent collective misjudgments by businessmen. He also believed that stabilization of prices was a key factor in reduction of business fluctuations, and he thought that an efficient monetary policy would be the most effective tool for reducing business fluctuations.

One of the people that Pigou met at Cambridge University was another talented economist by the name of John Maynard Keynes. What Pigou couldn't know was that this colleague of his would later on misrepresent what Pigou had advocated, then ridicule it, and at the same time steal some of his best ideas (Keynes created the impression that Pigou suggested that salary reductions should be used as a leading remedy for depression and that Pigou ignored the role of expectations in creating unemployment. This was in fact not true. Furthermore, Pigou had described a number of concepts that Keynes later on launched again — more successfully).

ROBERTSON: FOCUS ON CAPITAL INVESTMENTS

One of the people at Cambridge University that had the pleasure of working with both Pigou and Keynes was a young student called Dennis Holme Robertson. Robertson was born in 1890 in Lowestoft and had gone to Eton at the age of 12 and from there to Trinity College at Cambridge to study classics. He had been absolutely brilliant in these studies but had never the less decided to switch to economics after a while. He was taught by Pigou and had the seven-year-older Keynes as his tutor. Robertson gained a close friendship with Keynes that would last until the 1930s, where they began to disagree severely.

Robertson published his first book, "A Study of Industrial Fluctuations" in 1915 and followed up with "Money" in 1922 and "Banking Policy and the Price Level" in 1926. His first book was a major contribution to business cycle literature. One of the main suggestions in the book was that the chief cause of economic instability was changing demand for capital goods. He described the following scenario:

- Capital investments increased because of the need for replacement or because of innovations …
- The new capital would then lead to increased return on investments …
- And this would often not be matched by a similar increase in actual interest rates.

- The result would be a cumulative expansion that was much larger than the initial impulse.

These ideas were different from what many other authors focused on since they took capital investments as their basic focal point. Robertson didn't see monetary policy as the typical culprit. It was typically changes in the *natural rate,* caused by innovations and waves of replacement re-investments, that caused the discrepancy and the instability. He regarded the economy as basically unstable with instability intensified by changes in money supply and velocity of money.

While Marshall and Pigou were well-known capacities on business cycles during the first decades of the century, it was in fact Dennis Holme Robertson that many viewed as the greatest maestro. He was considered the leading authority on the subject of business cycles for half a century.

HAWTREY: A MONETARY VIEW

Ralph George Hawtrey, who was two years older than Pigou, provided other contributions to the understanding of business cycles. Having gained his insights not so much from reading and teaching, but from working in the City of London and in the English Treasury (where he served from 1904 to 1947), it is perhaps hardly surprising that he was very interested in monetary matters and their effect on business cycles. He published his first book about the subject in 1913, nine years after he had joined the Treasury. "Good and Bad Trade", as the book was called, essentially attributed business cycles to fluctuations in money supply. The frequent business cycles could, according to Hawtrey, evolve in two different ways:

- *External shocks.* An external shock could create accumulated economic fluctuations in the aggregate economy as the initial impact in one sector could create secondary effects in other sectors through the exchange of money between individuals and businesses. However, these fluctuations would be dampened and thus disappear some time after the initial shock had ended.
- *Inherent monetary instability.* Hawtrey believed that the monetary system was inherently unstable. There would at any given time exist a theoretical lending rate that would keep the economy more or less stable, if applied. However, what could easily happen was

> that the bank lending rates were lower than the "profit rate". This would create a vicious spiral that would drive the two rates further and further away from each other.

Hawtrey's explanation of the monetary instability was largely related to the role of bank reserves. Financial regulation required any bank to have financial reserves that were in a given proportion to its total exposure balance. Economic booms created confidence and increased investment activities, which meant that banks tended to lend out more aggressively. However, at a certain stage they would reach a point where they were close to the ceiling of lending that they were allowed to do given their limited reserves. When they reached that stage they would begin to increase interest rates so that they would attract more deposits and reduce the lending activity. This would eventually force industry to decrease stocks and production. However, it would take some time for them to adjust to the new situation, and the banks would thus continue to increase rates for some time. This meant that bank rates would drift further and further away from the lower rates that would have created stability.

One of the situations that Hawtrey was most concerned about was what he called a "credit deadlock". A credit deadlock occurred when the reduction of interest rates didn't seem to stimulate any lending. Such a situation could arise when an excessively restrictive credit policy had killed enterprise. The only thing to do in such a situation was to stimulate money supply through any means.

Hawtrey was very highly regarded as a leading capacity on business cycles and monetary policy during the 1920s, but he had one problem in common with Marshall, Pigou and Robertson: they needed more facts. More facts were needed in order to judge who provided the most realistic theories.

MAPPING THE PROBLEM

Exactly what the facts were was what interested the American economist Wesley Mitchell the most. Mitchell studied the newly discovered business cycle phenomenon as an archaeologist would study the layers in a kitchen midden: he measured them, noted down every detail he could find, and looked for clues, traces and patterns. According to his friend Schumpeter, Mitchell read a lot and was quite familiar with the various theories about what could drive the cycles, but his primary concern was not so much that of understanding them as it was of mapping them[2]. "If you don't know how they behave ...", he seemed to think, "... how can you know what there is to explain?" In 1913, he published his first book about the subject, "Business Cycles". The book started with a short description of the prevailing business cycle theories. He did that, as Schumpeter later described it, with "surprising detachment", almost as if he believed that any one of the theories might be as good as every other. Mitchell defined business cycles in the following way:

> "Business cycles are a type of fluctuation found in the aggregate economic activity of nations that organise their work mainly in business enterprises: a cycle consists of expansions occurring about the same time in many economic activities, followed by similar general recessions, contractions, and revivals which merge into the expansion phase of the next cycle; this sequence of changes is recurrent but not periodic; in duration, business cycles vary from, more than one year to ten or twelve years; they are not divisible into shorter cycles of similar character with amplitudes approximating their own."[3]

This definition contained two points of special importance. The first was that *oscillations are in aggregates*. Whatever drove the cycle, it seemed to influence the economy on a very broad scale. The second point was that *cycles are not periodic*. He repeated this important observation over and over again, fearing that people would exaggerate the regularity of the swings.

FORECASTING TOOLS

In 1920, Mitchell cofounded the National Bureau of Economic Research, NBER, an institution for international business cycle research, in New York. Here he came to work closely with Arthur Burns, who later became director of research of NBER, its president and, after Mitchell's death, its chairman[4]. Mitchell was often criticized for his "naive empiricism", but as years passed, people gained more and more respect for his team, and eventually NBER became an internationally respected center for business cycle research (which it still is)[5].

The scientists at NBER soon discovered that many economic and financial indicators could be grouped as "leading" the cycle, others as "coincident" with it, and still others as "lagging" the cycle. A leading indicator, for instance, would tend to rise somewhat before general activity picked up — and fall somewhat before activity leveled off. These indicators stood the test of time: They remained reliable after they had been established. One surprising feature of the system was that lagging indicators turned out to be useful for economic forecasting[6].

CONFLICTING RESULTS?

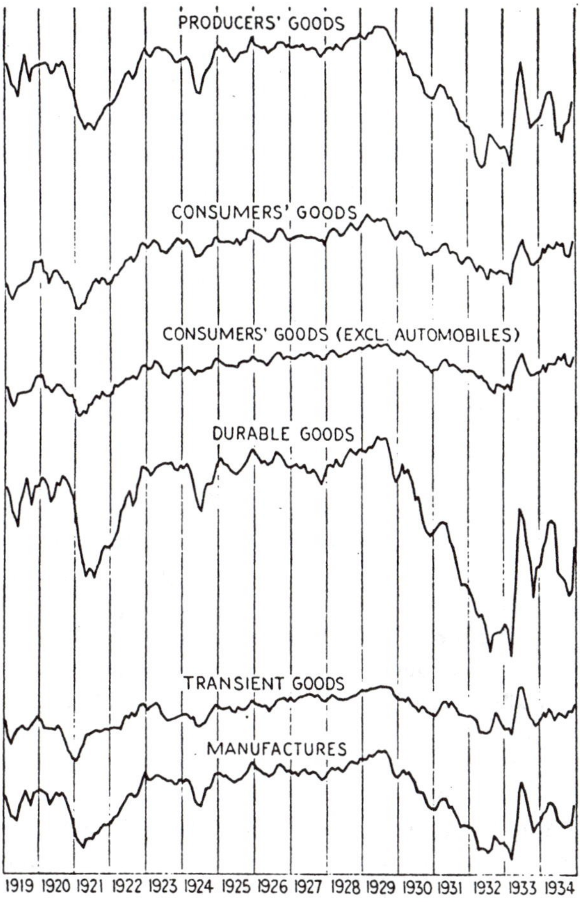

Figure 6.1: Production of producer and consumer goods.
The staff at NBER found that the production of producer goods was more pro-cyclic and more volatile than the production of consumer goods. Source: Mitchell, 1951.

The Americans were not the only ones trying to map the cycles. In 1923, the German scientist Joseph Kitchin published an article with analysis of English and American data covering 31 years. Kitchin found a cycle in them, but there was something funny about it: their wavelength was different from Juglar's — very different, in fact. Kitchin found an average duration of 40 months — little over 3 years — for the cycles: less than half of what Juglar had observed. Kitchin did not discuss this difference in his presentation, but the results were important. One possible explanation was, that the behavior of the economy had changed. Another was more dramatic: *Maybe there were several cyclical phenomena in action ....*

And this was where Simon Kuznets entered the story[7]. If Mitchell collected many figures, Kuznets collected even more. Kuznets was a pupil of Mitchell and did much of his work under the auspices of NBER. Kuznets would publish brick-sized books containing hundreds of tables and graphs covering such fascinating subjects as:

"Number of patents issued for typewriters in the United States", or

"Crude Zink Production, Belgium", or

"Tonnage of Freight Moved on the Eire Canal".

No stone was left unturned. One of his major works was the measurement of national income. Such a figure is almost taken for granted these days, but to calculate it for the first time was something of a nightmare. Kuznets did it, however, and without these figures, many theories developed in the following years would have been impossible to verify. But having developed a method to calculate national income, he turned to its oscillations. There he found a cycle, and he was able to substantiate its presence with much more thorough research than Juglar or Kitchin had used. But the funny thing happened once again: Kuznets' cycle had a wave-length of neither 40 months, nor 10 years. His cycle had an average duration of some 20 years. Very strange!

When the staff at the NBER investigated the different time-series, they found a clue to Kuznets' as well as a Kitchin's phenomenon: *There was very strong correlation between Kitchin and inventory fluctuations, and between Kuznets and capital investment fluctuations.* So it really seemed to be several distinct cycles ...

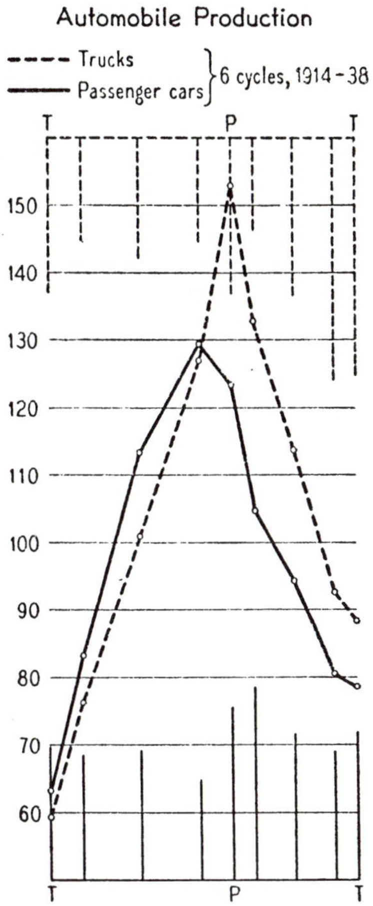

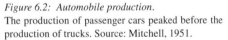

Figure 6.2: Automobile production.
The production of passenger cars peaked before the production of trucks. Source: Mitchell, 1951.

GIANTS AS WELL?

Just as an ant crossing your shoes is hardly aware that it is walking on somebody else, so can human beings be part of something that they do not see because of its size. It was in 1910 that an 18-year-old student in Russia thought he had found such a phenomenon. Nikolai Kondratieff had studied the behavior of capitalist economy and believed he saw an oscillation in the economy of extremely low frequency — with a wavelength of more than 50 years. Nine years later, he began a scientific study

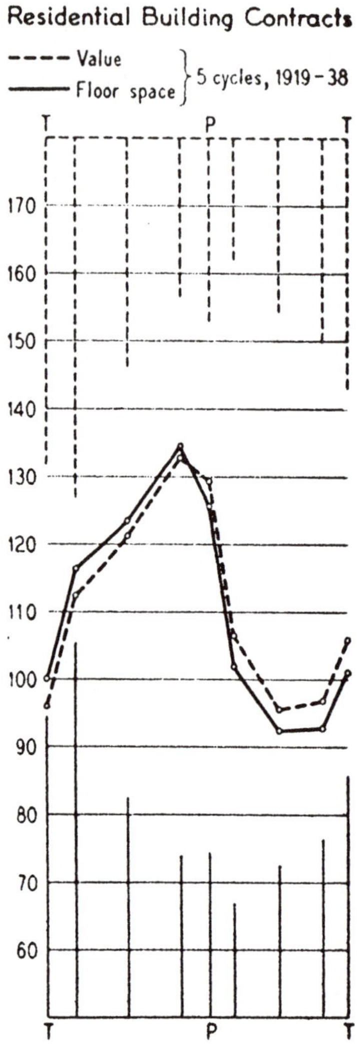

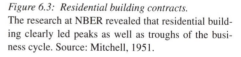

Figure 6.3: Residential building contracts.
The research at NBER revealed that residential building clearly led peaks as well as troughs of the business cycle. Source: Mitchell, 1951.

of the phenomenon[8]. In 1924, he completed an 80-page report, in which he concluded that capitalist economy had gone through two "long waves" with an average duration of 53.3 years — and was well into the third. In 1926, he published his results in the German "Archiv fur Sozialwissenshaft", in which he concluded:

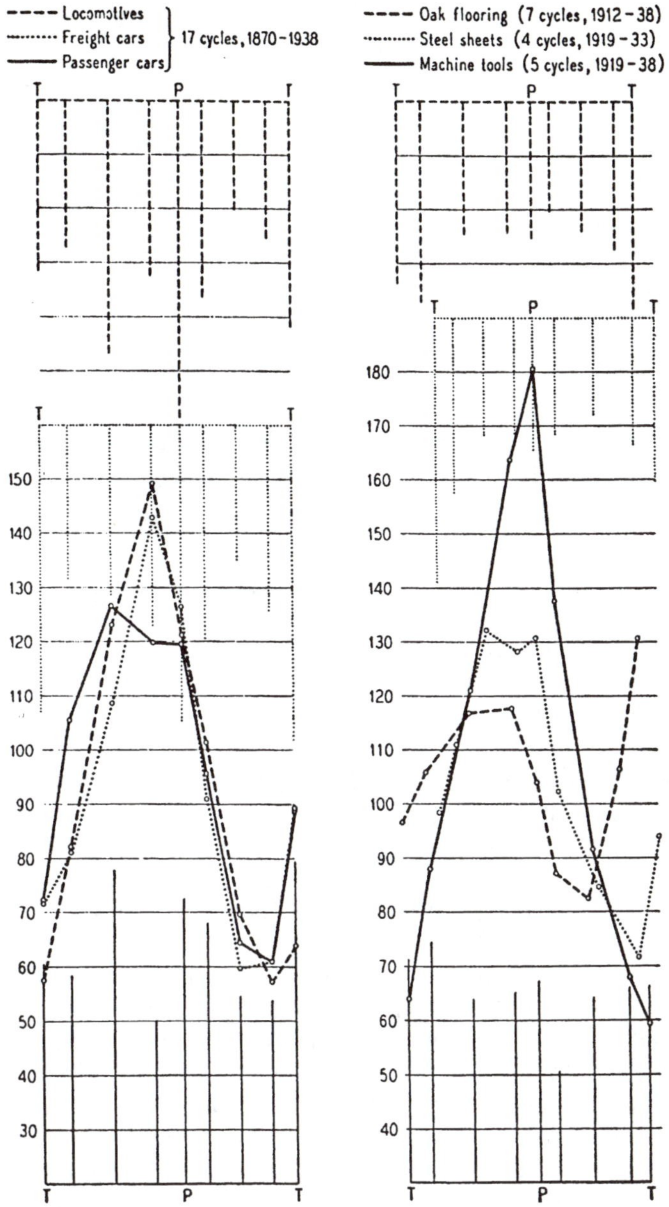

Figure 6.4: New orders for durable goods.
One of the most reliable leaders of the business cycle in NBER's research was orders for plants and equipment. Source: Mitchell, 1951.

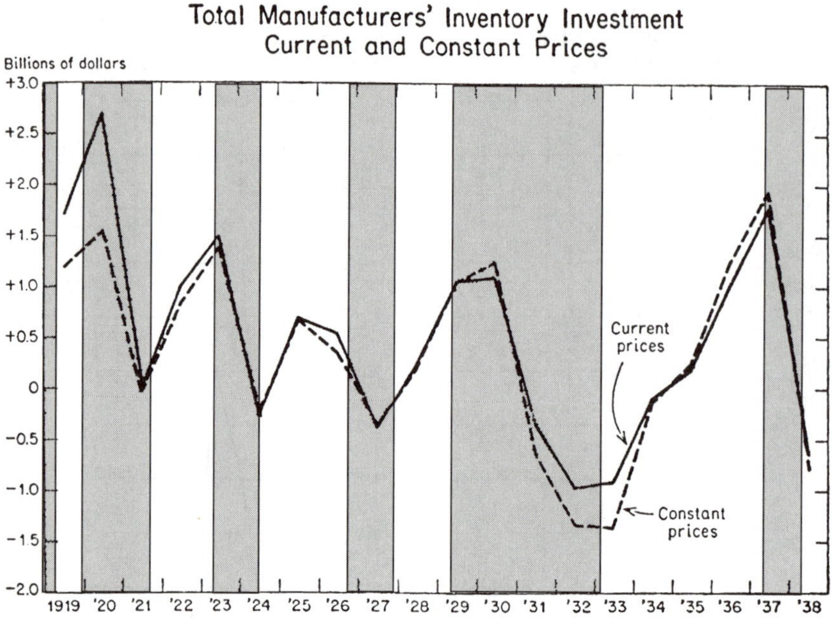

Figure 6.5: Total manufacturers' inventory investment.
This graph illustrates how fluctuations in inventory levels correlate with business cycles (the dark areas are recessions). Source: Abramovitz, 1950.

> "... the movements of the series which we have examined running from the end of the eighteenth century to the present time show long cycles. Although the statistical-mathematical treatment of the series selected is rather complicated, the cycles discovered cannot be regarded as the accidental result of the methods employed".

He had examined a number of time-series, of which many conformed to the cycle-theory, some did not, and one was counter cyclical[9]. The first cycle had started, you might say, on the hillsides in Adam Smith's Scotland. This giant cycle was fostered by the innovations of the industrial revolution; by the steam engines, waterframes and power looms[10]. The second came out of the railroad boom which started in 1843 and ended with Jay Gould's bear-raids in 1887. The third was ignited by the construction of electrical power plants, and later reinforced by the automobile-, steel-, glass-, road-, and textile industries. It started in 1893 and was supposedly nearing its culmination when Kondratieff printed his article in 1926.

Kondratieff explained the oscillations with over investment in capital, which would lead to a glut, then a recession, until the invention of new technology eventually led to a new spurt of investment. However, the invention of new technology was not the sole driving force of the upswing; it was merely the trigger:

> "If we are to form an idea as to the quantitative adequacy of innovation, we must bear in mind that all it should, according to our schema, be adequate for, is ignition."

The conditions for such an ignition to lead to a take-off were, he said, the following:

- High propensity to save
- Relatively large supply of liquid loan capital at low rates
- Accumulation of these funds in the hands of powerful entrepreneurial and financial groups
- A low price level

Kondratieff's theory was received with reservations by the economists in NBER. It was in fact possible to explain theoretically how "self-ordering" in the capital sector (that the capital sector depends on its own output to expand its production capacity) could lead to such an oscillation, but the critics were hardly being unreasonable when they claimed that two cycles and the alleged fraction of a third was a very meager evidence for a theory. On this basis, they claimed, you could neither prove nor refute the long cycle[11].

THE RIGHT THING, THE WRONG PLACE …

Juglar discovered the continent and Mitchell, Burns, Kitchin, Kuznets and Kondratieff did much of the pioneer work of mapping it. Mitchell became honored and respected for his books and for the institution he built; Juglar, Kitchin, Kuznets and Kondratieff all had their cycles named after them, and two of these cycles, Kitchin's and Kuznets', are today regarded as proven facts by most economists. Burns was appointed Chairman of the Board of Governors of the Federal Reserve System in 1969. And Kuznets was given the Nobel Prize in 1971.

But Kondratieff was less fortunate. He had been considered suspicious by the communists after he opposed elements of the Soviet 5-year plans. The conflict reached a critical stage when he wrote a rather unfortunate remark:

> "… each consecutive phase is the result of the cumulative process during the preceding phase, and as long as the principles of the capitalist economy are conserved, each new cycle follows its predecessor with the same regularity with which the different phases succeed each other."[12]

You could easily interpret this as a suggestion that capitalism would stay alive. This was in contrast to what Karl Marx had written in his "Das Kapital" from 1867–94, which predicted that each new crisis would become more severe until eventually the system would collapse altogether, paving the way for a communist take-over. Nikolai Kondratieff was sent to a working camp in Siberia where he stayed until his death. His theory was later described in the Soviet encyclopedia as follows:

> "Theory of long cycles, one of the vulgar bourgeois theories of crises and economic cycles …"[13]

Metzler and Abramovitz on inventory cycles

Lloyd Appleton Metzler is known for descriptions of the effects of inventory fluctuations on inventory cycles. Key factors in his models were the companies' failure to forecast the cycle correctly. His most famous contribution was "The Nature and Stability of Inventory Cycles", which was published in Review of Economic Studies in 1941.

Another great contributor on this and many other issues was Moses Abramovitz, who worked as a scientist at the NBER on the movements of inventories and their different components over the business cycle. He showed that shifts in inventories tended to be very significant, in particular over the shorter cycles. His most important contribution about inventories is perhaps his "Inventories and the Business Cycles" from NBER in 1950.

Some essentials of business cycles

- *Business cycles have been evident throughout the history of capitalist economy.*
- *They are very much alike in industrialized countries. Indeed, it has been shown that identical indicators are efficient forecasters in all major, industrial countries.*
- *Their behavior has not changed much over history.*
- *There are a very large number of processes responsible for business cycles.*
- *Many of the human processes contributing to business cycles are rational, seen from the individual's point of view.*
- *Involved phenomena tend to work in concert and according to a fairly regular sequence (but not frequency).*
- *There are at any given time several cycles of different duration at work. The archetypes are the "Kitchin", "Kuznets" and "Kondratieff" cycles, although more oscillations are present. The short "Kitchin" seems especially correlated to fluctuations in inventories. The longer "Kuznets" has high correlation to credit and capital investment. However it is not yet possible to prove statistically that the Kondratieff cycle really exists.*
- *None of the cycles are periodic. While impulses are important in deciding amplitude, the duration of a cycle is closely related to its propagation mechanism. The duration of one cycle is not correlated with the duration of the next in any reasonably predictable way.*
- *Prices and production of durable goods are more volatile than of non-durables, whether it be goods for industry or for private consumption.*
- *Profits, prices, inventories, short interest rates, quantity of money and velocity of money are very strongly pro-cyclical.*
- *Business profits fluctuate much more than income, inventories much more than sales and short interest rates much more than long rates.*
- *The amplitudes of the cycles are very irregular, but if several of these oscillations reach their trough at the same time (and there are inherent processes that make that likely), then you risk a major depression. This is apparently what happened in 1825–30, 1873–78, 1929–1938, and in the early 1990s. Amplitude is also highly influenced by impulses (external shocks).*

7
Fisher, Babson and the Quantity Theory of Money

"The first panacea for a mismanaged nation is inflation of the currency; the second is war. Both bring a temporary prosperity; both bring permanent ruin."

Ernest Hemingway

What a message to get! He was only 31 years old, healthy and strong to this date, a talented mathematician educated at Yale, happily married, and at the beginning of what looked like a promising career. And now the doctor had told him that he suffered from Tuberculosis, a diagnosis that was virtually identical to a death sentence. Was Irwin Fisher's life to end before it had really begun?[1]

Fisher took up the battle and commenced on the only known cure: fresh air and healthy living. He moved to Colorado, where many patients were seeking a cure for the same disease. Among these people was an interesting individual: the 22-year-old engineer Rodger Ward Babson. Fisher and Babson soon realized that they had much in common. Both were fascinated by economics, and especially by the business cycle problem and the role of the monetary sector. They were both absorbed with the stock market and its calamities. And they were both creative characters, with an urge to advise people about all kinds of problems. It was symptomatic that they both created an invention to facilitate the treatment of their common disease. Fisher designed a small tent for Tuberculosis patients, for which he was later given a reward by the New York Medical Society. Babson's invention was an electrically heated coat and some small rubber hammers.

AN UNUSUAL OFFICE

Babson decided that there was no reason why he shouldn't work while he was taking his fresh air cure. He hired a secretary and set up an open air office, where he would analyze business cycles and their consequences for the stock market. Soon you could see the energetic young man working in the cold air, wearing his heated coat, while the secretary, wearing mittens, pounded on the typewriter with the small rubber hammers. Gradually he recovered from the disease, and could eventually return to more traditional surroundings. In 1910 he published his first version of a book about business cycles, "Business Barometers used in the Accumulation of Money". This book contained a thorough analysis of historical crises, and his main thesis was that excessive investment and increase of the money supply would always lead to a counter reaction. The purpose of the book was, as the title hinted, to advise stock market speculators. In this advice, he laid great emphasis on his standard 10 phase business cycle model:

Phase 1: Increasing money rates
Phase 2: Declining bond prices
Phase 3: Declining stock prices
Phase 4: Declining commodity prices
Phase 5: Declining real estate prices
Phase 6: Low money rates
Phase 7: Increasing bond prices
Phase 8: Increasing stock prices
Phase 9: Increasing commodity prices
Phase 10: Increasing real estate prices

Babson's book became an immediate best-seller, and it supported his sales of various investment newsletters. These newsletters were based on his business cycle model, the "Swing-charts", which measured a number of economic indicators. His method was in essence quite simple: he estimated the long term growth trend and calculated accumulated deviations around this. Every deviation in one direction would be compensated by a deviation of similar magnitude in the opposite direction. To him, business cycle analysis became a considerable source of income.

IRWIN FISHER'S EARLY WORKS

Almost miraculously, Irwin Fisher also recovered gradually from the disease, and in 1901 he was declared completely cured. Fisher chose a more academic career than Babson. During the first years of his illness, he had still considered himself a mathematician, and it was not until the year 1911, when he was searching for a subject for a doctoral thesis, that his favorite professor, William Sumner, asked him:

"Why don't you write on mathematical economics?"

Fisher answered:

"I have never heard of such a subject."

Sumner explained the concept, and Fisher decided to pursue this particular discipline. In 1911, the year after Babson had published his "Business Barometers", Fisher published the book entitled "The Purchasing Power of Money". The main theme was the destabilizing effects of inflation and fluctuations in money supply. The book contained a popularization of a small equation that Simon Newcomb had described in 1885:

$$MV = PQ,$$

where

M = money supply
V = velocity of money
P = prices of goods
Q = quantity of goods

This was called "The Quantity Theory of Money". Fisher's main thesis was, as he expressed it, that "the levels of prices varies in direct proportion with the quantity of money in circulation, provided that the velocity of money and the volume of trade which it is obliged to perform are not changed."

What his monetary business cycle theory stated was that *increase in the money supply would first lead to a fall in inflation-adjusted interest rates, stimulating growth in the quantity of goods produced (which is nice), and later to rise in inflation and then in real interest rates (which is unpleasant). A large growth in the money supply would, in other words, first have pleasant effects, but then some nasty ones.*

One of the basic conceptions which preceded these theories was a new understanding of what banks really did. Until the end of the 19th century most economists had tended to view banks as merely traders in money.

They would receive deposits and lend to somebody else; money would simply change hands. But now the economists realized that behind the respectable walls of these institutions, something else happened; something vitally important that was largely beyond the control of governments or central banks. *The banks did not only trade money. They created it.*

Keeping this in mind, one of the key elements of Fisher's business cycle theory could be expressed largely as follows:

- The key to business cycles is bank credit, as it is the banks that create money in a modern economy.
- During the beginning of a growth period, sellers see their stock of inventories diminish, so they order more.
- This leads to a general increase of production, which according to Say's law stimulates demand further …
- … and this means, that in spite of increased orders, inventories don't rise, so for a time the merchants keep ordering still more. As producers have trouble filling this increased demand, deliveries may even be rationed, encouraging sellers to order more than they really want. During all this time, the quantity of money expands as banks supply credit for the increased business activity. The initial effect of this expansion of money supply is a fall in the discount rate, which leads to further rise in the activity.
- As some of the banks increase their lending, it increases the reserves at other banks (bond prices go up, people deposit more money), stimulating a tendency for them to increase lending too. At the same time, velocity of money accelerates as business starts to use idle reserves.
- But Say's law is not a perpetual mobile. Some of the additional income generated by increased supply is saved up. At this point, sellers will finally see their inventories up at normal level and will reduce orders accordingly …
- … which means that now they can start paying back their debts to the bank. As they do that, money supply starts to shrink in a cumulative process which eventually leads to a slump.
- As money supply shrinks, the prices of assets such as real estate etc., but also inventories, start falling, and as the liquidation of debts can't keep up with the fall of prices, liquidation defeats itself. This means that *the very effort of individuals to lessen their*

> *debts actually increases it*, because of the mass effect of the stampede to liquidate in swelling each dollar owed.

So the monetary system was unstable, as he expressed it:

> "*The more debtors pay, the more they owe*. The more the economic boat tips, the more it tends to tip".

If you would stabilize the economy (expressed as Q), he thought, then you should first and foremost focus on stabilizing the prices (P):

> "... it is always economically possible to stop or prevent such a depression simply by reflating the price level up to the average level at which outstanding debts were contracted, and then maintain that level unchanged."

But in order to do this, you needed methods for measuring the inflation. As nobody else had developed such methods, Fisher decided to do it himself. In 1922 he published a long and boring book about the subject, "The Making of Index Numbers", which to his own great surprise became a best-seller.

THE STABLE MONEY LEAGUE

In 1920 he published "Stabilizing the Dollar" and asked the publisher to insert a postcard in each copy with a request that the reader return it in case he was interested in the formation of an organization devoted to stabilization of prices and money supply. On New Year's Eve the same year he held a dinner for 254 people (Irwin Fisher had style), where he could announce that he had names of about 1,000 persons interested in the project. The decision to form the "Stable Money League" was subsequently made. Stabilization of prices could obviously be achieved through various methods, e.g. by making money convertible to metal (David Ricardo's philosophy), or stabilizing the quantity of money via central bank operations (Henry Thornton's philosophy). Another and less conventional method, which some of the League members preferred, was the "Compensated Dollar Plan", a system where the dollar should be revalued by 1% every time prices had risen 1%, and devalued by 1% whenever prices had fallen by 1%.

The Pigou effect versus the Debt-deflation theory

Prices tend to fall during depression. So does this make the depression worse, or does it contribute to the final turning point and subsequent recovery? Two important theories show two opposite (but not conflicting) effects. One is the "Pigou Effect" and the other is the "Debt-deflation Theory".

The Pigou Effect is named after Arthur Cecil Pigou, who in his article "The Classical Stationary State" from 1943 described how falling prices may help the economy to get out of a recession or depression. What he noted was that falling prices mean that whatever people have saved up will gradually represent more and more purchasing power. Sooner or later they will feel so safe (or wealthy) that they can start spending more (even though some might postpone spending for some time in anticipation of further price falls). Furthermore, the amount of products that need to be produced when they loose their purse has increased since unit prices have fallen.

The "debt-deflation theory" points in another direction. It claims that falling prices create a credit squeeze for producers. What happens is simple: companies have borrowed during the upswing to invest in business enterprises. However, during the economic downturn the prices of their output and assets begin to fall, and the nominal value of their debt increases. Thorstein Weblen touched on this phenomenon briefly in his book "The Theory of Business Enterprise" from 1904, but it was Irwin Fisher who brought it to wide attention as he made it central to his explanation of the depression of the 1930s. He substantiated this postulate by calculating that nominal debts had been reduced by 20% from 1929 to 1933 (where it was virtually impossible to lend any money). However, during the same period the real value of the dept had actually increased by 40%! So people and companies paid back parts of their debt and became more indebted anyway. Fisher even suggested that a great depression would be unlikely if the debt-depression phenomenon was not in force: "if debt and deflation are absent, other disturbances are powerless to bring on crises comparable in severity of those of 1837, 1873, or 1929–33" (Fisher, 1933). Hyman Minsky has later incorporated the Debt-deflation theory into his theories of financial instability, which Kindleberger has applied to his financial history.

So which of the theories is most important? Firstly, it depends of course on the initial conditions. The debt-deflation theory is, for instance, obviously most relevant when initial debt levels are high. James Tobin published in 1980 an analysis of the combined phenomenon where he proposed that Fisher's negative debt-deflation effect typically would be much larger than Pigou's positive effect. The main reason was people and companies who borrowed obviously must have had a larger propensity to spend than people/companies who saved. The combined effects would increase the purchasing power for those who had saved while reducing it for those who had borrowed. However, since the net savers didn't tend to spend much they wouldn't react much to the change (except by saving even more). The borrowers, on the other hand, would be forced to reduce their spending proportionally. Many modern econometric models that have both Fisher's and Pigou's effects built into their equations tend to show a fast return to natural output levels after a small shock. However, larger shocks will trigger a debt deflation spiral.

A TOUR TO EUROPE

In 1922 Fisher left for Europe to lecture on "Business Depressions and Instability of Money" at the London School of Economics, and incidentally to study some very strange developments, which were taking place in the German economy[2]. Before the First World War, the German economy had been among the strongest in the world, and the Deutschmark had been steady on the foreign exchange markets. The mark had been backed one-third by gold and two-thirds by commercial papers/T-bills issued by the state and by credit worthy companies and individuals. If, for instance, the state wished to spend more money, it could issue T-bills to the central bank, which would pay for these with freshly printed marks. The state could then spend these marks and thus, at least temporarily, increase money supply. But when it did so, the gold stores had to be increased proportionally: the system had build-in controls.

A year before the war, four German marks were required to buy one dollar on the foreign exchange. But just before the hostilities broke out, a lot of Germans rushed to change their marks to gold, and the country had to abandon its gold standard.

The war lasted far longer and was far more expensive than expected. In order to finance it, the government started issuing T-bills like never before, and all for nothing; Germany suffered a humiliating defeat in 1918 and was saddled with horrendous war reparations.

The mark had fallen 50% relative to the dollar during the war, and the fall accelerated afterwards — as Thornton would have predicted. At first the fall was moderate, but then it accelerated until it eventually grew into an uncontrolled selling-spree. In February, 1920, the exchange rate reached 100 marks to the dollar — 25 times the pre-war rate. But it continued on and on as the money supply kept growing. To those who had saved up money, the inflation was of course a disaster. But in many ways, there was something quite nice about accelerating inflation: unemployment fell sharply, reaching less than one percent in the spring of 1922, and disappeared almost completely during the summer.

MONEY ILLUSION

All that money seemed to breed a lot of activity, but as Fisher and his colleague, Professor Roman, found, it was activity based on a total illusion. To Fisher and Roman, everything was very cheap in Germany thanks to the low price of the mark vis-à-vis dollars, but to the Germans, everything seemed incredibly expensive. As the two professors asked two female shop owners about the high prices, their answer was the blockade by the allies, wage increases enforced by the unions, freight rates, and inefficient government. But when Fisher asked them if it could be because the government was simply printing too much money, the idea had seemed entirely new to the women. He concluded that the Germans thought of commodities and the American gold dollar as rising, while the mark was all the time the same mark. He called this absurd tendency to have faith in your own currency irrespective of its quantity "the Money Illusion".

WHY INDEED …

The mark continued its free fall, however, and in the spring of 1923, a parliamentary committee was asked to investigate why the exchange rate had fallen from 18,000 marks to 30,000 during the first month of the year. When the committee held its first meeting in the middle of June, the problem had to be re-phrased, however. Now it was why the exchange rate had fallen to 152,000 marks. In July, the question had changed again:

> "Why is it, that the exchange rate has changed from 18,000 to 1,000,000 marks for a dollar during little over six months?"

Could it possibly be, by any chance, because the government was financing only 3% of its expenditures through taxes etc., and 97% through issuing T-bills?

It was during 1923 that the price of eggs reach a level 500 million times as high as when the war stopped in 1918. It was also in that year that it became common for employees to demand salary payments twice daily. When they were paid, a truck would often come to the factory, loaded with bills. The cashier would climb to the top of the pile, read up the employees' names, and throw down bundles of bills to each as he responded. The employees would then rush out to buy anything they could think of — like a newspaper for 200,000,000,000 marks, or a cup of coffee for … well, did it really matter? At this stage it wasn't fun anymore. Unemployment came back, and there were riots in the streets. Fisher's nasty effect was showing its ugly face. He left Europe and went home to continue his work, and also to write a book about world peace.

During these years, he was prospering. He was beginning to receive large income from an index machine he had invented, and his shares in the Remington Rand Corporation soared. As his personal wealth reached into several million dollars, he bought a chauffeur-driven Lincoln in 1925, a luxury rather unusual for a university professor.

Fisher decided to return to Europe in 1928, partly because he wanted to meet Benito Mussolini whom he wanted to give some advice. At this time, Fisher was known as the most famous American economist, and also for his frequent advice to stock traders.

A STRANGE MEETING

Mussolini wasn't a pretty man. He was bald, with a fattish face and two front teeth far apart. But he radiated an aggressive energy that would impress many visitors. And if this wasn't enough to generate respect, then it might help to consider that the wall carpet behind him was generally assumed to cover a row of soldiers armed with machine-guns. During the day of Fisher's appointment Mussolini had received several delegations. There had been a large group of students, a team of athletes, and about 100 very young cadets. But shortly after 5:30 pm, it was Professor Fisher who entered the room. Mussolini opened the conversation with the following question:

> "Is this Professor Fisher?"

Fisher answered:

> "Yes, is this Mr. Mussolini?"

Mussolini was apparently baffled by this question, so his next sentence became total nonsense:

> "Yes. Do you not speak English?"

After this odd exchange of words, Fisher started to lead the conversation on track, however:

> "You are one of the few great men in the world who are interested in the subject of inflation and deflation, unstable money and stabilization."
>
> "Ah! Stabilization! And you have made a special study of this?"
>
> "Yes, for twenty years. I wrote you in April for this appointment. Meanwhile you have already done one thing I wanted to suggest — stop your deflation. I think that was wise. I am glad you have stopped. But there are other suggestions I would like to make …"

Fisher explained various measures that he would recommend for the Italian economy, and delivered a written analysis of the country's situation. That Mussolini some years later should choose to declare war against Fisher's country must have seemed completely grotesque to Fisher, if he could have known it.

Shortly after this strange meeting Fisher embarked on a boat heading for New York. As he returned, he found his secretary on the dock, who told him that a brief slump in the stock market had required her to use the full hundred thousand dollars in her agent's account to reduce bank loans. This was the very first warning of events, which would later change Irwin Fisher's life …

How private banks created money

Imagine that Fisher had inherited 100,000 dollars, which he then deposited in his local bank. (He hadn't but had married a quite rich girl). Depositing the money in the bank would surely not change his perception of how much money he had. But what would the bank do? If banking regulations required that banks kept 10% in reserve, they would rush to lend 90,000 dollars to another person, so they could collect maximum interest. Whoever borrowed this amount would surely have a purpose, and would spend the money on something — giving the money to somebody else. Now this "somebody else" would receive the money and place it in his *bank — which would again lend out 90% (81,000) to a customer. And so on until the 100,000 deposited had grown to 1,000,000 dollars. In other words: When Fisher's bank received 100,000 dollars, this would enable the banking system to create 900,000 dollars of credit! And credit and money were the same, because both enabled people to spend. So* money supply is largely in the hands of the private bankers, not only the central banks.

8
Keynes and Von Mises

"A monetary system is like some internal organ: it should not be allowed to take up very much of one's thoughts when it goes right, but it needs a great deal of attention when it goes wrong."

D.H. Robertson

There is a difference between making a mistake and repeating it. The Austrian economist, Ludwig von Mises could understand why the Duke of Orleans had made mistakes, but it was a wonder to him why people never learned anything from the past[1]. When there had been so many recessions, why didn't governments or central bankers identify for once and all the basic errors and prevent them from happening again? Actually he had his own explanation: Politicians and bankers were simply led to temptation.

INVISIBLE INFLATION

Mises' explanation of the recurrence of the cycles was that politicians and central bankers tended to lower interest rates below the "natural rate" during periods of recovery, where the banks had ample liquidity and wanted to expand their own business. This meant that time after time, they allowed the development of over investment, which eventually led to credit squeeze and then to crisis. The natural rate term was really an expression from Swedish Knut Wicksell, whose proposition could be expressed as follows:

- It is well known, that low interest rates stimulate business, and that high rates inhibit it. But what is "low" and what is "high"? ...

- We can solve that question if we identify a normal or "natural" rate. Such a rate can be defined as equalling the rate of return which businessmen expect on newly bought capital equipment.
- If the bank rate drops below that "natural" rate (or the latter soars above the former) then it becomes very profitable to do business. Consequently, businessmen will be more busy, commodity prices will be bid up and eventually all prices will rise in a cumulative process.

Von Mises believed that Wicksell had missed an important point, however. According to Mises, the injection of new money into the economy would first lead to inflation in the capital industry, where the initial expansion took place, while consumer prices might still fall. Later on the process could reverse, so that prices of consumer goods would rise while those of capital goods would fall. So it was quite possible that *real rates could be below natural rates without this causing a generally visible inflation before it was too late to react*. Wicksell's and Fisher's theories were in other words too simple.

During the 1920s von Mises felt that exactly this phenomenon was taking place. While Irving Fisher said the expansion of the 1920s was sustainable because it entailed no price-inflation, Mises said the economy would break down because of the dramatic credit expansion — or credit inflation. The left side of Fisher's equation had gone berserk and was due for a correction due to inherent instability in the monetary system. When the correction came, it would hurt the right side. Or as he put it:

> "There is no means of avoiding the final collapse of a boom brought about by credit expansion. The alternative is only whether the crises should come sooner as the result of a voluntary abandonment of further credit expansion or later as a final and total catastrophe of the currency involved."

Every Wednesday afternoon from 1924, he met with the economist Fritz Machup and walked with him past the great Austrian bank, Kreditanstalt in Vienna. And every time they passed the bank, he gave the same remark:

> "That will be a big smash."

A STRANGE QUESTION

A few years earlier the English economist Austin Robinson had been taking a walk with one of his fellow students, when he suddenly came to think of an odd question:

> "If somebody spends an additional pound, why does it not keep on being spent by successive recipients until it puts all the unemployed back to work?"[2]

Assume we did add such an additional pound. The government could for instance borrow it from abroad and use it to pay somebody to clean up the doorsteps of the Parliament. Whoever got the job — and the pound — could then spend it to buy something from somebody else. Who could again spend it to buy something from somebody else. Who could again …

Each time this happened, it would mean employment to the seller of the product or service in demand, and as the pound kept circulating, the derived employment would be infinite. Or would it? Well, of course not. Surely you couldn't get infinite effect with one pound. But why was it that you couldn't?

A part of the answer had really been given by Quesnay two hundred years earlier (the money would be "saved up"), but the standard answer of the economists of the day was the "Treasury View". One example of this was a White Paper, published by the English government in 1929, which stated:[3]

> "Apart from its financial reactions, a big programme of State aided public works has a disturbing effect upon the general industrial position. If it is a long programme with continuity of work promised to the personnel, it draws off labour which would otherwise find employment, though perhaps with less regularity, in normal industry without being able to secure replacement."

So according to the Treasury View, government spending of an additional pound wouldn't help. But this answer was obviously weak if there was high unemployment. There had to be more to the matter. The additional pound had to have an effect on employment that was more than zero, one should think, but less than indefinite. But how much, then?

An early indication of the real answer was to be found in a pamphlet released by the Liberal Party in the same year as the above mentioned government paper. Its title was "Can Lloyd George do it?" The pamphlet was part of a program in which an increase in government spending to combat unemployment was proposed. The party would release not just one additional pound, but quite a few. According to the pamphlet, the consequence would be reduced unemployment:[4]

> "The fact that many working people who are now unemployed would be receiving wages instead of unemployment pay would mean an increase in effective purchasing power which would give a general stimulus to trade, moreover, the greater trade activity would make for further trade activity; for the forces of prosperity, like those of trade depression work with a cumulative effect."

The pamphlet went on to supply an answer to the standard objections from those holding the Treasury View:

> "The savings which Mr. Lloyd George's schemes will employ will be diverted, not from financing other capital equipment, but (1) partly from financing unemployment. (2) A further part will come from savings which now run to waste through lack of adequate credit. (3) Something will be provided by the very prosperity which the new policy will foster. (4) And the balance will be found by a reduction in foreign lending."

It stated, in other words, that fiscal spending could be self-financing to a high degree and could stimulate much more than the initial effect. *The spending of an additional pound could be not only an effective cure, but also partly self-financing*.

CHAMPAGNE AND MONEY

This pamphlet had two authors. One was Hubert Henderson; the other was the well-known economist, John Maynard Keynes. Keynes believed that the capitalist economy was inherently unstable — a view that had become generally accepted with the vast amount of new business cycle literature. But he also thought that the economy was prone to falling into permanent unemployment equilibrium, and this view was very much in contrast to that of classical economics.

When the pamphlet was published, Keynes was 46 years old and an eager participant in the debates of the day[5]. He had been educated at Eton and Cambridge, worked in the India Office and later as a journalist, a lecturer, the manager of an insurance company and as Senior Treasury official of Great Britain. He had advised the government on numerous occasions and had participated in the negotiations with defeated Germany after the First World War. Keynes was a successful man in most senses. He was married to a Russian ballerina, made lots of money and drank lots of champagne. Like Adam Smith before him, Keynes was a master of the spoken word. Like Law, he loved to play cards and roulette. Like Thornton, he had many good friends he could trust.

And then of course there was the stock market. Like Cantillon, John Maynard Keynes was an eager stock market investor — an activity which contributed to his understanding of economic instability. He was known for making his investment decisions in the morning while still in bed, but if his research was somewhat laid-back, this can hardly be said of his actual dispositions: they were aggressive and daring. His pet market was currencies, where he believed his experience at the Treasury would secure him a competitive advantage.

In April 1920, two years before Irwin Fisher went to study the hyperinflation in Germany, Keynes went short German marks on margin. The currency was indeed in a down-trend when he did it, but as it counterreacted in a brief rally, he lost 13,125 pounds for himself and 8,498 for his fellow investors. When he received a margin call for 7,000 pounds from his broker, he was unable to pay; only two loans secured him from bankruptcy. But that experience did not stop him. In 1924, he was appointed first bursar of Kings College, where he had persuaded the board to open an investment fund, which he managed.

DIFFERENT OPINIONS

While Keynes' views gained popularity, so did the Austrian school, which gradually gained more adherents as students from Vienna University grew up and got important jobs. One of these was Felix Somary, who had studied under Mises. As a student Somary had been especially interested in business cycle theories, and in 1901 he had won a prize for a paper on Juglar's theories and economic crises. Somary became an investment banker in Zurich. On September 10, 1926 he gave a speech at the University of Vienna. It was a very strange experience for some of his audience, because although the economy was booming and everything appeared as rosy as ever, Felix Somary predicted that the boom would end "with the bankruptcy of governments and the destruction of banks."

In 1927 he met Keynes. Keynes asked Somary what he was recommending his customers to do. Somary answered:

> "To maintain the best possible protection against the coming world crises and to avoid the markets"

But Keynes was very bullish and responded:

> "We will not have any more crashes in our time"

Then he asked Somary about several specific stocks, and added:

> "I find the markets very interesting, and the prices low. So where should a crisis come from?"
>
> "From the difference between expectations and reality. I have never before seen such clouds approaching in the horizon."

But the stocks market kept climbing. In the year 1928 Keynes wasn't very happy with his own investment performance, however. Whereas the English stock index had yielded 7.9%, his fund was down 3.4%[6]. Obviously it would be most welcome if 1929 went better. And many things indicated that it might. First there was the fact that Wall Street, the world's leading stock market, was booming. Stocks had risen almost constantly since 1924. Secondly, the economy had been just as impressive. Partially thanks to the archaeologists at the National Bureau, Keynes had some pretty good statistical tables to consult. Here are some of the key figures he could look at:

American key figures, 1922–28; 1922 = 100

	Industrial production	Durable consumer goods	Non-durable consumer goods	Consumer price index
1922	100	100	100	100
1923	120	146	116	103
1924	113	130	102	100
1925	127	176	113	104
1926	133	143	116	104
1927	133	143	117	98
1928	140	156	117	99

Over seven years, industrial production had risen 40%, consumption of durables 56%, and non-durable consumer goods 17%. John Ford was putting Say's law into practice by paying the workers partially with their own products, and the stock brokers in New York saw too that money was always allocated to the strongest and the fittest. Indeed, stock trading had never been so popular before. During the preceding years, tickers, quotation boards and brokerage services had been installed on ocean liners, and radio programs had begun broadcasting stock prices at intervals throughout the day[7]. In one factory stock prices were posted on a blackboard from hour to hour to please workers. And one prospering market operator was supposed to have complained, with some exaggeration of course, that to keep a good cook he had to install a ticker in the pantry, that his valet refused to come on duty before the market closed, and that the street cleaners in Wall Street would pick up only the financial papers. In fact, as stocks kept rising and rising, stock trading was now considered so easy that it was almost impossible to lose. A popular joke was about a gentleman who called the manager of a brokerage house and asked:

"Does William Jones have an account here?"

"What right do you have to ask?"

"I am attorney and guardian for William Jones. He is in an insane asylum."

"His account shows 180,000 USD profit."

So joking apart, if people had ever doubted the virtues of capitalist economy, this, in most people's view, was the time to give in. You could treat the system rudely like the Germans after the First World War, or like the French during and after the Sun King, and it would fail. But if you played it by its own rules, like the Americans did, it worked wonderfully. With one pillar in Detroit and the other in Wall Street, the house of capitalism seemed to be standing firmer than ever before. So Keynes was bullish on the stock market, just like Irwin Fisher. There could be no doubt about the soundness of the economy.

Or so, at least, everybody seemed to agree. Everybody except "the Seer from Wellesley", Roger Babson, who for some time had warned his customers of an impending crash. And of course the ever-sceptical Austrians. In 1928 Felix Somary had spoken to a group of economists and warned them of the large disparity between the loan rates and the very low yield of stocks, which he called "an unmistakable symptom of a crash." He later described his surprise to see that none of the economists present, although they represented "at least a dozen theories", believed in his prediction. In the February issue of the economic journal of the Austrian Institute of Economic Research, Friedrich von Mises joined in with a new forecast of an imminent crisis in the USA.

Nobody would listen to either of them, but as Somary was on his way through France to spend his holiday in Spain in late August, he received an urgent call from Dr. von Mautner in Vienna, who sought advice on behalf on Baron Luis Rothschild. The problem was that Bodenkreditanstalt, Austria's largest financial institution, was in serious trouble and that the Austrian government insisted that Kreditanstalt should merge with it to save it from bankruptcy. Von Mautner asked what Somary would advise them to do?

> "It will be the safest way to the ruin of Kreditanstalt."
>
> "That is what I believe, but the government insist on the merger; if we pass, then they will do not do anything to help Kreditanstalt, when we should need assistance."
>
> "Let the problem of Bodenkreditanstalt be left with the government; you cannot help, when that assistance can cost your own existence, and definitively not when you are stumbling yourself."

During the summer of 1929 the Kreditanstalt offered von Mises a very well paid job, which made his girlfriend (and future wife) ecstatic. But much to her surprise, he didn't take the bait. When she asked him why not, he answered:

> "A great crash is coming, and I don't want my name in any way connected with it."

Both von Mises and Somary knew that something wasn't right. It wasn't right at all …

The Austrian school

The "Austrian school" of economics had tended to oppose almost any government interference, including any attempts to fine-tune the aggregate economy. Mises and his pupil Friedrich von Hayek were among the leading exponents of this philosophy. Von Hayek elaborated on Mises' theories in a number of books and articles. To him the root of the problem was that the financial sector reacted to an increase in the demand for money by producing more credit rather than increasing its price, i.e. the interest rate. *His thinking took the Wicksellian natural rate/real rate concept as the starting point. It can be expressed like this:*

- *We know by now that if the real interest rate drops below the natural rate, a cumulative investment and growth process will start, which will allow the economy to drift further and further away from its equilibrium growth path …*
- *… and this process will be facilitated by the banking sectors' ability to produce more credit at unchanged prices (unchanged interest rates).*
- *But we have forgotten that this process can happen for several reasons. Mises suggested that this can take place as banks lower the real rate. But another possibility is that new inventions or other new business opportunities* raise the natural rate *because they raise potential business profitability.*
- *And we have also ignored the fact that when the economy grows, then money supply has to expand with the expansion in activity. This means that the real rate can be permanently below the Wicksellian rate without leading to inflation. But in that case, the interest rate level, which stabilizes inflation, may be too low to ensure that voluntary saving equals investment.*

So according to Hayek, money supply could influence production for a time even if it didn't create inflation. *An increase in money supply could in other words stimulate production without anybody really noticing the process, because there was no disturbance in prices. Interest rates could be too low, so that saving was too small to match investment, without releasing warning signs in the inflation. And so,* credit inflation could sneak in and precipitate a crash, *he warned. (Actually Thornton had reached the same conclusion in 1802).*

Another point in Hayek's business cycle theory was that low rates would encourage many "grand schemes", or lead to what modern economists call "a deepening of the capital structure". Eventually, interest rates would be forced up, however, partly because consumer demand revived and consumers and consumer goods industries started to compete with capital industry for money, and partly because the savings rate had been too low because of the low interest rates. Higher interest rates would now force producers to shorten the investment period again. In many cases, it could force companies to abandon ambitious long-scale projects — leading to large write-offs and to losses in complementary industries. So interest rate fluctuations would lead to an alternating lengthening and shortening of the possible investment period. *During the late 1920s, Hayek became convinced that this process was unfolding again, and that a crash was inevitable.*

9
The Great Depression

"No real Englishman in his secret soul was ever sorry for the death of a political economist; he is much more likely to be sorry for his life."

Walter Bagehot

Jesse Livermoore lived on the top floor of the Heckscher Building on Fifth Avenue[1]. Visitors coming to see him would meet a doorman, who would categorically deny the existence of his office. If you had an appointment, you'd be taken by elevator to the 18th floor, where an oversize Irish bodyguard would check you before allowing you in. Once inside, you would find a select team of some 20 clerks and 30 statisticians who assisted Livermoore in gathering and interpreting market intelligence from all over the world. Livermoore used this information exclusively to trade his own money — a fortune which had grown from 3 dollars and 12 cents to 30 million dollars over 38 years. During the summer of 1929, the assistants had informed Livermoore that while the much followed Dow Jones Industrial Average (which was based on a few large stocks) was still performing well, 614 out of a selection of 1,002 stocks, which the staff monitored, had actually fallen since the beginning of the year. Livermoore saw this "lack of breath" as a warning sign for the bulls. Should he prepare for a bear-raid? — he was looking for further clues.

DECISIONS, DECISIONS …

Such a clue arrived during the afternoon on September 4th. One of his informants said that a "high official" at the Bank of England had told associates during lunch that day that "the American bubble had burst,"

Figure 9.1: Roger Ward Babson.
"The Seer from Wellesley Hills" graduated as an engineer in 1898, but soon went into stock broking. As he developed tuberculosis a few years later, he set up an open air office and founded his "Babson Statistical Office". In the fresh, cold air, Babson wore a coat with an electrically heated pad in the back, and his secretary, wearing mittens, used small rubber hammers to hit the typewriter keys. His company became very successful, and many stock-traders subscribed to his forecasting service.

and that Montagu Norman of the same bank was considering raising interest rates before the end of the month. Livermoore stayed at the office until midnight, trying to figure out what was going to happen. Then he went home, slept a few hours, and was back even before his staff showed up next morning. That morning, he called everybody he could think of to discuss the situation.

At 8 a.m., a contact in Boston reminded him that the speaker at the forthcoming annual National Business Congress was Irwin Fisher's friend Roger Ward Babson. Livermoore knew what that meant. According to Babson's "Swing-charts", the boom since the early 20s had deviated considerably from the long term growth trend. Thus, the time was due — no, overdue — for a very serious recession. But Babson also used the monetary sector as indicator. If money rates started rising, then bonds and stocks would fall soon after. In March of the same year, the money rates had risen first to 14 percent, and later, on the 26th, to 20 percent. Just as the 20 percent rate had been posted on the electric announcement board, a fuse had blown out, and everybody had laughed[2]. Although stock prices had rebounded, Babson saw this as another clear warning sign.

Livermoore knew that Babson would repeat something like that in his speech. Not that he thought much of Babson's analytical skills, but that mattered less. His concern was what would be the people's *reaction* to Babson's words. Livermoore asked a secretary to bring the file on Babson, looked it over and put it aside. Then he called for the newspapers. He read his newspapers in a different way than almost everybody else — he had developed a feel for journalists' psychologies. Instinctively, he knew when the journalists got tired of sticking to the same attitudes. Once they did, they could suddenly swing around and take their readers with them. Livermoore felt that they were ready for just such a turn: there was a lack of news and people had gotten enough economic success-stories. The press was likely to cover Babson, and people were likely to listen. Livermoore went short 300,000 dollars of stock.

He was right. Before the conference, a tense atmosphere developed. As reporters called Babson for a summary or print of the speech, he refused to give it. This convinced the editors that the speech could be important, so the "Herald-Tribune" called Irwin Fisher to ensure that he would be available for a commentary to the speech. At noon, on September 5th, Associated Press sent out the news flash:

> "Economist predicts 60- to 80-point stock market crash."

It got extensive coverage on the radio and evening newspapers. Herald-Tribune called Fisher who denied that a crash would be coming. Babson's speech and Fisher's comments were displayed on the same page in the next day's paper. Meanwhile Livermoore called his brokers to increase his short positions.

THE MELTDOWN

This was the beginning of the great crash of 1929. Despite a bullish statement by Fisher on October 15th ("I expect to see the stock market a good deal higher than it is today, within a few months"), it kept falling.

On October 21st, Jesse Livermoore became furious, as he read a headline in *The New York Times*:

> "J.L. Livermoore reported to be heading group hammering high-priced securities."

Almost everything in the article was untrue, but instead of attacking the newspaper, he decided to get the best out of the situation. He called one of *The Times*' editors and told him that he was going to hold a press conference to "set the record straight". What he didn't tell the editor was that nobody else was invited to the conference[3]. At 10:00 the journalist was shown in to his office, and as he sat down, he started scribbling his observations:

> "Sphinxlike, imperturbable and rigid … he reached for the telephone resting on a ledge to his left, and carefully covering the mouthpiece with his delicate fingers, began to whisper market orders to an unidentified ally, somewhere deep in the financial district."

Only after his telephone conversation did Livermoore acknowledge the presence of the reporter, giving him a friendly smile. The journalist asked if Livermoore could confirm that he was leading a bear consortium, and Livermoore handed him a written statement, where he denied this allegation. Then the reporter asked him why stocks were declining, and Livermoore answered that stocks for a long time had been "selling at ridiculously high prices". The journalist reminded him that Irwin Fisher had claimed that stocks were cheap. Livermoore's answer to this came promptly as he slammed forward in his chair:

> "What can a professor know about speculation or stock markets? Did he ever trade on margin? Does he have a single cent in any of these bubbles he talks are cheap? Beware of inside information — *all* inside information. How can he possibly rely on information coming from a classroom? I tell you the market never stands still. It acts like an ocean. There are waves of accumulation and distribution."

He was of course unfair to Irwin Fisher, who was in fact very exposed in the market. But on October 24th, panic exploded and the market started a nosedive never before seen in America. One broker employee described the days like this:

> "The telegraph operators handling our out-of-town business went without sleep for 30 and 35 hours, time and again. Trays with sandwiches and coffee were passed around every two hours. None of the

The New York Times.

FRIDAY, OCTOBER 25, 1929. TWO CENTS

WORST STOCK CRASH STEMMED BY BANKS; 12,894,650-SHARE DAY SWAMPS MARKET; LEADERS CONFER, FIND CONDITIONS SOUND

FINANCIERS EASE TENSION

Five Wall Street Bankers Hold Two Meetings at Morgan Office.

CALL BREAK 'TECHNICAL'

Lamont Lays It to 'Air Holes' —Says Low Prices Do Not Depict Situation Fairly.

FINDS MARGINS BEING MET

Sees Market 'Susceptible of Betterment'—Mitchell, Potter, Wiggin, Prosser at Talks.

Wall Street gave credit yesterday to its banking leaders for arresting the decline on the New York Stock Exchange at a time when the stock market was being overwhelmed by selling orders. The conference at which the steps were taken that reversed the market's trend was hurriedly called at the offices of J. P. Morgan & Co.

The five bankers who met at the headquarters of the famous private banking house at noon yesterday and again at 4:30 P. M., follow-

Wall Street Optimistic After Stormy Day; Clerical Work May Force Holiday Tomorrow

Confidence in the soundness of the stock market structure, notwithstanding the upheaval of the last few days, was voiced last night by bankers and other financial leaders. Sentiment as expressed by the heads of some of the largest banking institutions and by industrial executives as well was distinctly cheerful and the feeling was general that the worst had been seen. Wall Street ended the day in an optimistic frame of mind.

The opinion of brokers was unanimous that the selling had got out of hand not because of any inherent weakness in the market but because the public had become alarmed over the steady liquidation of the last few weeks. Over their private wires these brokers counseled their customers against further thoughtless selling at sacrifice prices.

Charles E. Mitchell, chairman of the National City Bank, declared that fundamentals remained unimpaired after the declines of the last few days. "I am still of the opinion," he added, "that this reaction has badly overrun itself."

Lewis E. Pierson, chairman of the board of the Irving Trust Company, issued last night the following statement:

"Severe disturbances in the stock market are nothing new in American experience. The pendulum always swings widely and it would seem as though the long-expected break should bring about an equilibrium.

"The position of the Federal Reserve Bank is unusually strong and the borrowings of member banks are moderate.

"Considering the record-breaking earnings in many industries, we may well remember that whenever fundamental values are lost sight of by the unthinking majority it is time for courage on the part of those investors who have a real sense of basic worth."

Because the clerical facilities of brokerage houses are overtaxed as a result of the recent phenomenally heavy trading, an agitation was started yesterday in favor of a suspension of trading on the New York Stock Exchange tomorrow.

It is thought possible that the governing committee will take action today, without waiting for a petition from the membership. In many brokerage houses the posting of books has fallen far behind and some relief will have to be afforded according to brokers unless the market quiets down shortly.

LOSSES RECOVERED IN PART

Upward Trend Starts With 200,000-Share Order for Steel.

TICKERS LAG FOUR HOURS

Thousands of Accounts Wiped Out, With Traders in Dark as to Events on Exchange.

SALES ON CURB 6,337,415

Prices on Markets in Other Cities Also Slump and Rally —Wheat Values Hard Hit.

The most disastrous decline in the biggest and broadest stock market of history rocked the financial district yesterday. In the very midst of the collapse five of the country's most influential bankers hurried to the office of J. P. Morgan & Co., and after a brief conference gave out word that they believe the foundations of the market to be sound, that the market smash has been caused by technical rather than fundamental considerations, and that many sound stocks are selling too

Figure 9.2: New York Times front page, Oct. 25, 1929.
It is characteristic of the media coverage of the crash that optimism prevailed almost all the way down.

clerks went home at all during the worst. My brother didn't sleep for 27 hours. He had been working 18 hours a day for weeks, and he was only one of hundreds of clerks. Girls at the adding machines and typewriters fainted at their work. In one odd-lot house 34 keeled over in one afternoon from sheer exhaustion. In another, 19 had to be sent home …."

An observer in one of the boardrooms wrote:

"I saw them sold out, dozens of them, scores of them. I watched their faces when the customers' men gave them the news. I saw men's hair literally turn white. I saw a woman faint dead away; they carried her out cold. I heard a middle aged doctor say: There goes my son's education."

Figure 9.3: Jesse Livermoore and wife.
During the 1920s, stock manipulations organized by investment pools were very frequent, and the most famous participant in these pools was Livermoore. With a particular taste for bear-raids, he did well during the 1929 crash, and at the start of 1931, the total of his fortune was approximately 30 million dollars. But he lost his grip, possibly because he discovered that his wife, who was an alcoholic, was having an affair with a prohibition agent. In March 1934, he filed for bankruptcy.

The crash was a reality, and it soon spread to the European markets. The English stock-market ended down 6.6% for the year and Keynes' fund netted a meager 0.8% in 1929. As regards Irwin Fisher, he lost around 10 million dollars, or all the money he had made on his filing machine and his stock market investments[4].

HAS ANYBODY SEEN THE INVISIBLE HAND?

The stock market crash of 1929 was just a beginning. After a brief revival in the spring of 1930, the market started falling again and went on in a vicious spiral until, in 1933, it had lost 85% of its value. With it went the economy. During these three years, the entire capitalist marketplace seemed to be falling apart. Industrial production fell not by 5%, not even by 10%, but by a third. Consumer purchases of durable goods fell by almost 75%. At the beginning of the contraction, many families tried to keep their assets, but as the situation worsened, they had to start selling whatever they could — at whatever price they could get. One example was the sales in November 1934 following the bankruptcy of the Chester H. Johnson Gallery. During this sale Picasso's "Supper Party" was sold for 400 dollars and a Juan Gris for 17 dollars and fifty cents. The best expression of the severity of the collapse, however, was not that people sold their assets at incredible prices, but the fact that purchase of non-durables (like food) dropped to half.

Many people blamed the banks because of their increasing reluctance to lend out money. Public officials urged the bankers to ease their credit policy, for example Atlee Pomerene, who in November 1932 gave the following message to the reluctant bankers[5]:

> "... the bank that is 75 per cent liquid or more and refuses to make loans when proper security is offered, under present circumstances, is a parasite on the community"

But no matter what people said, the bankers wouldn't do their special trick; now that the world really needed it, they wouldn't create any money. Soon the press started referring to them as "banksters", and Clifford Reeves went even further, when he wrote in the magazine *American Mercury*[6]:

> "The title of banker, formerly regarded as a mark of esteem in the United States, is now almost a term of opprobrium ... and we may even see the day when to be called the son-of-a-banker will be regarded as justifiable grounds for the commission of assault and mayhem."

As money supply imploded, and the Federal Reserve did nothing to prevent banks from failing, businesses defaulted by the day, and many

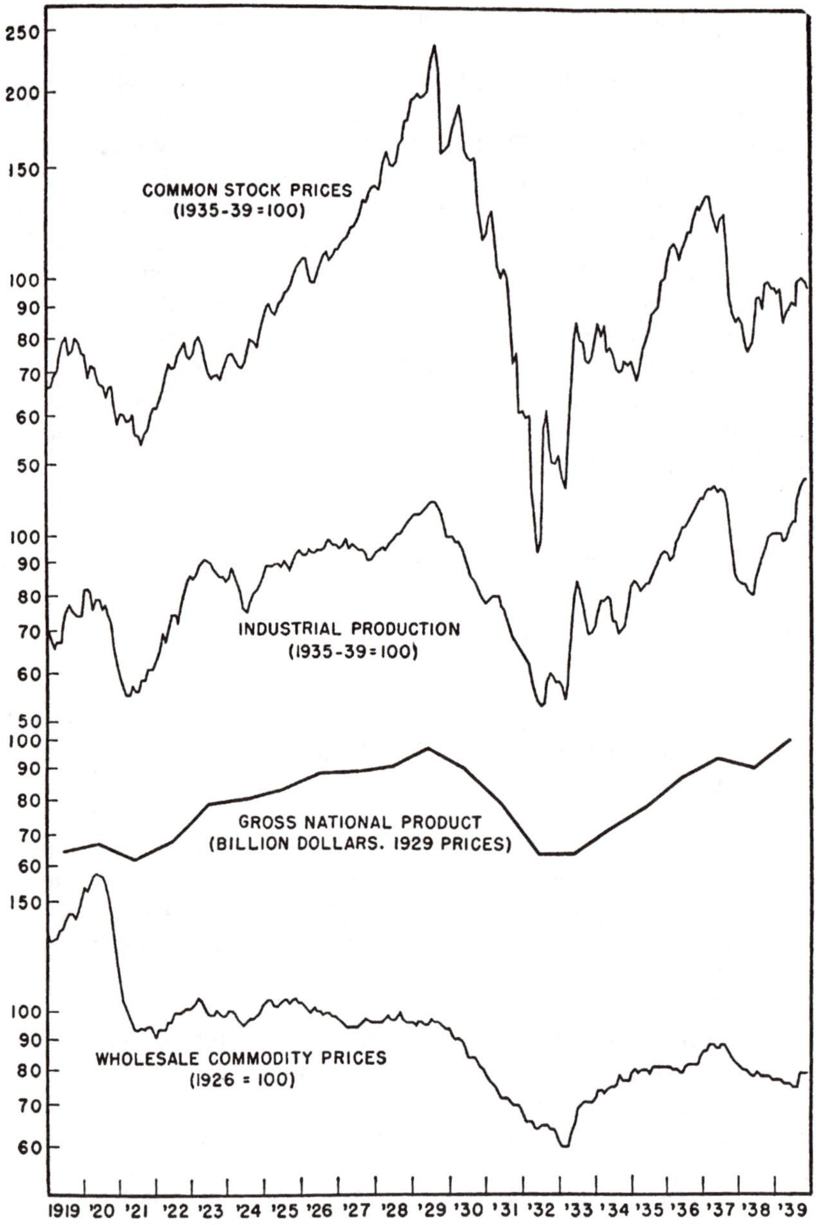

Figure 9.4: The Great Depression.
The four graphs illustrate stock prices, industrial production, GNP and commodity prices from 1919 through 1939.

people were freezing or starving. By 1932, unemployment had increased from 1.5 million to 13 million, or about 25% of the work force. Along the Hudson Riverfront, squatters building cardboard and tin-roofed huts to protect themselves against rain and cold could be seen. Could this really be the end of capitalism?

Many thought so. It was well known that Karl Marx had predicted that recessions in capitalist countries would become gradually worse and worse until the system eventually collapsed altogether. In 1917, the Bolsheviks had seized power in Russia, and in the following years, a number of similar coups had been attempted in Central Europe. During the period of the hyperinflation in post-war Germany, Soviet Republics had been declared in Berlin (1919), Bremen (1929), Hungary (1919), Bavaria (1919), Slovakia (1919), Leipzig (1921) and Hamburg (1923). All had lasted only a few weeks, however. In 1932, a great famine had set in in Russia, and uncounted millions were starving to death, so the revolution wasn't setting its best example. But people outside Russia were largely unaware of this, and some Westerners hoped that this capitalist depression was the very end, the one which Marx had predicted.

KEYNES STRIKES BACK

John Maynard Keynes was not one of them. Keynes thought there was a technical mistake in the way politicians had run the system; a mistake that could be corrected. He was convinced that the key to the solution was in the "additional-pound" problem[7]. In scientific terms, his idea was still more a hunch than a theory, but this didn't bother him. He knew that great scientists had often started with a hunch and afterwards moved backwards looking for the consistent theory. Indeed, he liked to quote Newton for saying once:

> "I have known that for years. Give me a couple of days, and I will find the proof."

Keynes' problem was that his hunch was contradictory to standard theory. Some economists might propose such a hunch anyway, based on partial reasoning and leaving the ensuing mess of fitting things together to somebody else. Keynes worked differently. He began working backwards through time; through the foundations of accepted theory to find out where the basic errors might be. Only having found those errors could he demolish what was wrong and reassemble a new, coherent theory. But it was not a "give-me-a-couple-of-days-and-I-will-find-the-proof" problem. He battled with the problem for a number of years.

Meanwhile he was also busy as a teacher, as a member of the MacMillan Committee of Finance and Industry, and writing about numerous other subjects. In 1936 a number of documents written by Isaac Newton were put on an auction, and Keynes bought many of these with his brother in what must have been one of the best bargains in history (the whole auction fetched only GBP 9,030). He studied the documents carefully and used them as the basis for a paper about Newton. But he was also busy with managing Christ's College funds. During 1930, the fund lost 32%, and in 1931 25%. But then it got into gear, earning 45% in 1933, and 35% in 1934. But while Keynes' fund was very healthy in that year, the economy was definitely not, and people were now beginning to get desperate. Would this crisis never stop? When would Adam Smith's "invisible hand" come and restore order? What was wrong with the system? The depression had now lasted four years, and the figures spoke for themselves:

American key figures 1928–33; 1922 = 100

	Industrial production	Durable consumer goods	Non-durable consumer goods	Consumer price index	Money supply (M2)
1928	140	156	117	99	144
1929	153	185	119	98	145
1930	127	143	97	91	143
1931	100	86	78	80	137
1932	80	47	56	73	113
1933	100	50	60	73	101

Although Keynes did not yet have a complete theory, he wanted to convey his message. Many theorists of the time had ridiculed him before, but now they were forced to listen! He managed to get a meeting with President Roosevelt in which he tried to convince him. The meeting was far from successful, however; afterwards, both of them doubted the sanity of the other[8]. So Keynes went back home to write and study, and to manage his job and his fund, which was now consistently successful — in 1935, it had a return of 33% and in 1936, 44%.

Figure 9.5: John Maynard Keynes.
With an exceptional lack of modesty, Keynes was not reluctant to describe himself as the greatest living economist. Before publishing his "General Theory" he wrote that he believed his book would "revolutionize" within 10 years "the way the world thinks about economic ideas." And so in fact it did.

THE SOLUTION

It was in 1936 that Keynes could finally publish his book, and thus the answer to where the classical economists had been mistaken. "The General Theory of Employment, Interest and Money" contained 400 pages, which were written in an elegant and entertaining prose of which he was a master[9]. The book was difficult to understand, however, partly because it was so different, and partly because it was sometimes a bit, well, blurred. But it came at a time when the capitalist economy was apparently falling apart and when nobody (but the strange Austrians) seemed to have an answer.

Keynes' book gained fame mainly for three reasons. One was that it introduced a number of new methods for analyzing the economy. The second was that it contained a frontal attack on the conventional wisdom that recessions would automatically be corrected, because real money supply — the purchasing power of money — would rise as wages, prices and interest rates fell. According to this assumed "Pigou-effect", a high or rising inflation reduced effective money supply and thus eventually created the conditions for recession. Falling prices, on the other hand, would after a while increase real wealth because of increased purchasing power. It was here that Keynes believed classical economists made their most important mistake. The third reason for its fame was that it recommended a shift of political priority from price stabilization (which was logical, if you believed in the "Pigou-effect") towards direct stabilization of employment and aggregate income through active use of the state budget. The central theme of the book can be summarized in this way:

- If you add up the expenditure for *investment* and for *consumption* in a country, then you get an aggregate called "national income".
- If this national income is too small for the given population (with a given average productivity), unemployment results.
- The consumption part of national income is fairly passive in the sense that it is determined by investment. If investment goes up, consumption goes up — the question is only by how much.
- An investment (our "additional pound") keeps circulating from hand to hand, where each receiver saves a fraction and passes on the rest until it's all saved up. This increase in the value of an additional pound invested is called "the multiplier". So the relationship between investment and consumption is determined by this multiplier.
- The system is out of balance if people save more than society invests. If, say, they save 20% of their income, then their income has to be five times as big as investment. There is, in other words, a relationship between income, saving and investment which may or may not be in balance.
- Assume now that investment has dropped below the savings that people make with their present income. In that case, income will start to drop as it is dragged down by the multiplier effect (which can also work in the reverse).
- As consumers' income drops in this way, they find themselves unable to save the fraction they did before. This means that savings fall until they match the low level of investment.
- In other words: society falls into an unemployment equilibrium …

- … which can last for many years due to the durability of existing production equipment (capital) and to the cumulative effect, when companies try to lower their inventory stocks.

Any classical economist would immediately object to this theory. He could put it more or less this way:

> "The concluding part of the argument is completely wrong. If investment goes down, then three things happen, which will automatically halt the downswing. First, interest rates will fall because too many people try to save and too few invest. Lower interest rates encourage new investment and make saving less attractive. This is in other words a stabilizer. Secondly, during recessions, wages fall, which makes new business ventures more profitable. This will also stimulate new investment. And thirdly, the fall in prices of real estate, consumer goods, capital goods, etc., means that the real purchasing power of the money stock increases. This will eventually persuade everybody to start buying again."

Keynes' answer to those arguments would be something like this:

> "You make two mistakes. First, you think of economics as a mechanical machine. It isn't. It's human beings with human emotions — if not animal spirits. When the economy goes down, people get scared stiff and extrapolate the trend. They don't try to buy at the bottom because they don't have a clue where the bottom is. Long-term expectation is almost an illusion — people are much more influenced by short-term reality. When they extrapolate present (bad) conditions, then we can say that they see "marginal efficiency of capital" as falling. So when business gets bad, people hoard their money as liquidity — "under the mattresses" if you please. This "liquidity preference" presses interest rates up, not down, in times of uncertainty. Your second mistake is that you assume that a cut in wages will initiate the next upswing. You forget that it will undermine the very saving that should finance equilibrium growth. If investment fails, then we shouldn't allow consumption to fail too."

Regarding the last argument, that real purchasing power of money increased as prices fell, Keynes ended up agreeing that it was true. But he thought that this phenomenon, which was later called the "Pigou effect" after A.C. Pigou, was too slow to be considered a solution.

HOLES IN THE GROUND

Keynes had one great advantage in the debate: the economy had collapsed, and people didn't know why. If Adam Smith and Jean Babtiste Say were so smart, how come America was no longer rich? His prescription for a cure was additional government spending to fill the investment gap. This could be done in more or less meaningful ways. More meaningful measures could be to counter a downswing through

- Tax cuts
- Increased transfer payments
- Increased or accelerated public investment and maintenance expenditures

Keynes noted, moreover, that his philosophy would work even if the government projects were completely silly. The government could fill money in bottles, bury them, and sell companies the right to dig them out. Because of the multiplier effect, this would lead to an aggregate effect on employment, which was much larger than the initial effect.

Keynes' book had a tremendous impact. He stressed short-term management of the economy, a view which was in sharp contrast to the laissez faire concept. Equally important was his overall method of analyzing aggregates in an operational and verifiable way. His theory was such that you could test many of its theorems and quantify its parameters. Take, for instance, the marginal propensity to consume. Using American data computed by Kuznets, he calculated this to be around 60–70%. Or take the multiplier: Using Kuznets' data again, you could fix it at around 2.5[10]. So this was at least one answer to the additional-pound question: it had an aggregate effect equal to 2.5 pounds.

Almost any book written after the publication of "The General Theory" was distinctively different from earlier literature. To the policymakers, the most important aspect of the book was that of flexible fiscal policy. In classical economics, thrift had always been regarded as a virtue, but what Keynes suggested was the use of public expenditure as an active stabilizer, as a tool, a fiscal pendent to the monetary tool which Thornton had devised 134 years before.

Keynes never expected that people should read his book as an economic Bible — even as he did the proof-reading, he found that it could be much improved. Nor did he think that his ideas should be used uncritically. He was convinced that he was a great economist, but not that he had found final wisdom. Once, when he had spent an evening in discussion with a group of economists in Washington, he told his friend, Austin Robinson, the man who raised the additional-pound problem, that: "I found myself the only non-Keynesian present." He believed that a thinker should not postpone publication eternally like Marshall had done. Better publish interim, so that other people could absorb your thoughts and elaborate. If this was what he wanted, he had no reason to complain. It is doubtful that any academic book has ever been a subject of so much discussion and so much research. The scientists treated it as a pack of sledge-dogs would raw meat, and much of what Marshall, Pigou, Robertson and Hawtrey had published on business cycles was soon forgotten.

The most important analytical innovations in "The General Theory"

Four analytical concepts in "The General Theory" were especially important:

- *The "propensity to consume" and "propensity to save", which were dependent on the income level*
- *The "multiplier"*
- *The point that human investment decisions are influenced by "liquidity preference" combined with "animal spirits" (as Keynes called it), and uncertainty*
- *The suggestion that the economy could run into a "liquidity trap", where interest rates would not fall below a given level, no matter how much money was injected, because people were scared and bearish on bonds*

10
Schumpeter's Synthesis

> *"... I published a few other studies on points of theory and my second big (in size) book, which seems to enjoy the most widespread obscurity though I myself thought some of the results it aimed at explaining new and not entirely void of importance."*
>
> Joseph Schumpeter

It was in the fall of 1935, when the depression had lasted for five years, that the Canadian graduate student Robert B. Bryce arrived in America from London[1]. With him on the boat, he carried manuscripts and notes from Keynes' lectures in Cambridge. Even though Keynes' book had not been formally released, most economists knew at least something about its contents. One day a "Keynes seminar" was held in Winthrop House, in which Bryce could explain the new ideas. Now they had a chance to ask young Bryce what exactly this Mr. Keynes was trying to say. But although people were generally enthusiastic about Keynes, at least one man present didn't like what he heard. He didn't like it at all, in fact.

A MAN OF AMBITIONS

This man was not just anybody. Once he had set three goals for his life: to become the best lover in Vienna, the best horseman in Europe, and the best economist in the World. He might have failed in his first goal, and he surely had in his second. But he tended to think that he had succeeded in the third. To him, Keynes was wrong; wrong in the conclusions he drew, wrong in his methodology, and wrong in his very attitude to the science he was practicing. How could normally intelligent people fall for this stuff?

Joseph Alois Schumpeter was born in Vienna in the same year as Keynes.[2] As a child he went to school in Graz, where he did well, and was allowed in continue in a demanding school, the "Maria Theresa Academy of Knights", where he soon realized that his formidable memory and his ability to concentrate gave him an important advantage over many fellow students. In 1901, Joseph Schumpeter entered the faculty of Law in Vienna, and on February 16th, 1906, only one week after his 23rd birthday, he received his law degree.

He was the kind of person who pretended to be relaxed, but who in reality worked like a beast. Often he would sit at the coffee houses in Vienna and talk for hours as if he had nothing else to do; but when he came home, he would read half the night, eager to know everything about the subject that had caught his interest. That subject was economics.

Figure 10.1: Joseph Schumpeter (right) and Irwin Fisher (left).
In his analysis of business cycles and of the future of capitalism, Schumpeter emphasized in particular the role of the entrepreneur. It was the entrepreneur who more than any other factor was responsible for each revival after a recession. Like Karl Marx, Schumpeter foresaw the eventual fall of capitalism, but for an entirely different reason. Businesses and the state would grow larger and larger, and as this happened, the entrepreneurs would disappear, and renewal in society with them.

Joseph Schumpeter's first job was in Egypt, where he was to rationalize a sugar refining factory. He did that with great success, and was able to observe how his technological innovation led to increased profitability — an impression which was probably important in shaping his later theories. When he came home from his daily work, he would continue on another project. He had decided to write a book about economics, which should be nothing less than the German language match to English classics.

Written over just a year and a half, the book was published in 1908. Schumpeter was now 25 years of age and decided to quit business to pursue an academic career. He returned to Vienna and started preparations to earn the right to teach political economics at the university level. In June 1909, at the age of 26, he received the "venia legendi", with the title of "privatdozent". At that time, he had already published 22 book reviews and 9 journal articles in addition to his 657-page book. He was more than ready for the academic world.

But maybe the academic world wasn't quite ready for him. People found the young Schumpeter irritating and offensive. For one thing, he dressed up like a Count. Another thing was the way he spoke in public. Like an experienced old professor, he always spoke without manuscript, typically with a gracious smile and often with an arrogant attitude. So when the young "enfant terrible" got his first job, he was sent to the place usually preferred for troublesome old professors: the remote Czernowitz.

THE CZERNOWITZ YEARS

Schumpeter left Vienna in September 1909, and soon after his arrival in Czernowitz, the dean of the Faculty held the first meeting of the teaching session with the professors. They all arrived wearing dark woolen suits and high collars, and sat down to wait for the meeting to be called to order. But one chair was empty: that of the young, new professor from Vienna. Finally the door opened and Joseph Schumpeter entered, wearing not a dark suit, but boots, jodphurs and hunting jacket. He was late because the meeting was too close to his daily ride, he explained — was it possible that the dean could make the next meetings a little later, so he could get time to change?

They didn't send him back, and eventually he gained many friends (and girlfriends) in Czernowitz. He stayed for two years, and none of his colleagues ever forgot him. Which other young professor had ever insisted on eating in white tie and tails in his own, humble place? Once Schumpeter became very upset at the university librarian who wouldn't allow his students to borrow books about political economics. They ended up in a shouting-match until the librarian finally challenged him to a duel with swords. Schumpeter accepted, and they had their seconds arrange for the contest. Schumpeter was well trained in sword-fighting, and after a short fight, he nicked the librarian's shoulder. The seconds immediately intervened, and the fight was over: Schumpeter apologized for the whole affair, the librarian apologized as well, and after that the students were allowed to borrow books about political economy.

CLUSTERS OF INNOVATION

The Czernowitz years were not only fun and games, however; Joseph Schumpeter was writing his second book, "The Theory of Economic Development". The book was published when he was 29 years old after he returned to Vienna. It contained an original theory about economic growth and business cycles: In the capitalist economy, he claimed, *innovation arrives in clusters, and these clusters explain the business cycles.* Many thought this sounded unlikely: "Why should new ideas arrive in clusters?"

Schumpeter's answer was that it is not ideas themselves that matter, but putting them into practice. During a depression, it was easy to get access to production factors:

> "One favorable circumstance, which always facilitates and partly explains a boom, must be particularly remembered, namely the state of affairs created by every period of depression. As is well known, there are generally masses of unemployed, accumulated stocks of raw materials, machines, buildings, and so forth offered below cost of production, and there is as a rule an abnormally low rate of interest."

Such a situation was ideal for entrepreneurs, who merely pieced these factors of production together in new and more profitable ways, which opened new markets. So during hard times, there would be more innovations that would lead not only to local prosperity, but to a general boom. One reason for this was that innovation typically happened in new companies:

> "… it is not the owner of stage-coaches who builds railways."

> "... the vast majority of new combinations will not grow out of the old firms or immediately take their place, but appear side by side, and compete, with them."

This meant that innovations would not only change the nature of activity, but increase its total level. A second reason why innovations created business cycles was that once the entrepreneur had broken the new path, more and more would follow:

> "... the successful appearance of an entrepreneur is followed by the appearance not simply of some others, but of ever greater numbers, though progressively less qualified."

Thirdly, the development of new industries meant increased demand for capital, raw materials, services and new by-products, and thus a general spread of derived demand to other industries. Eventually this would lead to over investment and distress as the prime effect of the innovations dried out and old companies were forced out by increased cost and competition.

Schumpeter was strongly opposed to socialism as he believed that such a system would have very few innovations and would suppress its people.

Creative destruction

Joseph Schumpeter used in "The Theory of Economic Development" from 1934 a term that would become famous. He talked about "creative destruction" when describing processes whereby old structures are destroyed to free production resources for new and more efficient structures. What happened during these phases in the business cycle was that entrepreneurs with new and more productive ideas used credit to build up their businesses. Once they were able to take their new products to the market they would obviously compete against suppliers of older products. The result was that the more old-fashioned producers were forced out so that factory halls, office space and people that were previously employed in the old structures became available for the entrepreneurs. The economy could not grow very fast or at all if this destruction process didn't take place.

One day he met with Felix Somary and the economist Max Weber at Café Landmann in Vienna, and soon they came to discuss socialism. Schumpeter said that the debate over socialism would now cease to be a paper discussion, as there would be a real experiment to observe. Weber agreed, but worried that the Russian experiment would lead to incredible human suffering and would end in a catastrophe. "That may very well be ...", answered Schumpeter, "but it will be a nice laboratory for us." Weber was shocked over this cynical attitude and a discussion followed, which became louder and louder until the other guests stopped talking and started staring at the combatants instead. Finally Max Weber ran out of the café, and Schumpeter laughed to Somary and said "How can you argue so hard in a coffee house."[3]

ROUGH TIMES

In 1919, a new socialist cabinet was formed in Austria, and the social democrats' leader, Dr. Otto Mayer was looking for a state secretary of finance. Apparently unaware that Schumpeter nourished strong sympathies for the laissez faire philosophy, he suggested him for the post. Schumpeter accepted and immediately after proclaimed his new policy. He would:

- Reduce money supply through a one-time capital levy
- Adopt a fixed exchange rate policy
- Establish an independent central bank
- Put emphasis on indirect taxation, and
- Promote free trade.

He rented a suite at the Vienna Waldorf Hotel and a countryside castle with a stable of horses — to get ready for the battle of his life. But the battle could not be won; the rest of the government had completely different views than Schumpeter, and one of their first steps was to establish a commission to nationalize a number of industries. Schumpeter successfully prevented many of these nationalizations, but after only six months he was forced out of government.

After this disappointment he went into private business. It started when some conservative MPs struck a deal according to which Schumpeter was given a banking concession. He now made an alliance with the Biedermann bank, which was a private bank in need of a concession to go public. The bank had the money, and as Schumpeter had the concession, he became partner — with an attractive salary as well as a large credit-line. Eager to make it big in a hurry, he rushed to invest in various industries, and after a few years, he seemed to be very well off. But in 1924, Austria had been hit by recession and almost every investment he had made turned sour. Before the year was through, he had lost his job, was deeply indebted, and was left feeling that he had wasted a lot of time in his academic career. After some university years in Bonn, he accepted in 1927 an offer to teach at Harvard, and borrowed most of the money needed for the boat ticket. Then, seven years later, he found himself sitting in Winthrop House listening to this young Canadian student telling about the supposedly ingenious theories of Mr. Keynes.

Schumpeter felt that Keynes underestimated the inherent stability of capitalism, and that he was wrong in letting too high savings take the blame for recessions — it was these very savings which permitted entrepreneurs to innovate and create new growth, Schumpeter thought. And further, Keynes was wrong in his very attitude to economic science. Schumpeter believed scientific economists should stick to analysis only — and leave policy matters to politicians. In "The General Theory", Keynes did not only give recommendations, but it was clear to Schumpeter that he had decided upon these first and then developed a theory which could justify them afterwards. Not very scientific …

THE UNIFYING THEORY

When the seminar took place, Schumpeter was himself in the process of writing a book about the instability problem; a kind of Grand Unifying Theory of business cycles. He had embarked in 1933 on this "Krisenwerk", as he called it in his diaries, and had believed it could be finished by 1935. But as the work progressed, it swelled, and when rumors of Keynes' book stole the spotlight in 1935, Schumpeter wasn't even half finished (he was beginning to tell his friends that it had turned him into a "Galley slave"). In fact he had to continue his work for several more years until it was finally published in 1939 — at a time when any non-Keynesian theory was considered almost irrelevant.

The 1,095-page book (in two volumes) was impressive. The first 219 pages dealt with pure theory. First he discussed behavior according to the equilibrium theory[4], and then he introduced his entrepreneurs, which were responsible for innovation — much like he had described in his "Theory of Economic Development". Clusters of innovation were responsible for the "first wave" — the initial business cycle movement. The next step was to introduce "the secondary wave". He wrote:

> "There is no need to emphasize how great a mass of fact now enters our picture. Indeed, the phenomena of this secondary wave may be and generally are qualitatively more important than those of the primary wave. Covering as they do a much wider surface, they are also much easier to observe; in fact they are what strikes the eye first, while it may be difficult, especially if the innovations are individually small, to find the torch responsible for conflagration."

So the secondary wave amplified the initial impulse so much as to almost hide it from the eye. This amplification was created by the multitude of phenomena described by other writers, such as debt-deflation, forced liquidations, group-think, etc. After the first impulse had arrived, less entrepreneurial people believed that they could benefit from the growth created by the entrepreneurs — a belief which was deceptively self-fulfilling in the short term. In the longer term, however, *everything gained during the secondary wave would be wiped out, and only the benefits created by the first wave would remain.* So the first wave was "evolution", while the second was tremors around this evolutionary path. But the timing of those tremors dictated when innovations would surface: the downswing in the secondary wave created the conditions necessary for the entrepreneurs. *Because of the secondary wave, the primary evolution occurred in steps.*

SIMULTANEOUS CYCLES

His third step was to introduce several, simultaneous cycles:

> "There is no reason why the cyclical process of evolution should give rise to just one wave-like movement. On the contrary there are many reasons to expect that it will set into motion an indefinite number of wave-like fluctuations which will roll on simultaneously and interfere with one another in the process."

He had believed from the outset in a single-cycle hyphothesis, but as he analyzed the problem still closer, he realized that there had to be several cycles in action as innovations had very different propagation patterns. In reality there could be an indefinite number of simultaneous oscillations,

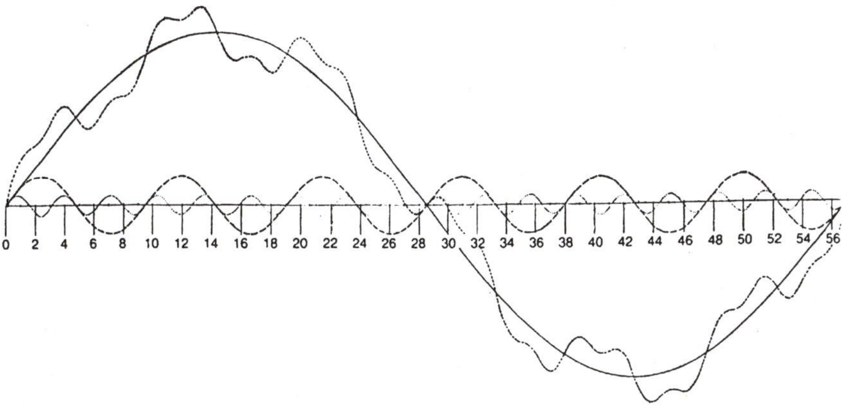

Figure 10.2: Schumpeter's three-cycle schema.

but he chose to simplify this scenario by assuming the presence of three dominant cycles: Kondratieff's, Juglar's and Kitchin's — all of these with very irregular duration.

From page 220, the book contained a thorough analysis of business cycles through history. He dated capitalism from the 12th or 13th century, when mankind had introduced the first credit instruments, but he concentrated his analysis on the most recent 300 years — including John Law, whom he regarded as an entrepreneur who created his own credit. This analysis also suggested a theory to explain occasional deep depressions:

> "... it is clear that the coincidence at any time of corresponding phases of all three cycles will always produce phenomena of unusual inten-

Schumpeter's historical approach

Schumpeter had a historical approach to economic theory. He would, for instance, classify periods with great waves of innovation as prosperity, even if the economy as a whole was in fact turning down during the same time. On May 6, 1937 he wrote to Michell that: "I strongly feel that we must thoroughly get rid of the prejudice that our phenomena are simple and can be directly handled by simple methods either theoretical or statistical."

> sity, especially if the phases that coincide are those of prosperity and depression. The three deepest and longest "depressions" within the epoque covered by our material — 1825–1830, 1873–1878, and 1929–1934 — all display that characteristic."

So Schumpeter explained the American Great Depression of the 1930s by the coincidence of downswings in Kondratieff, Juglar, and Kitchin. But the fact that the depression lasted so long needed an additional explanation: Why didn't the Juglar pull the economy back up in 1935 like it had in 1879?

His answer was the accumulated effect of anti-business policies. First there was a rise in direct taxation of the highest brackets. Schumpeter believed that this was generally accepted as an intermediate measure "as a sacrifice to be made in a national emergency", but later it was regarded as a permanent deterrent against initiative. Secondly the government imposed a tax on undistributed corporate income, which stimulated an immediate distribution of corporate income as dividends, but which Schumpeter believed had "a paralyzing influence on enterprise and investment in general". He believed that companies were much more willing to invest reserves, which they were now impelled to distribute instead:

> "One of the causes of the efficiency of private business is that, unlike the politician or public officer, it has to pay for its mistakes. But the consequences of having to do so are very different according to whether it risks owned or borrowed "funds", or whether a loss will only reduce surpluses or directly impinge upon original capital."

And later:

> "All this, it is true, vanishes from the economist's mind as soon as he buries himself in the mechanics of aggregative theory."

A third reason for the failed revival was, according to Schumpeter, that minimum wages were forced up, making it more difficult for industry to "repair its damaged financial structure". A fourth reason was competition from government industries. And a fifth reason was new anti-monopoly policies. Schumpeter believed that all such anti-business measures "obviously tended to reinforce each other." As he expressed it:

> "It is surely not too much to ask economists to realize that behavior in human societies differs from behavior in animal societies or in physi-

> cal systems, in that it not simply reacts to "disturbances", but to interpretive and anticipative — correct or false — diagnosis of them."

He believed that the sum of all the anti-business measures had a disastrous psychological effect on business. Not only *were* businessmen objectively threatened, but they *felt* threatened. Later he continued:

> "... it is only necessary to reflect that any major change in the relations between the individual and the state, including any major shift in favour of the latter of the shares in total private revenue earned, involves changes in the fundamental habits of mind, the attitudes to life, and the valuations at least of those who are immediately concerned."

As Schumpeter attributed the pivotal role in revival to entrepreneurs — and not to consumer spending — it is quite obvious why he didn't think raising salaries was a wise thing during a depression. But what about the increased government spending which was the potential positive effect created by increased taxation? You could sense a clear address to Keynes (who was only mentioned twice and in 7 footnotes in the entire book) when he wrote:

> "... the writer entertains no doubt that slump will give way to recovery as the new spending program within the 4 million deficit budgeted for 1938 unfolds during the fall of 1938, but also that tapering off will again be attended by the symptoms of — according to the way in which it is effected — recession or depression. This should make us both envious and thankful: envious because fellow economists will be able to enjoy so delightful a verification of their views, thankful because in other fields — medicine, for instance — people do not reason like that, or else we should all be morphinists by now."

Even as the book was published, Schumpeter knew that he was too late. The whole world had turned towards Keynes, and the name of the game had become fiscal stabilization measures. During the first 18 months in print, Schumpeter's book sold only 1,075 copies. Just two American professors used it as a textbook, and only for one year. The academic community was not interested in Schumpeter's micro-economy. Now the scene was in fact set for something entirely different. It was set for the simulators.

The most cited macroeconomists on monetary issues and business cycles, 1920–39

The success of economists is sometimes measured by how often they are cited by other scientists. Patric Deutscher constructed these figures by scanning all articles classified under the headings "Aggregative and Monetary Theory and Cycles ..." and "Money, Credit and Banking" in the Index of Economic Journals. The table illustrates the clear dominance of Keynes, which was steadily increasing during the period (in the years 1920–30, Keynes ranged 10th with Fisher and Mitchell as the most frequently quoted). Joseph Schumpeter ranked 17th to 18th for the period illustrated.

Rank	*Name*	*Number of citations*
1	*J.M. Keynes*	*200*
2	*D.H. Robertson*	*104*
3	*I. Fisher*	*73*
4	*A.C. Pigou*	*72*
5	*R.G. Hawtrey*	*66*
6	*F. von Hayek*	*58*
7	*A. Marshall*	*43*
8	*W.C. Mitchell*	*42*
9	*G. Cassel*	*40*
10	*J. Hicks*	*35*
11	*R. Harrod*	*35*
12	*G. Haberlar*	*34*
13	*A. Hansen*	*32*
14	*K. Wicksell*	*31*
15	*J.M. Clark*	*25*
16	*W.S. Jevons*	*23*
17	*C. Snyder*	*22*
18	*J. Schumpeter*	*22*
19	*J. Robinson*	*20*
20	*S. Kuznets*	*19*

Source: Deutscher, P.: R.G. Hawtrey and the Development of Macroeconomics, Macmillan, 1990.

A Hidden World

"A really naked spirit cannot assume that the world is thoroughly intelligible. There may be surds, there may be hard facts, there may be dark abysses before which intelligence must be silent, for fear of going mad."

George Santayana

11
The Simulators

"Mathematicians are a species of Frenchman: if you say something to them, they translate into their own language and presto! It is something entirely different."

Goethe

It is every economist's worst nightmare to publish a new epoch-making theory at exactly the same time as somebody else. But this was exactly what happened to Henry Schultz, Jan Tinbergen and Umberto Ricci. In 1930, these three economists each published his own description of a theorem that was later named "the Cobweb Theorem." All three published their theorem in German and two of them, Tinbergen and Ricci, even published them in the same issue of the same magazine![1]

SHERLOCK HOLMES AND DR. MORIARTY

The idea is rather simple. Imagine a number of farmers who have to decide what proportion of their land should be dedicated to the production of potatoes. If the price of potatoes is very high one year, then everybody will rush to plant more potatoes. But the next year, when they all bring a mountain of potatoes to the market, oversupply depresses the price. Disappointed, they skip most of their potato production — only to see that the consequent lack of supply in the following year forces the price back up. And so on, they keep trying to adjust, but never can make it. The problem is a bit like when Sherlock Holmes gets off the train to see his enemy Moriarty rushing by in the next passing train. "If Moriarty only knew what I was going to do …", thinks Holmes, "… then he would have done otherwise."

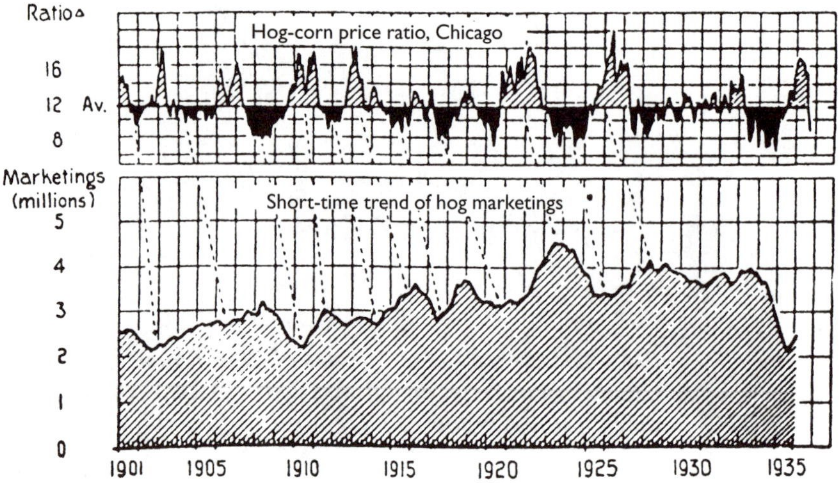

Figure 11.1: The cobweb theorem.
This graph illustrates how the number of hogs brought to the market always lags after increases in the hog-corn price ratio. It appears that the poor farmers are tricked repeatedly by letting present conditions decide future supply. Source: Ezekiel, 1938.

It is quite clear that the cobweb assumption could add more than a twist to Adam Smith's invisible hand hypothesis. Adam Smith assumed correctly that businessmen would quickly identify attractive niches in the market and fill them to gain profits. But just two factors can make the whole system begin to oscillate: one is the time-lag between investment and production, and the other is incomplete information about what the competition is planning to do. And both assumptions seem quite realistic, don't they?

The cobweb was described as a phenomenon in the commodities market. But if you think of it, it was really very similar to John Stuart Mill's thesis from 1826 about the general economy. An "economic cobweb" can occur if too many competitors, dissatisfied with a market, simultaneously decide to cut their production. Or if many companies, attracted by an unexpectedly high price, say in a new market, decide to invest in production equipment for this market. This mistake is called "competitive illusion" and can obviously lead to partial overproduction. After the introduction of the cobweb-concept, it could be said that a local cobweb-phenomenon might pull the entire economy with it; crowd psychology gluing people and industries together, trapped in one giant web.

NORWEGIAN SWELLS

The important aspect of the cobweb theorem was not really the assumption of insufficient knowledge — after all, such an assumption is quite trivial and penetrates almost any business cycle theory. (If everybody knew everything, speculators would soon eliminate cycles by arbitrage). The important aspect was that of time lags. The theorem showed that even some very simple time lags in a very simple system could lead to significant fluctuations. But cobwebs were not the only examples of such inherent instability with very simple explanations. Another example was the so-called “Sciffbaucycles”. In 1938, the Norwegian professor Johan Einarsen published a book, “Reinvestment Cycles and their Manifestation in the Norwegian Shipping Industry”. In this classic, he described a phenomenon that he had discovered in the Norwegian ship-building industry: after a boom in ship construction well-defined “echoes” seemed to occur in the construction level at certain intervals. His choice of the Norwegian industry for investigation was deliberate; first of all, it was well described statistically, second it was the world’s third largest fleet, and third Norway had lost about half its ships during World War One, and after that the reconstruction of most of the fleet had taken place over just two years, 1920 and 1921. His curves showed:

> “a distinct five-year-cycle with peaks in the years 1884, 1890, 1895, 1899, 1906, 1912, 1916, 1920, 1925 and 1929”

It seemed reasonable to assume that these echoes were due to either repair or sale — in both cases, the time interval depended on the average length of time it took for critical wear and tear to take place. To distinguish these events, he investigated which ships were bought by somebody who had just sold other ships beforehand. He called this category of investment “replacement”. Among replacements he found a clear pattern, which peaked at nine and again 19–20 years from initial purchase. The five-year cycle could in other words be generated by overlapping replacement echoes. So here you had a lag between investment and reinvestment, which was quite different from the cobweb phenomenon, but which could also lead to systematic fluctuations. Just like the cobweb phenomenon, such a lag could constitute at least a partial explanation of the turning points of business cycles. Einarsen wrote:

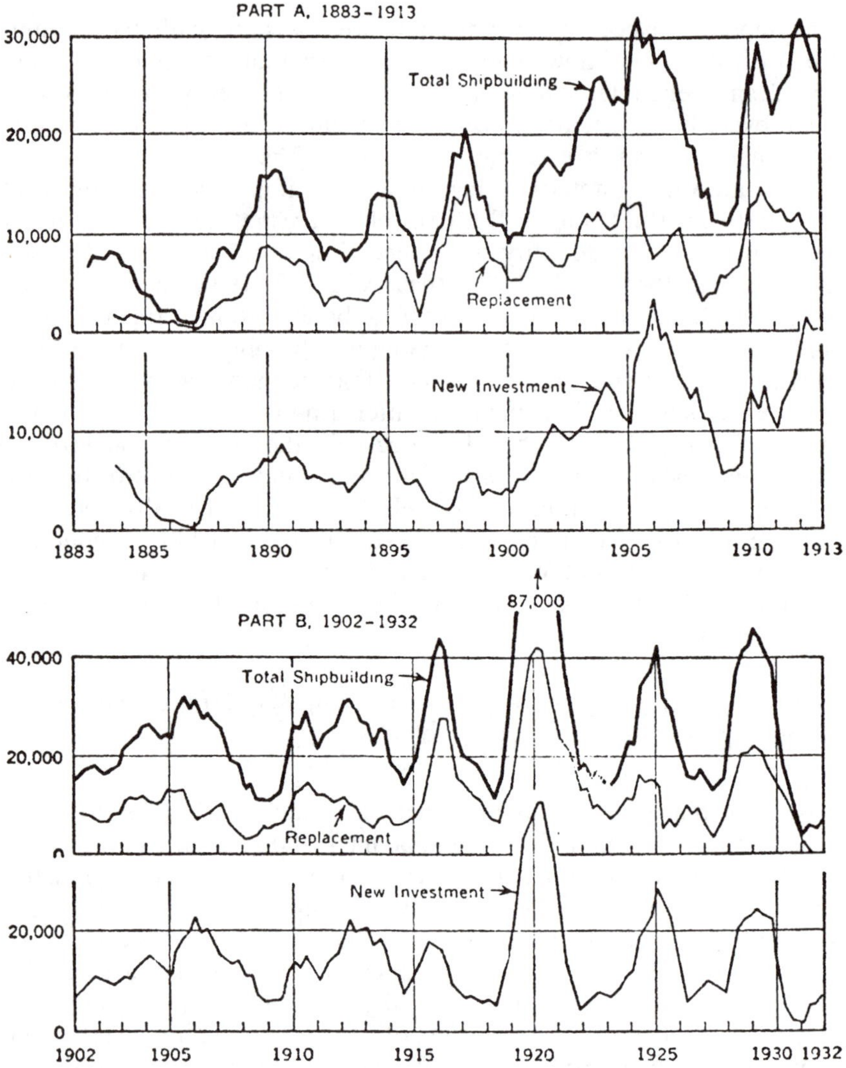

Figure 11.2: The echo phenomenon in Norwegian ship-building.
The graphs illustrate total ship building, replacement and new investment for Norwegian ship-owners. The upper graphs cover the years 1883–1913; the lower cover 1902–1932. There seems to be a clear 5-year cycle in replacement construction. Source: Einarsen, 1938.

"It seems to me that the theory of pure reinvestment cycles will give a satisfactory explanation of how this turning-point takes place, and how it takes place quite automatically."

The cobweb and echo theorems were proposed during a decade where the methodology of business cycle research started to shift. Before, most authors had put the emphasis on a Mitchell-style "exhaustion" explanation of the turning point; that the economy was subject to self-reinforcing trends, which continued until stopped by some exhaustion mechanisms. The upper turning point was explained by lack of capital (monetary theory), lack of saving (under investment), lack of production resources or demand (over investment), etc. The lower turning point was largely seen as the opposite phenomenon; that it had become so easy and profitable to invest and innovate, that people had come out of their holes for that reason. Now more and more inherent processes, which could contribute to turning points, were being described, and how all these processes could work was best demonstrated with small, mathematical simulations. Leon Walras, Wildredo Pareto, Thomas Moore, Alfred Marshall, Irving Fisher, and many others had already integrated mathematics in economics, but now almost any economist used mathematical simulations — at least from time to time. They were paving the way for "econometrics".

THE NIGHT TRAIN

Integrated, econometric simulation is an idea that is often associated with Dutch Jan Tinbergen[2], one of the three authors behind the cobweb theorem, and with Ragner Frisch.

What you do, when you model the economy in Tinbergen's and Frisch's "econometric" way, is that you first try to describe the governing rules of the economy. Instead of using words, you describe each rule as an equation. Such an equation can be an "identity", in which you simply define the building blocks of a variable — as, for instance, your definition of "gross national product". Or it can be a quantitative relationship like, say, the relationship between gross national product (GNP) and consumption. An equation for GNP could look like this:

"GNP = C + Ig + G + X — M",

where

C	=	personal consumption
Ig	=	private investment
G	=	government purchases
X	=	exports
M	=	imports

In this equation, GNP is an identity. When you have defined such an equation, the next step is to estimate parameter values. Let us say that you think you can forecast the following values from the information you have:

Private investment (I)	=	1000
Government purchases (G)	=	1200
Exports (X)	=	800

When you come to income and imports, you find it a bit trickier because they are most of all dependent on GNP — which is exactly what you wanted to estimate. So you define the *relationship* between each of these two and GNP. And that relationship is estimated simply by calculating what it *has been* on average for as many years back as you can, or as you find relevant. Let us say that you study Kuznets' and Mitchell's old figures (for the USA) and find the following historical correlations:

Consumption is 70% of GNP	or	"C = GNP * 0.70"
Imports are 15% of GNP	or	"M = GNP * 0.15"

Given these two relationships, you have in fact a total of three equations. To solve the problem, you simply have to merge them and insert the parameter values. Now it looks like this:

$$GNP = GNP * 0.7 + 1000 + 1200 + 800 - GNP * 0.15,$$

which means that

$$GNP = 3000 + 0.55\ GNP,$$

so that

$$GNP = 6666.7$$

Voila. But in reality, of course, it is much more complicated than that. To begin with, the number of important, initial equations of an economy is large, and some of them have exponents, square roots, and what not. Anyhow, when you have these, you start a step-by-step integration until you have a single, large equation left. This elimination process is called the "night train analysis" because you often find correlations under way which have never seen the light of the day before, but which must be true, if the rest is true.

The next step is to make the model dynamic. This is done by modifying the construction into differential equations, which relates leading, coincident and lagging elements of future conditions to each other. And the last step is to test the models against statistical data to try to find a pattern. This is where Ragnat Frisch, one of the two pioneers of economic simulation, really excelled.

THE STICK AND THE ROCKING CHAIR

Ragnar Frisch was born in Oslo in 1895, the son of the gold- and silversmith, Anton Frisch, and his wife, Ragna Fredrikke Kittilsen. Frisch had originally planned to follow in his father's footsteps, and did take this ambition as far as starting as an apprentice in the workshop of the famous Oslo firm, David Andersen. However, his mother soon got a strong feeling that the job would not be satisfactory for him, so she insisted that he at the same time should take up a university study. They sat down together and examined the catalogue of the Oslo University and found that economics was the shortest and easiest study, so that was what he chose. He received his degree in economics in Oslo, 1919, and the year after, as he had also completed his apprenticeship as goldsmith, he decided to leave Norway to study mathematics in France, Germany, Great Britain, the United States and Italy. Later on he returned to the Oslo University in Norway where he was appointed Assistant Professor in 1925 passed his Ph.D. on a mathematical statistical subject the year after and became Associate Professor in 1928.

Ragnar Frisch became more and more convinced that mathematics ought to play a much bigger role in the formulation of economic theory, and he thought that the discipline should be called "econometrics". In 1930 he agreed with Josph Schumpeter, Irwin Fisher and others to do something about it. The other scientists liked his term for the discipline and they decided to found "The Econometric Society". One of their first problems was to find funding to run the Econometric Society. The solution came from a surprising source: a stockbroker who wanted to understand the underlying nature of economic markets better. His name was Alfred Cowles.

Cowles was not only a stockbroker; he was also the second biggest shareholder in the Tribune Company. He had for a number of years published a newsletter where he provided stock market forecasts, but one day in 1931 he did something highly unusual: he wrote to his subscribers that he would close down the service because he didn't think that he was able to provide valuable forecasts of the markets! Nor did he think that anyone else could do much better; he had studied the track records of other newsletters and found them all to have poor records. So he decided instead to contribute to the development of economic science. Struggling with the complexity of his market models he one day picked up the phone to call Harold Davis, a mathematician working at the University of Indiana and asked him an unusual question: would Davis be able to create a mathematical model that described the behavior of a system with 24 different variables?

Davis responded that it wasn't clear to him why anyone would have a need for such a model, but yes, in principle he might be able to help. They decided to meet, and the meeting went very well. The outcome of their talks was that Cowles, who was well off, offered to sponsor the Econometric Society. Furthermore, he proposed to sponsor publication of a magazine that the society had considered to publish and also to set up a commission, called "the Cowles Commission", which would support the econometric work and arrange various scientific discussion events. The publication he sponsored, which would be called *Econometrica,* would have Ragnar Frisch as its editor.

The first issue of Econometrica was printed in 1933. Frisch wrote the introductory editorial where he stated that the main purpose of the magazine was to combine abstract theory with observation so that theory didn't lose touch with reality. The focus of the publication would be general economic theory, he claimed, as well as business cycle theory, statistical theory and statistical information.

Frisch had meanwhile become very interested in the fundamental causes of the business cycle problem, and he had, like many economists before him, spend hours poring over diagrams that illustrated past business fluctuations. One of the things that he observed was that most diagrams illustrating actual business cycles seemed to display some, albeit limited, degree of regularity. Not so regular that you could predict them by the calendar, but more regular than a purely random phenomenon. So business cycles didn't appear to be pure noise; they were independent "things"; phenomena that required their own explanation. The problem that he struggled with was why they displayed this relative regularity. Could it be because it simply had inherent dynamics that created recurring cycles, or did the economy receive external shocks at regular intervals (like proposed in Jevons's dubious "Sunspot" theories?). He didn't believe much in either explanation. But how could you then explain the relative regularity? He played with various models until he finally believed that he had the answer. So one day in 1933 he sat down and began writing an article.

Impulse and propagation

The name of his article was "Propagation Problems and Impulse Problems in Dynamic Economies". Published in 1933, this article has become one of the real classics in business cycle theory. This was not because it stated something very complicated or abstract (it didn't), but because it was the first to state very clearly how a series of random shocks could stimulate economic fluctuations that seemingly had some regularity. In other words: how the economy could generate order out of chaos. He invited firstly his readers to think about what happens when you hit a rocking horse randomly with a stick. The movement of the stick is fast and swift. However, the subsequent movement of the horse is completely different. It is cyclical and continues over a long period of time. He then continued to provide a few simple mathematical models with economic variables to illustrate how economic shocks ("impulse") would create cycles ("propagation"). Frish demonstrated often to his students how this worked. He would show them how you could add a series of completely random shocks to his model. The result was that it generated cyclical movements that were very different and much more structured than the shocks that caused them. The most interesting observation here was that:

- The *amplitude* of the cyclical fluctuations depended strongly on the shocks …
- … but the *duration* of each cycle was much closer related to the inherent propagation mechanism.

Frish disagreed with almost any other economist at the time on one issue: he believed that the economy in itself was stable: the rocking chair would only rock if there were external impulses to provoke it. No hits with the stick would mean no cycles, but there would in reality always be lots of hits with the stick; lots of external shocks, and the rocking chair would consequently rock all the time in a cyclical, but complex pattern.

SLIDE-RULE AND SQUARED PAPER

To Ragnar Frisch and Jan Tinbergen, the mathematical modelling methods had a number of clear promises:

- They would uncover whether existing theories were complete.
- They would force economists to state theories with absolute clarity.
- They would provide a good way to locate differences of mind between theorists.
- They would make it possible to test any theory.

One of the things Jan Tinbergen used his methodology for was to model the business cycle. If he had used Walras' original methods, he would have needed an enormous number of equations (His colleague Pareto once estimated that Walras would use 70,699 equations to calculate what happened when 100 people traded 700 different commodities). Tinbergen had the advantage that a number of macro-economic relationships had already been established with fair certainty; not the least by Keynes. This limited the necessary amount of equations dramatically.

His first attempt was on the economy of his own country. Equipped with a slide rule and squared paper, he set out to develop a mathematical simulation model for the Dutch economy. He knew that the task would be far from easy. First of all, to use the Wicksellian period analysis, he needed a deep understanding of the dynamic relationships. If e.g. consumption was dependent on income, was it then dependent on past income, the present or the anticipated future income? Second, he couldn't just use any mess of equations, even if they were all correct and relevant. The number of variables would have to be identical to the number of equations, so that he could isolate any one variable, and test its simulated run against reality. But the greatest challenge was in the essence of the holistic thought: if he made just one significant error some place — just a single one — then the whole construction would give a completely wrong result. It was like putting the science itself on the exam table. Did the economists or did they not understand all major aspects of the economic system? Econometrics would show.

A PROJECT FOR THE LEAGUE OF NATIONS

To posterity, it is clear that they did not. But his results, presented in 1936, were a scientific milestone nevertheless. The system consisted of 24 equations, out of which eight were identities. When you inserted your estimated parameter values, you could estimate the behavior of the entire system. This was of interest to the League of Nations, where a long-term research project to find solutions to the business cycle problem had been initiated six years earlier. They had picked two Dutch economists for the task. Von Haberlar was asked to examine and evaluate all existing business cycle theories, which he did in his book "Prosperity and Depression", dated 1937. Afterwards Tinbergen would test them statistically to see whether they conformed with reality.

Tinbergen grouped the phenomena together and tested the hypothesis surrounding each group. In 1939, he published his results in two articles. He concluded, among other things, that *fluctuations in profits were by far the most important explanation of aggregate investment fluctuations in most sectors* — a conclusion which could be seen to support Schumpeter's explanation of the durability of the depression of the 30s — that it lasted so long because new burdens were imposed on business.

John Maynard Keynes was asked to make a review of Tinbergen's first article. He was reluctant to write it, but once he did, it became one of the most quoted reviews in the history of science. An extract:

> "Prof. Tinbergen is obviously anxious not to claim too much. If only he is allowed to carry on, he is quite ready and happy at the end of it to go a long way towards admitting, with an engaging modesty, that the results probably have no value. The worst of him is that he is much more interested in getting on with the job than in spending time in deciding whether the job is worth getting on with. He so clearly prefers the mazes of arithmetic to the mazes of logic, that I must ask him to forgive the criticisms of one whose tastes in statistical theory have been, beginning many years ago, the other way around."[3]

He criticized the methods for a number of weaknesses; for instance that you had to know every important parameter, that spurious oscillations could be hidden in the real structure, and that assumptions about linearity could be unrealistic.

In essence he claimed that Tinbergen's models could only explain cycles if he assumed that they were pushed by other, exogenous cycles.

To explain inherent turning points, he would need to introduce non-linear correlations. Keynes concluded:

> "I have a feeling that Prof. Tinbergen may agree with much of my comment, but that his reaction will be to engage another ten computers and drown his sorrows in arithmetic."[4]

Which was exactly what he did. In 1939, Tinbergen published a business cycle model for the United States to analyze fluctuations in the period 1919–1932[5]. This time, he added a financial sector, with equations describing the behavior of bonds, shares, money rates and money supply. The model, which had 48 equations (twice the number in the Dutch model), tended to swing in a 4.8 year cycle, but only when continuously excited. Left alone, it would soon fall to rest. That, of course, was quite unsatisfactory if one wanted to explain the Great Depression.

Keynes did not fall to rest. When Tinbergen had published a reply to him in 1940, Keynes' comment was polite towards Tinbergen, but not towards econometrics:

> "There is no one, therefore, so far as human qualities go, whom it would be safer to trust with black magic."[6]

Keynes' basic education in economics had not been very extensive. His four years at Cambridge had mainly been dedicated to mathematics and outside interests, and it is likely that he was more influenced by his experiences in business and money management than by the prevailing academic schools. These experiences had taught him that reality was

Keynes on economic reductionism

Keynes attacked Edgewood (the man with the atoms of pleasure) for making gross mistakes in making economics mimic an old style physics:

"The atomic hypothesis that has worked so splendidly in physics breaks down. We are faced at every turn with problems of organic unity, of discreteness, of discontinuity — the whole is not equal to the sum of the parts, comparisons of quantity fail us, small changes produce large effects, the assumption of homogeneous continuum are not satisfied."

much too complex to be modeled correctly in a macro-economic system-of-equations. A very important hint of this complication appeared in an article the same year that Tinbergen published his model of the American economy. The author of that article was a 24-year-old graduate from Harvard.

TWO RULES COMBINED

It was one of the older professors at Harvard, Alvin Hansen, who had come to think about this question. Hansen had become America's leading Keynesian and was eager to integrate Keynesian thought with earlier, classical concepts. So he asked one of his brightest students, Paul Samuelson, if he could somehow develop an integration between the "Keynesian" multiplier and the "classic" acceleration principle.

The acceleration principle had been described by, among others, Spiethof, Robertson, Mitchell, Aftalion, Pigou, Harrod and Clarc. It can

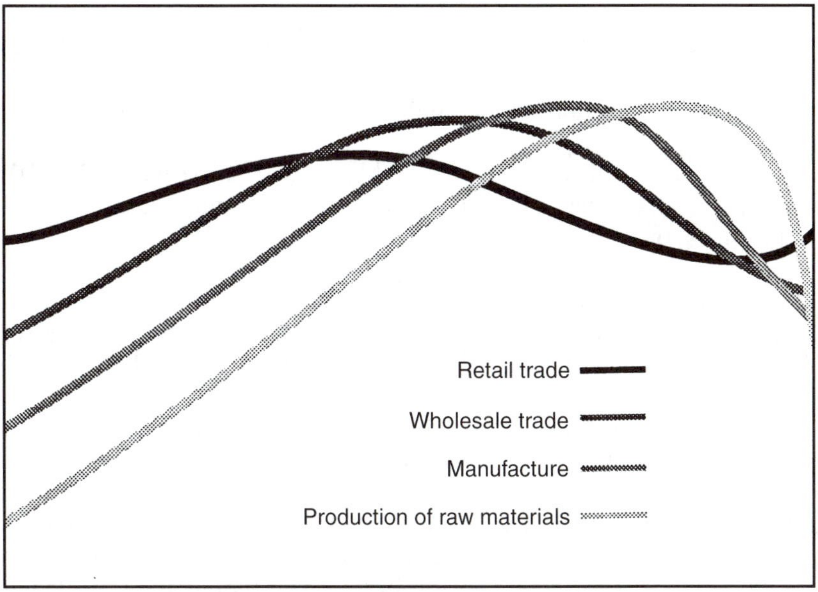

Figure 11.3: The acceleration principle.
Due to the acceleration phenomenon, a small amplitude in retail sales leads to larger amplitudes in wholesale, manufactured goods and raw materials.

best be illustrated by a simple calculation example. In 1914, Russia had a large wool industry with 700,000 spindles, 4,500 looms and 150,000 operatives. A wool industry makes clothes which people wear out — leading to a current and fairly stable demand. But let us assume that a loom lasts on average 10 years, so that the replacement sales in a steady situation is 450 looms per year. What would then happen if, during an upswing, people increased their demand for clothes by a modest 10%?

> Well, 45 looms would be sold to increase the capacity by 10%, and 45 would be sold as replacement of old looms. So the total sales of looms would be up 100% if the sales of the consumer product was up by 10%.

Assume now instead that the sales of wool wear *dropped* by 10%. How would this affect the loom industry?

> In this case, there would be no need for replacement sales, as the industry could do without the worn out machines. Sales of looms would drop to zero if sales of clothes dropped by 10%.

This simple (and simplified) example should clearly illustrate what the acceleration principle is. But the core of the principle is really what happens when consumption just stabilizes after a period of increase:

> If consumption in our example stabilizes after a period with a 10% increase, the sales of looms drops back to replacement of old machines, or to 45 looms. That is in fact a drop of 50%.

What the principle illustrated was that *stabilization in one sector could lead to a terrible shock in another*. It is easy to imagine how this derived shock may lead to a cumulative downswing and consequently explain the turning points.

What puzzled Alvin Hansen and his student was that with the accelerator and the multiplier you had two, in principle simple, dynamic properties. You knew exactly what to expect of each, "everything else being equal". But what would happen when you combined them? Would the resultant dynamics for instance exhibit dampened cycles? Or accelerating growth? Or something entirely different? And would it fit at all with observed reality? Because if not, then you had real trouble!

The first thing young Samuelson did was to set up a table combining the two effects in a model economy[7]. He gave it the following rules:

- Government expenditure was fixed at "1.00" every year (think of it as our "additional pound").
- Consumption was always half the national income in the preceding year (at that time, economists had discovered that "propensity to consume" was rather influenced by past income).
- Investment was always half the increase in consumption between the past and the present year (which fitted with Keynes' assumptions of investors using the rear mirror rather than the binoculars). This relationship between consumption growth and investment can be termed "the accelerator relation".
- Total income was the sum of government expenditure, consumption and investment.

Here is what happened in this simple model:

Period	Government	Consumption expenditure	Investment	National income
1	1.00	0.0000000	0.0000000	1.000000
2	1.00	0.5000000	0.5000000	2.000000
3	1.00	1.0000000	0.5000000	2.500000
4	1.00	1.2500000	0.2500000	2.500000
5	1.00	1.2500000	0.0000000	2.250000
6	1.00	1.1250000	–0.1250000*	2.000000
7	1.00	1.0000000	–0.1250000	1.875000
8	1.00	0.9375000	–0.0625000	1.875000
9	1.00	0.9375000	0.0000000	1.937500
10	1.00	0.9687500	0.0312500	2.000000
11	1.00	1.0000000	0.0312500	2.031250
12	1.00	1.0156250	0.0156250	2.031250
13	1.00	1.0156250	0.0000000	2.015625
14	1.00	1.0078125	0.0078125	2.000000

*Negative investment should be interpreted as marginal effect, implying that an additional government spending of 1.00 per year would mean that investment in years 6–8 would be *lower* than if the government had not tried to stimulate!

This table illustrates a time-journey in an economy with fixed parameters (a propensity to consume of 0.5; an acceleration relation of 1.0). It shows that the national income — given Samuelson's rules — can experience dampened cycles if subject to permanent fiscal stimulation (dampened cycles eventually fall to rest, in contrast to the behavior of cobweb systems). The basic reason for these fluctuations is that Samuelson inserted lags in the equation; he made investment and consumption dependent on the past, not on the present.

But Samuelson didn't stop there. He conducted a series of re-runs in which he experimented with the values of his parameters, that is, with marginal propensity to consume and the investment relation. This is called a factor analysis, and this is what he found:

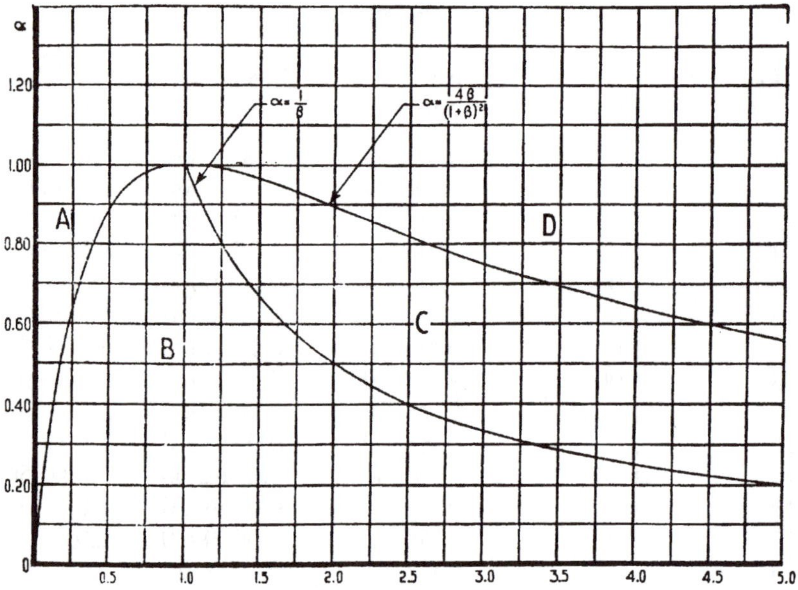

Figure 11.4: Factor analysis for Samuelson's simulation of the accelerator and the multiplier.
The horizontal axis represents values of the acceleration relation, and the vertical represents the propensity to consume. The graphs illustrate the boundaries between factor combinations with different behavior. Region A represents combinations leading to stability. Region B combinations with dampened cycles, Region C with explosive cycles, and region D with extreme growth. Source: Samuelson, 1939.

Propensity to consume	0.5	0.5	0.6	0.8
Acceleration relation	0.0	2.0	2.0	4.0
Behavior	Asymptotic stability	Dampened oscillation	Explosive oscillation	Exponential growth

So the answer to the professor's question was that, depending on the actual values of the two parameters, the income in this model society could either exhibit

- Stability,
- Dampened cycles,
- Explosive cycles, or
- Extreme growth.

The neoclassical synthesis

Samuelson's article was one of the works that stimulated the beginning of what would later be called "the neoclassical synthesis". This was a new line of thought that developed during the 20th century, and which made four basic, simplifying assumptions:

- All people (or so-called "agents") are consistently rational.
- The best way to model economic action is to model how individual agents behave to maximize their own gain and then aggregate the sum of this individual behavior to create macro-models.
- Free market mechanisms provide the best solution to achieve economic coordination.
- Free markets are generally inherently stable.

The neoclassical models were mainly inspired by classical models. It was about rational individuals (Adam Smith's self-interest) optimizing their atoms of pleasure (Edgeworth) to create a system that found its own balance (Adam Smith's invisible hand). The economy was modeled from individuals up: the sum of individual behavior created an aggregate behavior (Walras and Pareto).

The school had several scientific and practical advantages. A clear strength was the fact that it was based on a more elegant modeling approach than the Keynesian school. Any model that is based on simulations of how its smallest entities behave has the potential to be more correct and more flexible than a model that makes gross assumptions on the macro level. Secondly, the systems found their own equilibrium. You could change any parameter in the models, and the system would then find a new equilibrium after a transition period. This meant that you could derive a clear answer to any question like "which effect will it have if we raise taxes by 3%? The flip side was that the assumptions had to be really simple in order to make the models workable: it was, for instance, basically assumed that people were rational and that markets were efficient — something that Keynes had disagreed with. The neoclassical synthesis evolved over the years until it, according to Paul Samuelson (1955), was "accepted in its broad outlines by all but about 5% of the extreme left and the extreme right among writers".

The fact that neoclassical theorists assumed that markets were rational and efficient did not mean that they pretended that business cycles didn't exist. It would be absolutely coherent to assume that markets are efficient and people rational and at the same time observe business cycles if these were caused by series of external shocks. The shocks were like Ragnar Frisch's "stick". The basic assumption was that shocks that were external to the marketplace itself caused the fluctuations. But the neoclassicists explained these fluctuations with factors that were not inherent to the way a free market economy works.

Monetary or real factors?

The neoclassicists assumed initially, like Marshall, Wicksell and Hayek, that monetary factors committed by central banks were largely responsible business cycles (this doesn't make Hayek a neoclassicist since he didn't believe in rational agents and efficient markets). The early neoclassicists focused on monetary explanations for business cycles took two directions:

- *Assuming relative price confusion.* Increased money supply raised all prices. However, individual producers assumed mistakenly that they have a particular price benefit (a relative price increase), whereas the actual reality is that all prices are rising.

- *Assuming "permanent — transitory" confusion.* People do not understand changes in money supply and do therefore not know whether price increases are temporary or transitory.

However, the focus of the neoclassical school turned gradually more and more towards "real " factors ("real" basically meaning anything that wasn't monetary).

> ***Arrow, Debreu and the neoclassical tradition***
>
> *The neoclassical tradition reached a milestone when Novel laureates Kenneth Arrow and Gerard Debreu in 1954 published a famous article called "Existence of an Equilibrium for a Competitive Economy". This article provided something that almost looked like a proof of the existence of Adam Smith's invisible hand. However, many economists would later on question the realism of this assumption, and Arrow would even join their ranks. One of the methodologies that he became fascinated with was called "game theory". This theory dealt with situations where people who interact with each other were trying to figure out what the other party would do next. The theory which was first described by John von Neumann and Oscar Morgenstern could be used to describe a number of realistic situations where different players in a market had different (or asymmetric) knowledge. This was particularly relevant in financial markets, but also for situations where a central bank or government try to influence the economy.*

REAL BUSINESS CYCLE THEORIES

The concept of real business cycles was not new. Jevons had, for instance, proposed it with his somewhat dubious "sunspot" business cycle theories and Schumpeter with his waves of innovations.

The basic assumption of the neoclassical real business cycle school was that the main causes of business cycles were shocks caused, for instance, by new technical innovations, changing habits, wars, political changes, or nature (the focus was on supply shocks — a change in the output of something). These models were not assuming that the economy would respond proportionally to everything that hit it — and when it got hit. The assumption was that there were inherent propagation mechanisms that converted the effects of the external shocks into more regular, recurrent movements of contractions and expansions. However, the theoretical approach had a new and odd angle: it stated that *the economy always was in equilibrium, even when it fluctuated widely!*

The explanation was simple: markets are efficient and they will always move towards equilibrium. What happened was that the economy from time to time received a shock, and the markets would each time move through a step of transitory phases, all of which represented the best equilibrium possible at the time. The movement was smooth and "cyclical" simply because there was a natural, balanced propagation mechanism that played out as a response to the shock. You could call a real business cycle a "floating Walrasian equilibrium".

The attraction of this approach was that you could preserve the neoclassical equilibrium models and their foundation in micro-economics and yet explain business cycles.

The first significant attempt to describe modern real business cycle theory appeared in an article in Econometrica in November 1982. The article was written by Finn Kydland, a professor from Carnegie-Mellon University in Pittsburg and Edward Prescott, who was adviser in the Research Department of Federal Bank of Minneapolis and Professor of Economics at the University of Minnesota. The title of the article was called "Time to Build and Aggregate Fluctuations". This article described the so-called real business cycle model — the stick and rocking chair model previously introduced by Ragnar Frish, whereby business cycles were caused by external shocks and where the cyclical movements were created by the inherent propagation mechanisms as the effects of the shocks rippled through the economic systems.

Real business cycle models were nice from a theoretical/modeling point of view, but they generated an unusual amount of critical articles. A typical example came when Prescot presented an article about real business cycle theories ("Theory Ahead of Business Cycle Measurement") at a conference in 1986. One of the responses was an article ("Some Sceptical Observations on Real Business Cycle Theory") by Larry Summers, the Harvard professor who would in 1999 be appointed Secretary of Finance of The United States — possibly the most powerful economic position in the world. Larry Summer's response expressed a rather unfavorable view on real business cycle theories:

> "These theories deny propositions thought self-evident by many academic macro economists and by all those involved in forecasting and

controlling the economy on a day-to-day basis. They assert that monetary policies have no effect on real activity, that fiscal policies influence only through their incentive effects, and that economic fluctuations are caused entirely by supply rather than demand shocks."

And he continued:

"If these theories are correct, they imply that the macroeconomics developed in the wake of the Keynesian revolution is well confined to the ashbin of history. And they suggest that most of the work of contemporary macro economists is worth little more than that of pursuing astrological science."

Summers argued that the parameters in Prescott's model were not right:

"Prescott's growth model is not an inconceivable representation of reality. But to claim that its parameters are securely tied down by growth and micro observations seems to me a gross overstatement. The image of a big loose tent flapping in the wind comes to mind."

Other than concluding that the parameters were wrong (and that the whole thing reminded of a loose tent flapping in the wind) he concluded that it was difficult to identify the external shocks that should cause the actual business cycles people had experienced. Every growth era and every crash or recession should have an external cause, but they were very often nowhere to see. What seemed in most cases to be a much more obvious explanation was internal nonlinearity. He explained how real business cycle theorists could go wrong:

- Proponents of real business cycles would measure technical innovation through average productivity statistics …
- … but studies based on interviews with companies showed that productivity typically fell during downswings not because of an external shock, but because companies chose to keep their employees in order to have them stand by for better times.

Another element in real business cycle theories that Summers couldn't accept was that they claimed to be "tested" even though they did not involve price data. Price data would reveal whether it was supply or demand shocks that were taking place, but without them you wouldn't know. Finally he saw the assumption of efficient markets clearing (as the neoclassical approach suggested) during a depression as very unrealistic:

> "Read any account of life during the Great Depression in the United States. Firms had output they wanted to sell. Workers wanted to exchange their labour for it. But the exchanges simply did not take place. To say the situation was Pareto optimal given the technological decline that took place between 1929 and 1933 is simply absurd, even though total factor productivity did fall. What happened was a failure in the exchange mechanism."

Summers' alternative explanation was that there was convincing evidence suggesting mechanisms that often lead to breakdowns of the exchange mechanism and credit markets.

Proponents of the real business cycle approach claimed that its key strength was that it provided a microeconomics foundation to business cycle research and that this foundation was coherent with mainstream neoclassical economics. However, opponents like Larry Summers claimed essentially that the abstractions and simplifications that they had to make in order to fit the models were so many and so gross that the result had very little relationship to reality. What they had done was to remove anything that could create inherent instability from their models — any of the positive feed-back loops, echoes, cascade reac-

"Equilibrium" and business cycles in a neoclassical context

The neoclassical approach to business cycles comprises an original source of fluctuations and a propagation mechanism, which may amplify and transmit initial fluctuations to the rest of the economy.

The term "equilibrium" in these theories referred to the propagation mechanism while "monetary" or "real" referred mainly to the supposed sources of the fluctuations.

Ragnar Frish had initially introduced the concept of external shock and a propagation mechanism. The concept of monetary shocks as responsible for the fluctuations recalled the approach taken by, among others, Hayek, and the concept of real factors like innovation causing the fluctuations recalled the approach of Joseph Schumpeter.

tions, lags and disinhibitors that were popping up everywhere when you studied real events. They ignored most of the factors that created most of the fluctuations.

THE PROBLEM WITH EQUILIBRIUM

Samuelson had combined just two simple phenomena and showed how complicated their joint behavior could be. But the point was that the business cycle theories proposed so far contained descriptions of at least five different, non-linear categories of feed-back phenomena[8]:

- *Positive feed-back loops*. Vicious circles, in which a given event stimulated another, which in turn stimulated the first. Early theories such as those of Mill and Marshall, which suggested that people accelerated spending when they saw prices go up, belonged in this category.
- *Echoes*. Clusters of investments in durable capital goods (like ships) or consumer goods (like cars).
- *Cascade-reactions*. Chain reactions with a built-in amplifier effect. This was typical in "mass-psychology" theories, in which the sentiment in one sector spread through "social contamination", which was amplified by media through the chain.
- *Lags*. Phenomena in which an action or event appearing "now" had an effect that surfaced later in time. Cobwebs and accelerators were examples of such phenomena, as were e.g. many underconsumption and overinvestment theories.
- *Disinhibitors*[9]. Phenomena in which potential negative feed-back processes were temporarily blocked by positive feed-back processes. Many psychological theories incorporating tendencies towards conventional behavior could be described as such.

THE FEED-BACK CONCEPT

The non-linear feed-back phenomena showed that there was a complicated statistical dependency between past and present. The many feed-back phenomena that the economists had described over time came in two kinds, "positive" and "negative". Positive feed-back phenomena pushed the system away from the smooth trend movement. Negative feed-back phenomena, on the other hand, pulled the economy back towards the smooth trend. Adam Smith's invisible hand was a negative feed-back concept, and so were any explicit explanations of business cycles' turning points.

But the problem was the mere abundance of feed-back phenomena that had been discovered: there was something frightening about the rapidly rising number of theories and rules which seemed plausible. Given the complexity of the combined dynamics, how could anybody ever be able to develop a clear picture of the overall behavior — let alone be able to forecast it? Had the selection process in capitalism created a system so complicated, so improbable that nobody would be able to figure it out? Just imagine if loops fitted into chain reactions, some of which were amplified to form cascades, all of which were subject to echoes, and the whole damned thing equipped with a multitude of lags and disinhibitors! Damn!

It became increasingly clear that to understand business cycles, it was not enough to pile more and more mathematical rules for the economy on top of each other. As Samuelson simulations had indicated, there could be a very strange world hidden behind the neat logics of the simulators — a world which was about to surface. But the year the two articles by Tinbergen and Samuelson were published the Second World War broke out. More and more of the competent scientists would now be asked to switch from whatever they had been doing to military research.

Business cycles and their solutions

Business cycles may be compared to resonance in mechanical devices. If you have resonance in a mechanical device, you can look at three alternative ways to reduce it. The first way is to remove the primary source of instability. *If a windshield or a skylight creates resonance when the car is driving, you change its design until the problem disappears. The second way is to* produce counterwaves. *If, for instance, the movement of a fly-wheel causes the whole construction to shudder, then you can add a lever to produce counterwaves of similar magnitude. The third possibility is to* install shock absorbers *around the sources of oscillations, for instance over the wheels and around the engine. These devices may be clumsy, but you wouldn't want to drive a car without them.*

The Keynesian treatment of business cycles is really a counterwave-solution. *As in the car, you try to meet every movement with a counter movement. But politicians and their advisors can't know for sure what the next movement will be, and that's a complication. Although difficult to prove, it appears likely that many traditional policy measures, such as public investment management and active fiscal policy, actually often increase the amplitude of business cycles.*

A more promising approach is to modify the structural phenomena in the economy, primarily by removing primary sources of instability. *If the economy is equipped with a number of unnecessary, positive feed-back processes, then you can try to modify these processes — much like the car designer does with his critical parts. A classic example of a critical process is wage indexation, where wages are automatically increased to match inflation — which will rise when wages are indexed. Such a positive feed-back loop is powerful not only because of its simple mechanics, but because it creates self-reinforcing expectations, which amplify its effect further. You can also build in new negative feed-back where it is lacking. One example is to let unions co-finance unemployment aid.*

Monetary policy can play the role of shock absorbers. *Most central banks have fairly reliable statistics about its sector aggregates. Many also have some powerful intervention tools, which are effective even in the short term. When successfully performed, monetary measures stabilize the right side of Fisher's quantity equation simply by fixing the growth rate on the left side.*

12
Brains of Steel

"Then it took the next seven years after that to convince them that they hadn't all thought of it first."

Jay Forrester

Every day you could see the same scientists and technicians walk in and out of the former class room that had been sealed off at the Moore School, Philadelphia[1]. It was hardly a great secret to the students, that the room was now being used for the development of new war technology, but only a few people knew exactly what they were doing in there, and special clearance was needed to get past the inner sanctum's locked doors. But to those who actually did get inside, however, it was immediately evident that the machine that met their eyes was completely different from anything mankind had ever built before.

CHALLENGING THE GODS

What the scientists were trying to build in this room was nothing less than the machine Charles Babbage had dreamt about 80 years before. They were building it now because they had to. At first they had considered calling it "Electronic Numerical Integrator", but then they had added two more words: "... and Computer". "ENIAC", as it was abbreviated, was supposed to be the first artificial brain, a multi-purpose ultra high-speed computer based on, not steam power, cockwheels and falling weights, of course, but on something much faster and much smaller: electronics. It should repeat a complex calculation again and again in order to simulate the alternative trajectories of grenade shells fired from artillery. The army needed these new tables desperately as the Allied forces' firing tables were off in Northern Africa because the ground there was softer than in Maryland.

The first initiative to construct the machine had been taken by John V. Mauchly, head of the Physics Department at Ursinus College near Philadelphia. In 1940 he had written to one of his students that he hoped to be able to build an electronic computing device, which would have all the answers as fast as the buttons could be depressed. Few people had believed that it could be done, but one of his students, J. Presper Eckert, immediately understood the vision and gave support to the idea. On April 9, 1943, the project was officially approved, and fifty people were assigned to the task under the leadership of Mauchly and Eckert.

One day in April 1944, the men called in two women working on a differential analyzer to show them a breakthrough on ENIAC. They set up two accumulators with 500 tubes each, and as Mauchly pressed a button, the fifth neon bulb in the first accumulator lit up. Virtually the same time, the number "5" appeared to the fourth place on the second accumulator. The two women were shocked. Had this large team of scientists worked so hard to achieve so little? — to be able to transfer a figure from one unit to another? But then the two men explained. The "5" appearing at the fourth place in the second unit meant "5,000". The two units had multiplied five with 1,000. The machine had demonstrated that it could perform a multiplication in 0.0024 seconds!

Two months later, one of the engineers working on ENIAC, Herman Goldstein, spotted John von Neumann, a short heavy-set man, while he was waiting at a railroad platform for a train to Philadelphia. Neumann was considered the world's greatest living mathematician by many. Indeed, his intelligence was beyond dispute. He could recite books which he had read years before, ad verbatim. He could often within a few minutes solve mathematical problems in his head, that other mathematicians spent hours or days with. Goldstein indicated to Neumann that he was working on the construction of an electronic computer, and soon after, Neumann dropped most of the things he was working with to join the ENIAC project. The fact that the world's most famous mathematician had decided to join the project convinced many decision-makers that the electronic computer could have much more potential than they had formerly realized.

In December 1945, the team had finally assembled the whole machine. Dominating the room completely, it was 80 feet long, eight feet wide, and three feet deep. It had 40 panels, 4,000 knobs, and 4,000 red neon tubes to show the functions of various parts inside it. These parts included 10,000 capacitors, 6,000 switches, and 17,468 vacuum tubes. It was later said that when they turned this giant machine on for the first time, the lights dimmed in the state of Philadelphia …

PROJECT WHIRLWIND

It was at about the same time that Neumann and Eckert received a 27-year-old visitor, Jay Forrester, from Massachusetts Institute of Technology, M.I.T. Jay Forrester was a graduate in electrical engineering, and he came because he had a great task in front of him: he had been asked to build a real time flight-simulation computer. His visit in Philadelphia convinced him that the computer should be digital like ENIAC, and in January 1946 his project was approved under the popular name "Whirlwind".

The Whirlwind project became the largest computer program of the late 1940s and early 1950s, with 175 employees. When the central frame was erected in 1948, it occupied 2,500 square feet. Among the improvements were faster speed and less down-time (only a few hours per day). In 1953 a very important improvement was made as the computer was equipped with a magnetic ferrite core memory. Forrester's Whirlwind program became a major success, and the technology was later used for a sophisticated air defense program.

In 1956, Jay Forrester was approached by the president of M.I.T., however, who asked if he would be interested in coming back to M.I.T., to work at the Sloan School of Management. Forrester agreed, as he saw a very interesting potential for the new computers, which had implications in a number of sciences: their enormous capacity permitted vast, experimental simulations. You could use the computers to test an equation by checking whether the results looked reasonable, and then maybe modify the parameters a bit before trying again. He called this new discipline "Systems Dynamics."

BEERS AND BUSINESS CYCLES

Forrester was interested in business cycles, and soon he and his staff began looking at the old business cycle literature and started to play with small simulation models. One of their early studies was in a small board-game that simulated potential instability in a single business sector. The game was a kind of "Monopoly", a mini-world where players took turns in making their moves over an hour and a half, and where you had to earn as much (or, rather, spend as little) as you could. To ensure that the students at M.I.T. grasped the concept, the game was centered around beer distribution.

The players used an electronic play-board, which illustrated four sectors in the world of beer:

- Brewery
- Distributor
- Wholesaler
- Retailer

Sessions typically involved three to eight teams of four players, where each player was responsible for one of the four sectors. The players had full information on everything except for consumer demand (which was in a deck of cards). Only retailers knew consumer demands, and only as it progressed (when they took one card from the deck of cards for each new "week". The game lasted 40 "weeks"). They were not allowed to communicate, but they were all interested in optimization, as the price was given to teams, not individuals. Their tasks were to minimize costs in their own sector, given these simple rules:

- It cost $^1/_2$ dollar per week for each case of beer you had in your inventory.
- It cost two dollars per week for each case of beer ordered from you that you had not delivered in time.

The system had 27 variables and its dynamics were linear apart from the fact that you could not stop a purchase and your inventory could not be negative[2]. The system was more complicated than a simple cobweb, but obviously far more simple than a real business, let alone the entire economy. One would think it was piece of cake to manage.

WILD OSCILLATIONS

It wasn't. In the beginning they played the game at M.I.T., but later it spread to other universities in other countries, and was played by thousands of people, from high school students to chief executive officers of large companies. The experience was always the same: human behavior created instability. Many years later[3], Sterman of Sloan School of

Management, M.I.T., published the results from 48 games played over four years. The 192 participants had been business executives as well as undergraduate, MBA, and Ph.D. students at M.I.T. In every game, he had let consumer demand be identical, and very simple: four cases per week the first four weeks, then eight cases per week the last 36 weeks. There was instability and oscillation in all 48 trials. Between week 20 and 25, there was an average backlog at the brewery of 35 cases — *more than nine times the increase in weekly consumption*. Second, there was a clear "accelerator", as the initial disturbance of four cases per week in consumer demand was amplified through the chain. On average, *the initial increase had been amplified 700% when reaching the brewery.* So instead of stabilizing a system exposed to external shocks, the subjects ended up amplifying the disturbances. This is illustrated in Figure 12.1.

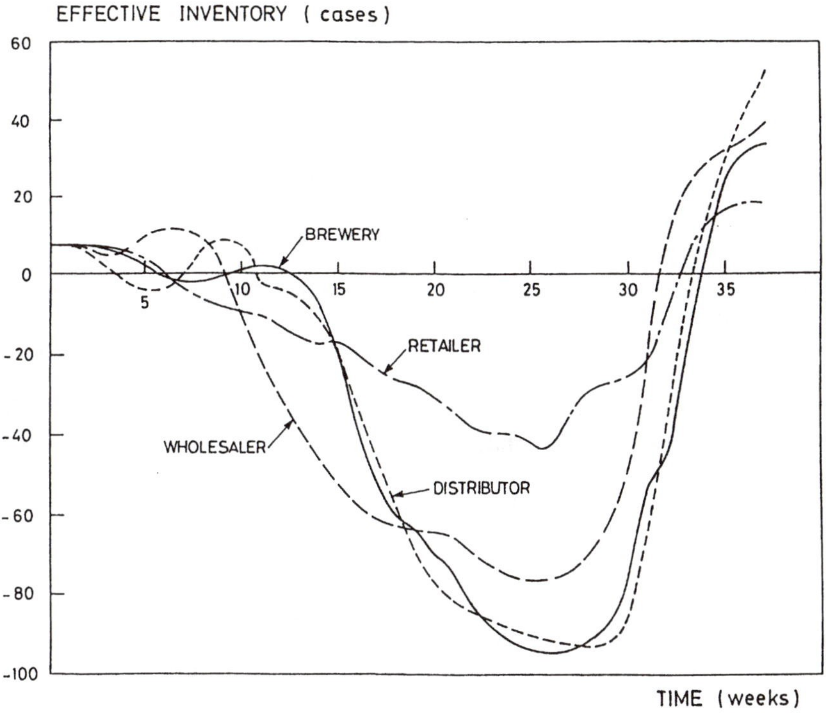

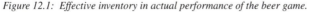

Figure 12.1: Effective inventory in actual performance of the beer game.
It can be seen that effective inventory in three of the sectors became very negative (large backlog) for a long period after the small demand shock, culminating in two sectors at levels corresponding to more than 10 weeks' demand. After 32 weeks, it finally caught up — only to become much too

After such early simulations, Jay Forrester and his team started building a dynamical multi-sector computer-model of the United States economy. The model was based on some core principles:

- Decision making in each sector was not based on mainstream theory of optimum economic equilibrium, but based on actual human behavior widely observed (not unlike in the beer game).
- Special attention was given to reservoirs/buffers such as inventories, goods in process, employee pools, bank balances and order backlogs.
- A number of non-linear relationships known from reality were incorporated.

The team started by investigating the behavior of the production sector alone, where they kept one factor, capital, fixed, so that production could only vary through various inputs of labor. What they found was surprising: the model created a wide range of periodic fluctuations, that, as Forrester concluded, seemed

> "… sufficiently diverse to simultaneously generate the business cycle, the Kuznets cycle, and the Kondratieff cycle."

The fluctuations are shown in Figure 12.2. In the next step, they expanded the model by (realistically) allowing fluctuations in capital. This created a behavior, where a new periodicity of some 15 to 25 years duration was added, equal to the Kuznets cycle. This behavior is shown in Figure 12.3.

Finally they made a simulation of some dynamic properties, that generated a Kondratieff-like behavior. Forrester wrote:

> "A sufficient cause for a 50-year fluctuation appears to lie in the movement of people between sectors, the long line to change production capacity of capital sectors, the way capital sectors provide their own input capital as a factor of production, the need to develop excess capacity to catch up on deferred demand, and the psychological and speculative forces of expectations that can cause over-expansion in the capital sectors."

Jay Forrester found that the conclusions could have radical implications for the understanding of the business cycle. Firstly they indicated that

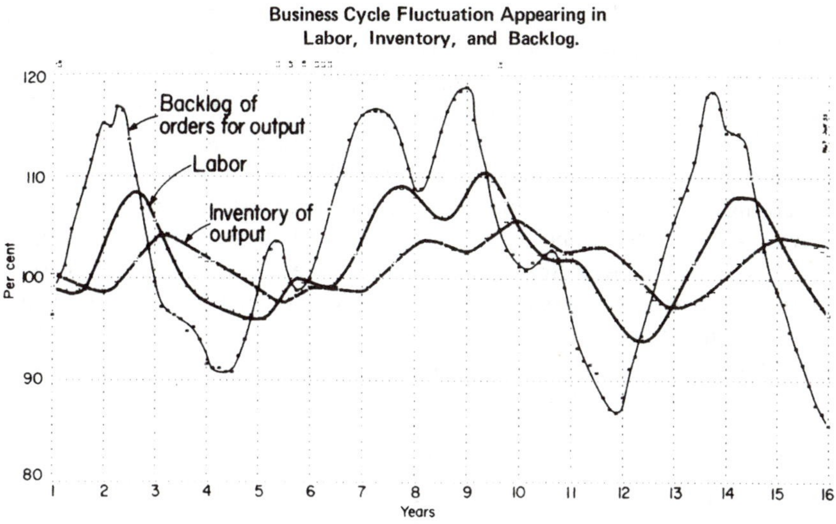

Figure 12.2: Effective inventory, backlog and labor in The Systems Dynamics National Model, M.I.T. Source: Forrester, 1976.

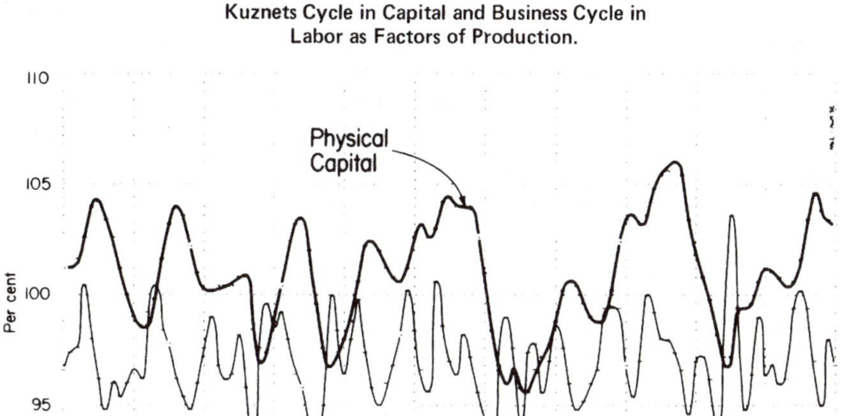

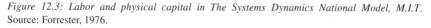

Figure 12.3: Labor and physical capital in The Systems Dynamics National Model, M.I.T. Source: Forrester, 1976.

the so-called "Phillips curve" could be wrong. Before the 1970s, the "Phillips curve" concept had been widely accepted. This curve expressed a simple trade-off between unemployment and inflation. If you wanted low unemployment, you had to accept a fairly high inflation. (In the United States, for instance, as late as in 1970, the major econometric models indicated that you could reach a low unemployment level by accepting an inflation of 4%). But what Jay Forrester's simulations had shown was that the economy could indeed be dominated by several business oscillations, like Schumpeter had suggested in 1939. If so, then there might not be any such simple relationship between inflation and unemployment. Instead it could very well be that the economy could have both, or neither of the two evils, depending on the mode of all three cycles:

> "Potentially, three different and largely uncoupled dynamic modes may exist. First could be the business cycle that yields a cyclic variation in both wage change and unemployment and gives rise to the Phillips curve relationship. Second could be the Kondratieff cycle that may be producing the increase in unemployment. Third could be the usual relationship between money supply and prices that is producing inflation. If these different modes are sufficiently separate, then money supply affects inflation without reaching the problem of unemployment."

Forrester suggested that economists were at a risk of misinterpreting current events if they were not aware of these potential independent cyclical phenomena. If his assumption was correct, then the econometricians might be missing some very vital points in their endeavors to make forecasting systems for the economies …

Macroeconomic models

Lawrence Klein was one of the first to introduce the term "macroeconomics" in his article "Macroeconomics and the Theory of Rational Behavior" from 1946. Klein introduced the team approach to macroeconomic model building, whereby large groups of scientists worked together to create large aggregate simulation models with several hundred or several thousand equations.

Large scale econometric models normally contain at least 100 equations that represent different aspects of macroeconomic behavior, with additional equations that represent definitions, external inputs, and constraints. They exist in all shapes and forms, but the typical modern model is non-linear and complex, and it will typically combine elements from neo-Keynesian models (assuming market inefficiencies) with elements from neoclassical models (assuming market efficiency). Some of the best known commercial models for Business Cycle research are Data Resources, Inc (The DRI Model), Lehman Brothers ("Sinai-Boston Model"), Chase Econometrics, Wharton Econometric Forecasting, Associates ("The Wharton Model"), and Lawrence Meyer and Associates (The LHM&A Model). The best known public models include the NBER model, and project LINK, which combines a number of local models to create an international super-model.

The LINK project expanded so that it as early as in 1987 included over 20,000 equations representing 79 macroeconomic models.

13
The Discovery of Deterministic Chaos

> *"I can stand brute force, but brute reason is quite unbearable. There is something unfair about its use. It is hitting below the intellect."*
>
> Oscar Wilde

The Whirlwind computer project was still very young and Jay Forrester had not yet begun his studies of economic instability when a small paper entitled "Long Term Storage Capacity of Reservoirs" was published in April 1950 by the American Society of Civil Engineers. The author of the paper was H.E. Hurst, a hydrologist who had worked on the Nile River Dam Project since 1907.

Judged by its title, it should have little relationship with the business cycle models that Forrester later developed, but actually it had. Hurst's primary object was to propose a method for dimensioning water reservoirs, or dams. And what happened in water reservoir systems had interesting similarities with the problems when you had economic reservoirs — like the beer inventories in the beer game.

Hurst's problem wasn't simple. The most important part was to forecast the natural fluctuations in the discharge levels from each river and lake involved. The Ugandan Government had proposed combining a large reservoir in Lake Victoria with two small, regulating reservoirs in Lake Albert and Lake Kioga. A simpler, alternative plan would include only Lake Albert. Obviously, there were many statistical problems, including rainfall, runoff and discharges of tributaries, etc.. Hurst had descriptions of the discharges since 1904, but how could he be sure that this limited period was representative for the future? What if it wasn't? What if the dams ran dry, irrigation ceased and people starved for that reason? Or if the dams were flooded?

THE FAT TAIL PROBLEM

Most people with a basic knowledge of statistics would probably start out with a simple approach to this problem:

> "Natural phenomena are usually subject to a Gaussian distribution pattern — a so called bell-curve distribution. Such must also be the discharge levels, and with more than 40 years of observation, you can easily calculate the average and the standard-deviation. Fill that into your Gaussian distribution equation, and you can calculate the likelihood that the fluctuations will exceed any critical level. According to the mechanics of Gaussian distributions, maximum fluctuations will grow with the square root of the time-span. We can call this the "square root N-rule". If over 40 years you have observed a maximum fluctuation (e.g. difference between highest and lowest discharge level)

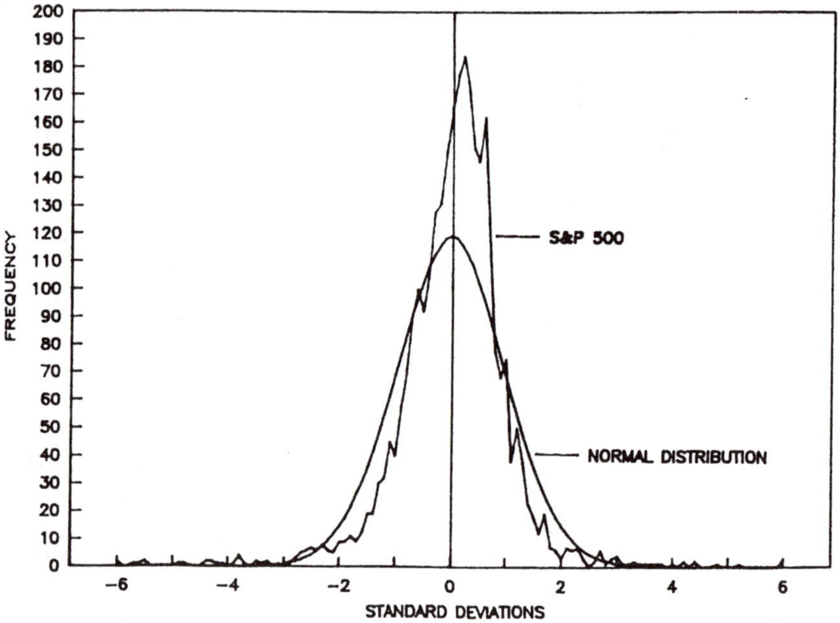

Figure 13.1: Gaussian- and Pareto distribution. Frequency distribution of S&P 500 5-day returns, January 1928 — December 1989: Normal versus actual returns.
Source: Peters, E.E.: "Chaos and Order in the Capital Markets", John Wiley & Sons, 1991.

of 24 billion m3, then over 500 years, the expected max. deviation is likely to be √500/40)*24 = 84.85. Given that information, you can reduce the problem to a cost/benefit analysis, where you compare the cost of any solution with the risk it bears, that the water-levels become too high or too low."

Neat and simple. But Hurst knew that such logic would not be exactly right — in fact, it could be fatally wrong. The reason was that many natural phenomena tend to have "fat tails"[1] and a higher than expected top, when compared to a Gaussian distribution.

A STRANGE GAME OF CARDS

Hurst didn't have access to any of the new computers, so to investigate the problem he made what he called a "probability pack of cards", which contained the following cards[2]:

Value	Number of cards
9	1
7	3
5	6
3	10
1	13
–1	13
–3	10
–5	6
–7	3
–9	1
Total	66

From this pack of cards, he drew one, recorded the number, put it back, and repeated this 1,000 times (a process which lasted more than three hours). He found that the standard deviation in the statistical distribution was 3.64, and the mean 0.03 (most likely theoretical value was 0.0). When the results were drawn graphically, they showed a standard bell-curve distribution, just as they should. But now he changed the game in the following manner:

- First he drew any card from the pack. Let's assume he drew a "–5".
- Then he put back the card, shuffled and divided the pack into two new packs of 33 cards each called "A" and "B", respectively. In "A" he put a joker.
- Then (assuming that the first card was "–5") he took the five lowest cards from pack B and put them in pack A. Afterwards he took the five highest cards out of pack A and put them in pack B. (Had his first draw been "+3", then he would have moved 3 high cards from B to A and low from A to B).
- Then he shuffled pack A, drew again and made a new transfer of cards between A and B accordingly.
- He kept doing so until he drew the joker. When that happened, he remixed pack A and B into one pack again and started all over. But he continously noted down the results.

This simple game, he believed, contained three characteristics which resemble many real, dynamic systems. First of all, it contained *positive feed-back*, in the sense that any initial random event tended to be "self-amplifying". If the first card you drew was negative, then the probability that the second card would also be negative rose to more than 50%. And the larger the negative figure in the first card, the larger the probability that the second card would also be negative. And the chances for the third being negative would be even bigger. And so on. Secondly, there was an element of *chance*: you could never be sure what card you would draw next. You only knew about the probabilities. And third, the joker represented a "*circuit breaker*", a tendency for the positive feed-back reactions to be occasionally broken off. (On average, this joker appeared in one of every 34 draws).

When Hurst made these experiments, he got a distribution which was not exactly Gaussian; it had fat tails due to the feed-back element. Inspired by his card games, he set out to find a simple method to describe how strong the feed-back tendency in any given system was. He used three basic variables:

- "N", the number of observations of, for example, days, years or whatever.
- "R", the distance ("range") between highest and lowest value recorded during "N".
- "S", the "standard deviation"; the average distance from each single observation to the average of all observations.

So *N*umber, *R*ange and *S*tandard deviations were the tools. He now introduced the following relationship:

$$R/S = (a \times N)^H$$

We have not defined "a" yet. This stands for a constant, an individual figure which is characteristic for any natural case you investigate.

But what is in this equation? Consider first this: *In a Gaussian distribution, the range is expected to grow with the square root of the number of observations.* To make this fit in our equation, H — our last variable — must be 0.5 (as an exponent of 0.5 is the same as a square root). So if the distribution is Gaussian, then H = 0.5.

Consider next the modified card game. Here you had positive feed-back leading to fat tails in the distribution pattern. *In positive feed-back systems, the range will grow by more than the square root of the number of observations.* So if you have self-amplifying processes, H will be higher than 0.5. The highest theoretical value of H is 1.0, as this means that observed maximum range can be expected to grow in direct proportion to the number of observations. Such a system would be, shall we say, "completely wild". On the other hand, if H is between 0 and 0.5, it means that the system has a tendency to dampen itself.

In Hurst's first card-game, H was 0.5. In the second game (with positive feed-back), it was 0.714. If he changed the rules so that an initial draw of a negative card would lead him to insert more *positive* cards in pack A, then H would be between 0.0 and 0.5. In that case, we would call the system "dampened" — or we would say that it contained "*negative* feed-back loops" — or shock absorbers, if you please.

Now one might ask what "S" did in his equation. It was there to make it "universal" or "dimensionless" — to make things comparable. Without "S" (and "a"), H would no longer be confined between 0.0 and 1.0. It would depend on the volatility and shakiness of the system — not only on the feed-back tendency. (An example: without "S" and "a", his second card-game would give a different value for H if you simply multiplied the value of each card by two. That would be unfortunate, as multiplying each card by any given number would not change the nature of the dynamics a bit).

Back to Nature. Hurst sampled a number of different time series from natural phenomena and calculated H. Here is what he found:

Evidence of positive feed-back in natural systems

	Number of "N" observations	Hurst exponent "H"
River levels, discharges, etc	99	0.75
Rainfall	168	0.70
Temperature and pressure	115	0.70
Varves (Lake Saki in the Crimea)	85	0.81
Annual growth of tree rings	114	0.69
Varves (Tamishaming, Ontario and Moen, Norway)	90	0.77
Sunspots and wheat prices	25	0.69
Total	690	
Mean		0.73

The H-values were more than 0.5 in all observations, so you could find a great deal of positive feed-back in the behavior of nature. And the average H-values were quite close to the value in his modified card-game. By the use of this system, Hurst could calculate a simple expression of the positive feed-back tendency in all the different phenomena which could influence the behavior of his reservoirs — whether it be created by loops, echoes, cascade-reactions, lags, or disinhibitors.

BENOIT MANDELBROT

One other scientist obsessed with fat tails was Benoit Mandelbrot. While Hurst was enjoying his sundowns in Egypt, perhaps overlooking the dusty streets of Cairo, Mandelbrot might be on his way to IBM's high-tech research center in Yorktown Heights, USA[3]. Mandelbrot was dabbling with mathematical problems of all sorts, and had come across exactly the same phenomenon as Hurst: he found fat tails in the most surprising places. One such place was on the blackboard in Hendrik Houthakker's office at Harvard[4]. Mandelbrot was invited to give a lecture there in 1960, and as he entered Houthakker's room, he saw on the blackboard a bell-shape drawing with two fat tails. Houthakker explained what the drawing illustrated: it was the statistical distribution of price-changes for cotton.

In a way, cotton was ideal for statistical tests, because the daily price data was both correct and available from far back in history. When Mandelbrot left after his speech, he carried with him a box with Houdhakker's cotton data on computer cards. Afterwards, he sent to the Department of Agriculture for more data, covering price movements back to 1900. Analyzing these, he found fat-tail distributions regardless of whether he was looking at daily or monthly data.

PHARAOH AND THE BUSINESS CYCLE

Mandelbrot distinguished between two dynamic properties:

- The "Noah effect" or "infinite variance syndrome", where the small movements were interrupted by violent, discontinous jumps due to disturbances
- The "Joseph effect" or "H-spectrum syndrome", which was the inherent tendency of prices to move in trends

The price movements he saw in cotton had to be a reflection of both; partly chance and partly necessity. The Noah effect took place when the economic system was pushed around by exogenous, unpredictable events. The Joseph effect occurred when you had, in Mandelbrot's words, "a very low decay of statistical dependence". The Joseph effect meant that during sustained periods of time, every observation was statistically dependent on a number of preceding observations, just like in Hurst's strange game of cards. In choosing a name for this dynamic property, Mandelbrot also let the Bible inspire him:

> "The term "Joseph effect" is, of course inspired by the Biblical story of the seven fat and seven lean years (Genesis 6:11–12). Pharaoh must have known well that yearly the Nile discharges stay up and then down for variable and often long periods of time, so they exhibit strong long-run dependence and a semblance of business cycles, but with either visible or hidden sinusoidal components"

SELF-SIMILARITY IN DYNAMIC SYSTEMS

Mandelbrot felt that he was on the track of something important. For a long time the bias of science had been "Euclidian" or "Newtonian". That meant that there was a tendency towards "reduction" and "linearity". Scientists looked for the straightest line, so to speak, for the steadiest behavior. It was not that there was anything wrong in Euclidian science, except that the bias towards it was just too strong. If you looked at reality, there were many things which were not at all linear. Mandelbrot used a coast-line as an example. If you look at a coast-line on a map, you can estimate with a ruler more or less how long it is. If you walk along it, you will find that it is in fact much longer, as you notice all the little bays within bays, and coves within coves. Get down on your knees and try with the ruler in real-size: it gets still longer. Take home a small sample and check in your microscope: still longer. The real world was incredibly complex. In almost all cases, you would find it full of "non-linear" phenomena containing feed-back of all sorts. One early example in economics appeared when Samuelson combined just two simple phenomena and showed how complicated their joint behavior could be, but there was obviously much more to it.

A traditional solution to this complication would be to assume linearity anyhow, and then brush off the remainder as statistical noise. Mandelbrot's interest was what happened if instead you assumed non-linearity in your simulations. He had already discovered one potential property of such non-linear behavior in feed-back systems: that of "self-similarity". *Non-linear systems often repeated the same behavior in different scales* — just as he had observed with the fat tails in his daily and monthly cotton data. He gave a special name to such self-similar phenomena. He called them "fractals".

COMPUTER MUDDLE

Mandelbrot was not the only scientist exploring non-linear behavior. At M.I.T. the American meteorologist Edward Lorenz had programmed his radio-tube computer to simulate weather forecasts[5]. The computer, a "Royal Macbee", did one of the things that computers are very good at: it made chain-calculations. First you fed into it the data describing the weather on a given day, for example wind speeds, atmospheric pressures, temperatures and humidity. Given this, the Macbee would calculate the weather for the next day, which it would again use as in-data for the third day, and so on. In about one minute, the Macbee could simulate the development of 24 hours.

One day in 1961, five years after Jay Forrester had started his system dynamics studies at the same institution, Lorenz looked at a simulation that he regretted having broken off too early. He decided to continue it, but with a small overlap period to check that it was indeed a continuation of what was already calculated. So he took the data printout and copied carefully the values for a given day into the computer. Then he put it to work, and went down the hall to get himself a cup of coffee. When he came back after an hour, he found something which was rather odd: in the "overlap" period of the two calculations, they did in fact not overlap as they should have. Everything in the system was completely predetermined: the in-data and the equation were entirely controlled by him, and they were entirely identical in the two runs. But the simulations diverged, in the beginning a little, and later a lot. What could be wrong?

The problem was the size of the print paper. The figures on this paper had only three decimals, as there wasn't space for more. He had copied figures with three decimals into the program although the program in fact operated with six figures. So the difference in the overlap calculation was due to differences starting in the fourth decimals of the initial data. The more he thought about this, the more incredible it appeared: Apparently you couldn't make a long-term weather forecast unless you knew, say, temperatures, with four or more decimals. It was not enough to know if the temperature in a given place on "day one" was 21.563 degrees or if it was in fact 21.563975 degrees. To have such figures for all the variables, covering the whole globe, was impossible. With little sense of publicity, Lorenz published his observations in "The Journal of Atmospheric Sciences", under the title "Deterministic Non-periodic Flow".

If anybody read the article, they didn't make much fuss about it. During the following 10 years, it was quoted less than 10 times by other authors. But then, in 1972, a scientist at the Institute for Physical Science and Technology at the University of Maryland came across it — and was delighted. He started copying it and giving it to anybody who cared. One day, he gave it to James York, a mathematician working at the same Institute. York understood the importance of the message, that long-term unpredictability could be a property inherent in a non-linear system. In 1975, he published his own article about the subject. It appeared in the popular “American Mathematical Monthly” with a title that no one could ignore:

> “Period Three Implies Chaos”.

That last word became the expression which people would afterwards use to cover deterministic, yet complicated and unpredictable phenomena. “Deterministic Chaos” would often be described as systems with a behavior that when tested by standard statistical methods appeared random, but which were in fact deterministic — and thus not random at all.

DON’T BLAME THE METEOROLOGISTS

It is clear that Lorenz had learned from York when he published a paper in 1979 with the title:

> “Predictability: Does the Flap of a Butterfly’s Wings in Brazil Set Off a Tornado in Texas?”

If readership is a success-criterion, this article worked. The chaos concept was catching on, and scientists started doing research about it everywhere. The flap-in-Brazil paper explained that a butterfly in Brazil could determine whether there would be a tornado someplace else six months later. Even if the meteorologists seized power in the world and, determined to make weather forecasting the primary objective of mankind, covered the entire surface of the earth with small weather stations one foot apart and up in the air to the outer extreme of the atmosphere — even then they would never be able to make long-term weather forecasts. Even if all these billions of weather stations continuously sent all their data to a giant central computer, equipped with perfect mathematical simulation software, even then it wouldn’t work. Because it just might happen that a butterfly flew between two of these measurement stations, releasing a small gust of wind that they couldn’t record with sufficient precision — and that the un-recorded effect of that movement of the air would amplify through positive feed-back and decide whether that tornado would come or not.

By now, Lorenz’s point was clear: *Feed-back systems could be very “sensitive to initial conditions*” — a property that would later be called

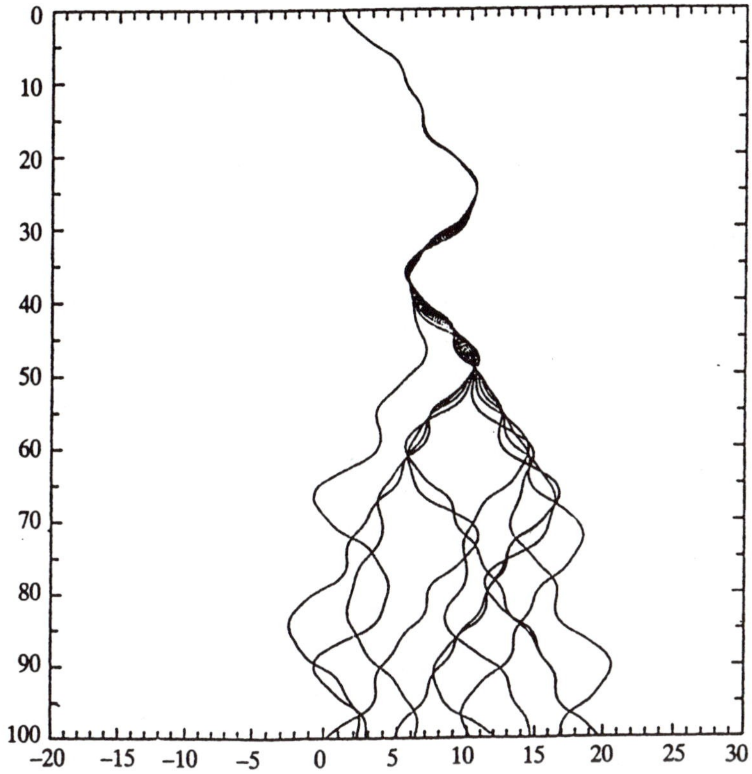

Figure 13.2: The butterfly effect.
The graph shows a mathematical simulation of 11 objects sliding down a 100-meters-long, uneven slope with peaks and troughs arranged in a sinosodial pattern. The objects start at point separated horizontally by only 5 millimeters. After sliding 100 meters, two of the objects are 20 meters apart. Source: Edward N. Lorenz, Center for Meteorology and Physical Oceanography, Cambridge, Massachusetts.

"the butterfly effect". This was an observation which was very much in contrast to Euclidian expectations, and to many layman assumptions. It was as unexpected as was Mandelbrot's observation that feed-back systems were often self-similar. By now, one knew at least two things about the behavior of such chaotic systems: as Mandelbrot had found, they were often self-similar. And Lorenz had discovered the butterfly effect. Feed-back systems could apparently create these two strange behaviors — but was that all?

SOMETHING FISHY

Far from it. Feed-back systems are notorious in not only economics and climatology, but also ecology. When Robert May developed a mathematical program for simulation of fish populations in 1971, he came across a peculiar phenomenon. His equation was designed to calculate how large a fish population would grow under various assumptions. When he had entered the chosen values for the variables into the computer, the model would simulate the ecologic behavior until the size of the population gradually settled down to some fixed level. If he changed a parameter, it would move on to a new equilibrium level.

One of his variables was fertility — the ability to lay eggs, so to speak. If the fertility was very low, the population would obviously die out. At higher fertility levels, it would reach a different equilibrium. But the peculiar thing was this: if he entered a very high fertility level, then the simulation never found an equilibrium; the population kept fluctuating endlessly and without any apparent pattern. The string of mathematical feed-back that created this chaotic behavior looked like this:

"X(n + 1) = r * X(n) * (1 – X(n))"

What this equation expressed is very simple. The left hand side of it simply means "the next value of X". And this next value of "X" is what we find on the right side: it is a constant, "r", multiplied by the present value of "X", multiplied by one minus the present value of "X". This little (and very simple) piece of feed-back mechanics created equilibrium at low parameter values, but chaos at high values of "r". This was interesting not only for the fun of it, but indeed because such equations were quite common in simulations of many kinds of dynamic systems — including economics. Like a small gene in a giant DNA molecule, such an algorithm could lie hidden in a giant simulation equation. And you would never notice the effect unless you made a multitude of factor analyses of the system dynamics with your computer. So like Charles Babbage had foreseen, the computer was really revolutionizing science.

BOUNDARIES TO CHAOS

An obvious question was how the boundaries between order and chaos might look. The only way to find out was to repeat the calculation again

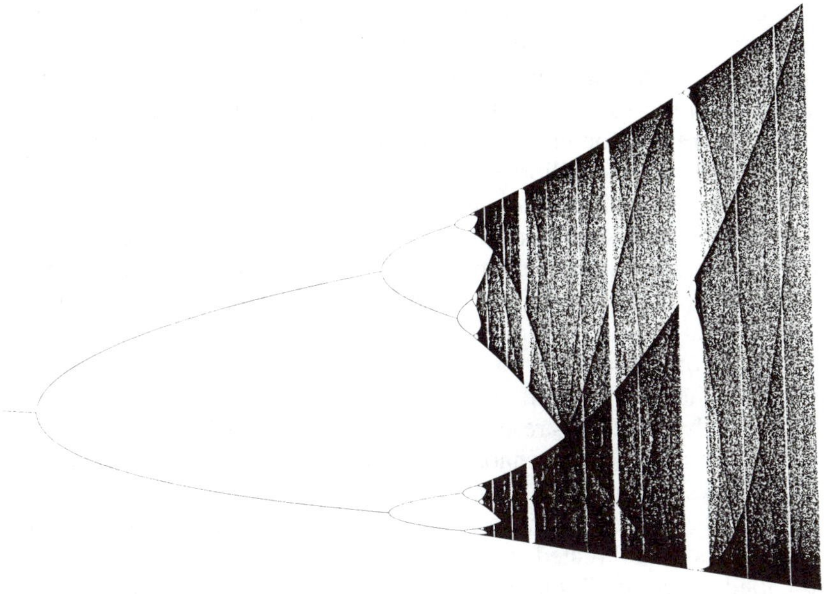

Figure 13.3: Bifurcations in a Feigenbaum Tree.
The diagram shows how a simple equilibrium (left) bifurcates into still more, finally resulting in chaotic behaviour. The simulation displays self-similarity, as fractions of the print resemble the whole. Source: Mosekilde & Thomsen, The Technical University of Denmark.

and again, each time modifying the fertility value (or "r") slightly. By doing so, May knew that he would eventually reach the transition phase between order and chaos, and see where it was. Starting from low values, the computer first drew a smooth curve, representing the gradually higher population equilibrium. But then the amazing thing happened: the curve split into two, which meant that the population, given this fertility level, had two alternative equilibria. That an equation could have two solutions was not unknown. (Take, for instance "((X * X) — 7X + 12 = 0). This has two solutions, X = 3 and X = 4). But then the curve split into four. Then to eight. Then to 16, 32, 64 … and then it broke into chaos. These concurrent splits on a road to chaos were called "period-doubling bifurcations", and the entire picture was called a "Feigenbaum Tree".

The Feigenbaum Tree conformed with the tendency towards self-similarity that Mandelbrot had described. Magnification of any area in the Feigenbaum Tree was a nearly exact copy of the whole; no matter how close you looked, it would keep on and on, developing into ever finer "fractal dust" — which kept copying the overall pattern. But the important message was that *such mechanisms could have multiple, alternative dynamic equilibria*. If this was the case in the real world, the actual size of the population (or it might be an economic variable) could be attracted to one equilibrium and stay there, or oscillate around several different levels as Halley's comet around many centers of gravity. Or it might settle at one equilibrium level until some external shock pushed it to start a cumulative movement process towards another equilibrium. Of course in reality, any social system as complicated as our economy would be subject to many more rules than expressed by this simple equation, but if only one small cockwheel in the entire machinery looked like this one, then the overall behavior could at least to some degree be subject to dynamic laws resembling the Feigenbaum Tree[7].

With the discovery of chaos, it became generally accepted that deterministic systems could be messy, and scientists started to devise new instruments to analyze these phenomena. An important group of such instruments was directed towards quantifying chaos and analyzing the so-called "attractors", the competing gravity centers, which could exert pull in a system. To understand these, it is useful to start by looking at the phenomenon called "phase space".

QUANTIFYING CHAOS

Imagine a friction-less spring nailed to the floor, which moves back and forth in a straight line. You can portray this movement by plotting its *position* against *time*, as shown in Figure 13.4. Or you can plot its *speed* against time — and the plot will look much the same. But these plots lead to a problem: to portray the total movement, the diagram should be extended horizontally forever, as the spring keeps moving. This problem can be solved by plotting the "phase space", which is simply *speed* plotted against *position* (Figure 13.5). Our spring has something called "attractors". There is a "point attractor" in its phase space; that attractor is the stable situation where the spring doesn't move at all. Without friction it would also have another attractor — a "limit cycle", which is the steady, circular movement. And another, where it moves along a straight line. We can also be more realistic and assume that the movement is dampened. In that case the phase space for the spring in a circular movement will look like Figure 13.6.

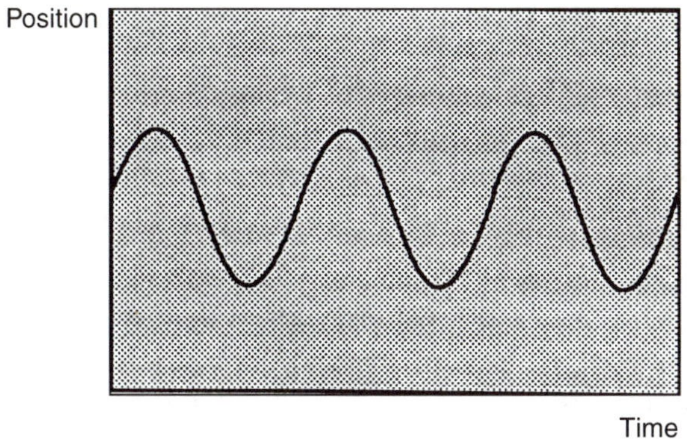

Figure 13.4: Position plotted against time for a moving spring.

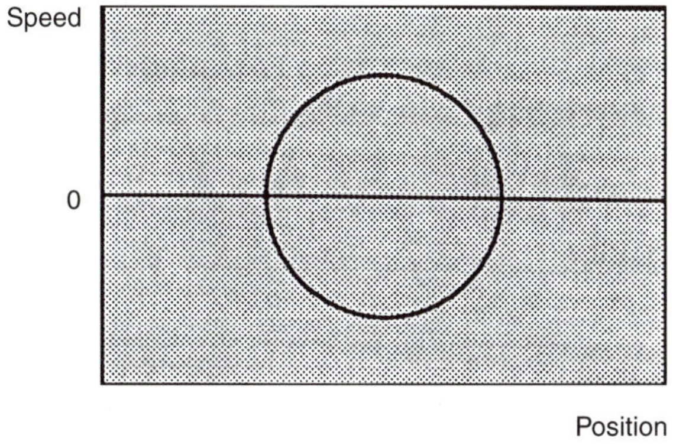

Figure 13.5: The undamped, circular movement of a spring plotted in phase space.

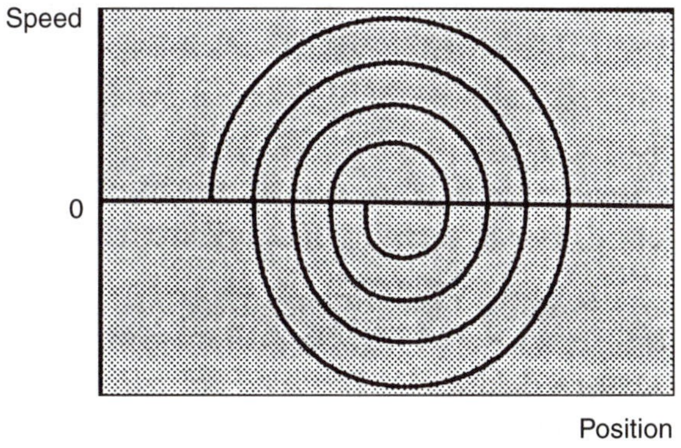

Figure 13.6: The dampened, circular movement of a spring in phase space.

In a sense, you can describe the whole potential behavior of a system simply by defining the attractor. Simple equilibrium economics can be said to focus on the presence of point attractors — of one, simple equilibrium. A naive business cycle theory could describe another attractor which would be a sinusoidal movement.

But then think about the situation with the Feigenbaum Tree. After the first bifurcation, you have two attractors. In the simplest situation, the object/variable we observe might try to circle around one of these attractors, but get interrupted when it gets near the other, circle around that, get interrupted again, and so forth. Its movements will be restricted by its initial energy, so the behavior in phase space will be limited — *but it is possible that it never follows the same path twice*. Such attractors, where orbits stay within a defined region in phase space but never repeat each other, are called "strange attractors". Strange attractors in two or three dimensions are not that difficult to grasp, but a system may have five, ten or many more dimensions, which you can not visualize at one time. The concept will be helpful anyway; you can draw up your portrait in three dimensions at a time and then have your computer print two-dimensional pictures of slices of the whole. If the system is completely random, then you will only find noise and no patterns, no matter how you slice it: The print will fill phase space completely. But if it is deterministic; if it abides to inherent, dynamic rules, then you will run into a structure, in which data "clump" together, because they are statistically correlated. No matter how well disguised the rules are, their presence will eventually be unmasked by this visual structure.

When you study something real — the economy for instance — you should of course never expect a single class of behavior — rather one with a mixture of some linear dynamics, some non-linear but not chaotic dynamics, some chaotic dynamics, and some Brownian noise[8]. Chaos usually pops up in the following situations[9]:

- When a marginally stable limit cycle moves through period doublings and attains chaotic mode, as it is pushed very hard (like in a hyperinflation situation or a speculation orgy)
- When two or more self-generating oscillators are coupled (like in a Kondratieff/Kuznets/Kitchin scenario)
- When an oscillating system is driven exogeniously by another force (like Wall Street driven by the business cycle, or vice versa).

But for a long time, these were all rules of thumb. The question was how could you measure the chaotic element?

A MEASURE OF THE BUTTERFLY EFFECT

The answer came from the Russian scientist A.A. Lyapunov, who had developed a method for quantifying one of the features of chaos, the butterfly effect. Through an enormous amount of computer simulations, you could find out whether the orbits diverged or contracted in phase space — in each dimension. Simply stated, he would calculate the movement from a given initial condition, then change that initial condition slightly and calculate the movement again. If there was a butterfly effect, then the small difference in initial condition would amplify over time; the geometrical distance between the two simulations in phase space would grow exponentially. So *a positive Lyapunov effect meant that the difference in initial conditions would be amplified over time* — and, consequently, that a change in initial condition would lead to a cumulative movement away from this condition. A negative exponent meant that the two diverging exponents converged. An example: if we bumped into a table with our spring nailed to it, it would soon revert to its former movement: the three dimensions in this simple system would all have negative Lyapunov exponents. We would express this (or a simple, dampened version of the business cycle) as follows:

(–,–,–)

A Lyapunov exponent of zero, on the other hand, would mean that the system would show neither butterfly effects nor inherent stability in the given dimension. A naive business cycle model expressed as a limit cycle had two negative and one neutral exponent, expressing that it contracted vertically and horizontally, but not over time:

(0,–,–)

Three-dimensional strange attractors had one negative exponent, which meant that it was sensitive to initial conditions; one neutral (it kept circulating forever) and one positive (its movements in phase space were limited within barriers; there was a negative pull to restrict its movements):

(+,0,–)

In 1979, O.E. Rossler had devised a system with four differential equations, that created behavior with two positive exponents in four dimensional space:

(+,+,0,–),

Such behavior had never been detected in real life, but it was given a name anyhow; he called it "hyperchaos".

THE QUESTION OF THE JOKER

Hurst had devised a method for measuring the net feed-back effect, and Lyapunov for measuring butterfly effects. But there was another problem: how could you measure the occurrence of turning points?

In 1950, Hurst had the key to this problem, but he never really used it[10]. The key was in a graphical design, the "Rescaled Range Analysis", which he developed to analyze his irrigation problem. What Hurst did was to insert his observations into a graph with the following values:

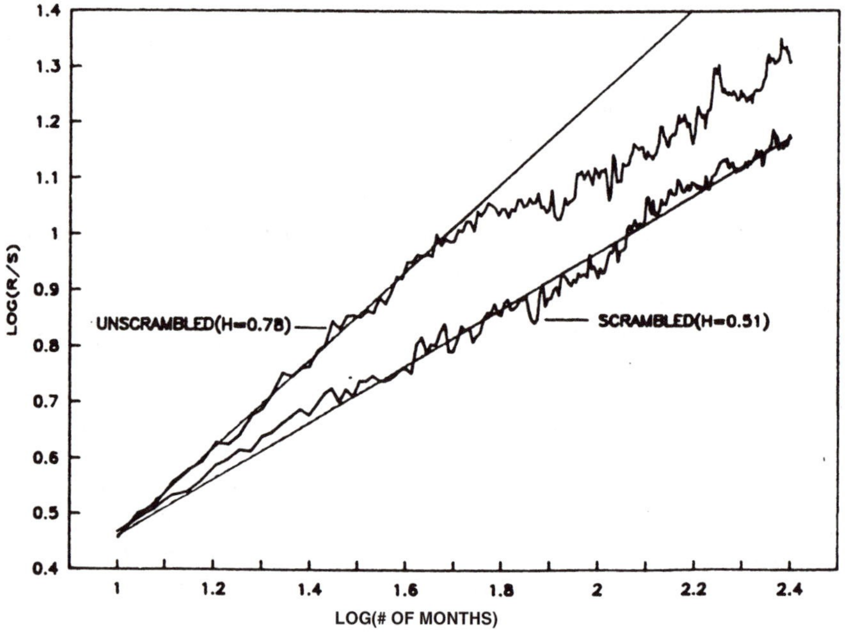

Figure 13.7: Scrambling test: S&P 500 monthly returns, January 1950–July 1988.
In the unscrambled run, the Hurst exponent is 0.78. When the figures have been mixed randomly, the exponent becomes 0.51. Source: Peters, E.E.: "Chaos and Order in the Capital Markets", John Wiley & Sons, 1991.

- The horizontal axis: the number of observations, N
- The vertical axis: R/S, or the maximum range divided by the standard deviation.

For practical reasons he used logarithmic values on both axis. As you plotted the results of different tests (with different numbers of observations) in this system of coordinates, the angle of the slope expressed the Hurst exponent, or Joseph effect, H. If it was more than 45 degrees, then it meant that H was more than 0.5, indicating positive feed-back.

That was as far as he went. But think it over: Hurst's card-game contained a Joker, which appeared at random intervals, but on average, in one draw of every 34. Every time it appeared, it destroyed the prevailing feed-back process. This meant that the cumulative tendency would be less for long term observations than for those of shorter term — the slope

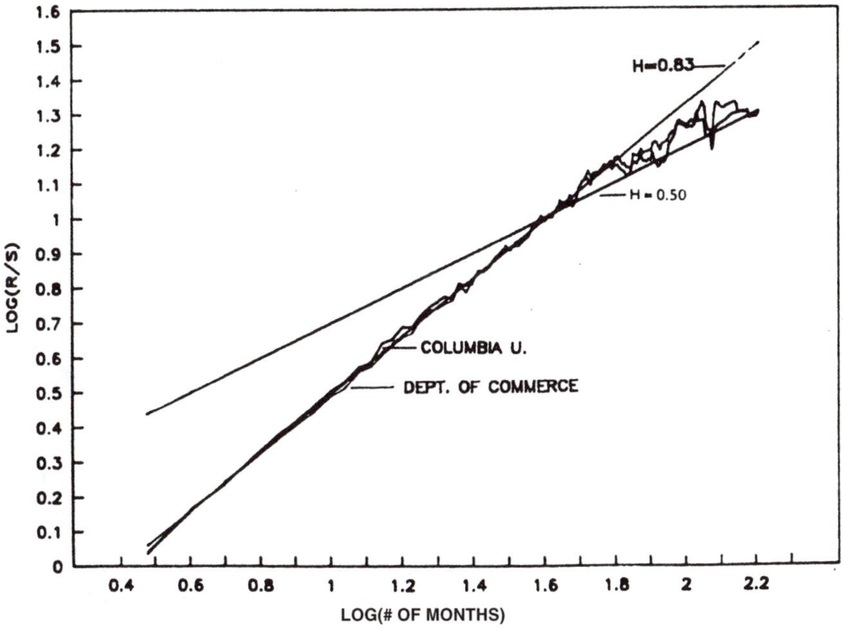

Figure 13.8: Leading indicators in the USA.
The graph is an analysis of leading indicators as measured by the Department of Commerce and Columbia University. In both cases the Hurst exponent (the slope) is 0.83, implying positive feed-back. The slope breaks to the neutral angle (0.50) after on average around five years (log 1.6 months). Source: Peters, 1991.

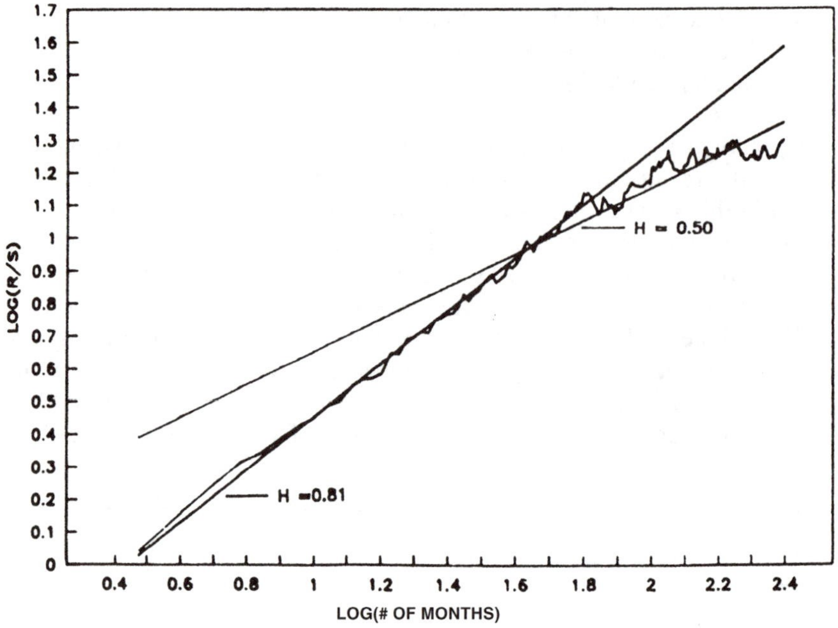

Figure 13.9: New business formation.
This graph shows an R/S analysis of the statistical data for new business formation in the USA for the period January 1950 — January 1990. The Hurst exponent is estimated to be 0.81. Source: Peters, 1991.

of the H-curve would in other words break off and flatten. It was this feature in Hurst's statistical diagram that Edgar Peters, a Senior Manager at PanAgora Asset Management in USA, had noticed, when he published his book, "Chaos and Order in the Capital Markets" in 1991.

Edgar Peters would fill in various time-series data in the computer, and then have them presented in the rescaled range graphs. To test the valid-ity of every run, he would repeat it, this time scrambling the data by changing the order of observations. When doing so, they should show an H-value of around 0.5 and thereby demonstrate that it was indeed the "memory", the order of the data over time, that mattered. If the H-value didn't change by scrambling, then the original data must have been as truly uncorrelated as the scrambled data.

Then he started filling in economic data covering the years 1940 to 1990. Each time, he would find on his computer screen a smooth line, which would then break off at some point; and this point would tell how soon the "Joker" arrived — when the feed-back tendency in average had been broken and thus the cycle had reached a turning point. Here is what he found:

	Hurst exponent	**Cycle length**
Leading indicators	0.83	appr. 5 years
Industrial production	0.91	appr. 5 years
New business formation	0.81	appr. 5 years
Housing starts	0.73	appr. 5 years

All the time the series showed net positive feed-back, and the cycle length was about five years — conforming well with the average upswing phase of the Kitchin cycle in the time span covered. So using Hurst's original platform, Peters had quantified cycle length and positive feed-back of the Kitchin cycle in America.

The practical implications of chaos theory

Chaos theory has taught us how non-linear systems can behave. It has also inspired the development of new tools in science, engineering, software writing, etc. But it is unlikely to produce many practical tools for economic and financial forecasting.

What it does give us, however, is basic understanding of the nature of some economic and financial systems. This basic understanding makes it easier for us to determine which groups of practical forecasting tools can have validity in various situations. An example: An econometric long term forecasting model is used. Testing its behavior over a policy space with tools associated with chaos theory reveals that it produces hyper-chaotic behavior. Conclusion: Either the economic system in question cannot be forecast beyond medium term or the econometric model is wrong.

THE MAIN FEATURES OF CHAOS

What the chaos scientists had discovered was that systems subject to even very simple feed-back rules could exhibit an extremely complicated behavior. They had also realized the fact that you could not analyze non-linear systems as you did linear ones, by breaking the system into details, which were analyzed one at a time. Non-linear systems had to be understood in their entirety. The most important features characteristic to such systems — when they were chaotic — were these:

- *Extreme sensitivity to initial conditions* (Edward Lorenz's butterfly effect). This meant that there was a distinct barrier against long-term prediction.
- *Self-similarity* (Mandelbrot's fat tails in different scales). Everybody knew that in nature and real systems, patterns would not copy themselves forever into endless fractal dust as in the "pure" equations, but there could be a tendency to repetition in at least many scales.
- *Multiple attractors in some parameter intervals* (the bifurcations in Say's Feigenbaum Tree). The potential existence of such competing attractors opened the possibility for much more complicated cyclic motions than simple sinusodial oscillations.

These were some of the incredible things that Samuelson had been unable to see for the lack of a computer when he opened the lid to the world of non-linear dynamics in 1939.

BACK TO SQUARE ONE?

It is a characteristic tendency in social sciences that you start by assuming that your systems can be explained by a few, simple rules. Then, as the research literature piles up, so do the number of dynamic rules. This was exactly what had happened in business cycle research. Before the appearance of computers, a large number of phenomena which could explain cycles had been discovered. What the system dynamics research and chaos theory indicated was that the behavior when you started to combine your rules could be much more complicated than formerly anticipated. Knowing this, one might get frustrated by the whole thing: would business cycle theory drown in complication?

That might have occurred if it were not for one rule which penetrates the complexity of many feed-back systems: that of mode locking. Mode-locking is a phenomenon that surrounds us in daily life. If you hang two mechanical clocks side by side on a wall, they will often synchronize because of the small mechanical impulses that travel through the wall.

When the audience applauds after a ballet, it will suddenly start clapping at the same rhythm, although nobody conducts them. Mode-locking happens when a number of initially uncorrelated processes lock into each other's rhythm to create a strong, aggregate movement. Given a vast multitude of processes in the economy which can contribute to instability, you would end up with something very similar to random noise, if it were not for mode-locking. Because of mode-locking, a boom can spread from one sector to many, as supply creates demand, activity creates money, and money creates supply. The business cycle is a movement in the aggregate; when the economy moves, almost everything moves in the same direction because of mode-locking. And we will even see that although there can be very different circumstances triggering the aggregate movements, and although there are at least two and maybe three major business cycle oscillations in action at the same time, the scenario of each of them ends up unfolding in surprisingly identical ways. As Lucas expressed it:

> "Though there is absolutely no theoretical reason to anticipate it, one is led by the facts to conclude that, with respect to the qualitative behaviour of co-movements among series, business cycles are all alike."[11]

Using computers for economic analysis

To gain a good understanding of the economy, a combination of analysis tools must be applied. The list below gives a brief and very simplified overview of the most important quantitative analysis tools:

Method	***What you typically do***	***Examples of what you typically achieve***
Statistics	*Statistical standard equations describe typical ways according to which statistical data ("observations") can relate to each other. The statistician can now test the actual data against any of these statistical templates.*	• *Classify statistical behavior* • *Measure parameter values, such as "mean", "Standard deviation", "H-exponent", etc.* • *Provide indications of the nature of the governing rules of the system* • *Detect, classify and measure correlations in the behavior of different time series*
Econo-metrics	*You describe the economy with a system of simultaneous equations (typically very large). You input present parameter values and calculate how the economy will evolve in the future. This is a chain calculation, where the output from one calculation (one time period) becomes input for the next.*	• *Forecast the economy* • *Simulate what will happen if you change policy (i.e. raise taxes, lower interest rates, etc.)* • *Test the validity of economic theories* • *Measure economic correlations* • *Detect, classify and measure repetitive patterns in given*

		time series • Detect economic correlations
System dynamics	You describe the economy, or parts of it, with a single equation. You input parameter values and calculate how they will evolve in the future. You repeat this calculation again and again, each time modifying initial parameter values slightly, until a "policy space" of parameter values is mapped. Expression of dynamic properties, such as Lyapunov effects are measured throughout the policy space.	• Understand how the dynamic behavior of a system may change, depending on initial conditions • Identify attractors • Identify chaotic and orderly areas of behavior • Test the practical validity of economic forecasting systems
Neural networks	You feed a number of financial/economic time series into a software program. This program will then continuously test for statistical correlations within and in-between economic time series. As it finds correlations, it will start building an econometric forecasting model.	• Forecast the economy • Forecast financial markets • Reveal the presence of patterns • Submit activity recommendations
Artificial intelligence	You observe (partly through on-site interviews) how human experts with a successful track record forecast economic and/or financial events. Their decision process is then expressed as an equation. As real data are fed into this equation, it will start generating forecasts and activity recommendations.	• Forecast the economy • Forecast financial markets • Develop theories

14
Instability and Money

"There have been three great inventions since the beginning of time: fire, the wheel and central banking"

Will Rogers

Hyman Minsky was born in America in 1919, the son of two devoted socialists. He grew up with his parents, went to school and followed the family tradition to join the socialist party. Later on he managed to enter the University of Chicago, where he eventually received a B.Sc. degree in mathematics. However, he soon realized that pure mathematics shouldn't be his professional focus; he was much more interested in society and economics. In 1942 he enrolled in the Littauer School of Administration at Harvard, but had to leave after just one semester to join the army. In late 1945 he was sent overseas; first to Newport in England and then to Paris, Frankfurt and finally Berlin.

Minsky's stay in Berlin provided him inspiration that would influence his research later on. He was assigned to work in the Reports and Planning Brigade of the Manpower Division under a man named David Saposs. Saposs was a labor economist with a doctorate from Wisconsin, and he was a leading member of the anti-Communist left. Many of the people who worked for him shared his political views, and so did Minsky. Minsky claimed later that his experiences working with Saposs led him to conclude that abstract models were helpful in developing thoughts and analysis, but that they were not the final goal. The final goal was to deduct *real* conclusions with a basis in *real* situations and events. This, he thought, could only be done if you had an understanding of the prevailing institutions and the relevant historical framework.

Minsky returned to the States after the war, and there he decided to study at Harvard rather than Chicago. However, after he had been there for some time he started to wonder about some elements in the teaching agenda. One was the way that his teacher Alvin Hansen (the leading disciple of Keynes) covered fiscal policy. Minsky found that Alvin Hansen used a very orthodox Keynesian program when addressing the rules of conventional and counter cyclical fiscal policy. Furthermore, the way Hansen interpreted Keynes was, Minsky thought, rather mechanistic. Hansen didn't address uncertainty, which Minsky had understood was a vital element of Keynes' thinking, and he was virtually ignoring money and financial markets.

Minsky studied at Harvard until 1949, when he accepted his first faculty appointment at Brown University where he stayed from 1949 to 1955 and wrote his doctoral thesis. Alvin Hansen expected that Minsky would work with him, but Minsky had at that time met Joseph Schumpeter and decide to work with him instead. The subject that he would explore was relation between market structure, banking, the determinants of aggregate demand, and business cycles. He was later appointed as visiting professor at Berkeley University in California, where he studied until he joined NBER in 1960. His stay at NBER became brief, however, since he was frustrated as he realized that the data that he needed in order to conduct his studies didn't exist. He returned to Berkeley and finally, in 1965, to Washington University where he would spend most of the rest of his career.

Minsky's approach to economics towards continued to develop further and further towards the attitude that Saposs had first inspired: economics had to be practical and realistic. Very theoretical constructions without roots in the actual realities were of little value.

Minsky was a good writer and he published rather a lot. His first really important article was probably "Central banking and Money market Changes" from 1957. He introduced here a distinction between two concepts of liquidity:

- The ability of the federal reserve to control the price of specific financial assets such as bonds and money markets because it deals with them directly
- Cash flows that drive other asset markets such as shares and real estate.

He argued further that you could distinguish between two price levels:

- The prices of current output such as food, cars and holidays, which were widely dependent on labor costs
- The prices of capital and financial assets such as stocks, bonds and art, which incorporate uncertainty and depend on yields. Since yields represented future cash flow the valuations depended on income that was expected over time.

Minsky would always use Keynes as his main theoretical reference, and one of his literary milestones was his book "John Maynard Keynes", which he published in 1975. However, he disagreed a lot with the way that most economists interpreted Keynes, and also to some degree with what Keynes himself seemed to have meant.

INHERENT FINANCIAL INSTABILITY

Minsky assumed like Keynes (and unlike the neoclassicists) that capitalism was inherently unstable. He observed that it mainly was private investment that drove the economy, and that these investments fluctuated much more than other components of the economy since they depended on investors' subjective evaluations of the future. Keynes had considered this aspect when he wrote about investors' short-term focus, their "animal spirits" and their tendency to hold on to cash during recessions and depressions, but Minsky found that his followers largely ignored this aspect. The financial sector was a main source of instability in a capitalist economy, he said, since this particular sector was motivated by many other factors than merely technology and market interest rates and these motivations could lead to instability. He saw himself as an expositor of "financial Keynesianism", and he talked about a "Wall Street View" and "Money-Manager Capitalism", to give a name to the approach that emphasized the problems created by the financial sector. The processes he described were common:

- Expansionary public policy created the basis for private investment booms driven by debts (an increase in federal debt would for instance add to private stocks of low-risk financial assets and decrease the risk-exposure of private balance sheets …

- … and this led to booms and overinvestments.
- The government would eventually intervene to avoid the potential resulting crash …
- … and this intervention meant that the financial sector didn't suffer the full consequences of their previous irresponsible credit expansion.

These recurrent cycles of irresponsible financial behavior followed by government bailouts created a more and more fragile financial sector, he claimed. Decisions about investments were taken in boardrooms, he said, and one of the main factors that were often considered there was the general conditions for financing, rather than the basic soundness of the projects. Increases in asset prices during a boom were here an important factor, since assets could be used as collateral for loans. This created non-linearity that could create considerable instability: increasing asset prices contributed to the creation of money (for instance when financial assets were used as collateral for loans). And all of this could happen while everybody (the "agents") all were acting rationally to optimize their own gain; they might even be *forced* to follow the prevailing trend simply to survive. He claimed that each phase of the business cycle created changes in the financial environment that led to the next phase.

Minsky's "Wall Street" paradigm was very different from the mainstream "barter paradigm" that was used by most economists (ignoring the financial sector). He declared war on the neoclassical approach, mainly by making three unorthodox statements:

- *Persistent employment can not be explained by market rigidity alone.* Assume that salaries actually did fall during a recession, as the neoclassicists would expect. The result would be that prices would fall as well, and companies would consequently postpone investments. Furthermore, they would be squeezed by the increasing cost of debt service (Fisher's debt-deflation theory).
- *The wide fluctuations in financial markets are relevant.* Neoclassicists ignore the financial sector, basically assuming that it is efficient. But it isn't. Central banks can control the prices of some bonds and of interest rates, but they have no direct control over the prices of any other investment asset.
- *Unemployment does not come from market rigidities.* It comes from uncertainty about the future among business executives; an uncertainty that is reflected by fluctuations in investments.

Inefficiencies in the financial sector could consequently be a key culprit for major economic disasters like the depression of the 1930s.

CHARLES KINDLEBERGER

Minsky had a fan and ally in a man named Charles Kindleberger. Kindleberger was working in the Federal Reserve Bank in New York during the late 1930s, and he experienced there how complex a task it is to re-ignite an economy once it has run into a deep depression.

He would later on leave the bank to work in the State department, where he was involved in the Marshall Plan after World War II. In 1948, when he was 38 years of age, he decided to leave government altogether and instead join the world of academia. What he wanted to study and teach was all the complex phenomena that took place during crashes and panics. He wanted to understand completely what had happened when the economy collapsed in the 1930s.

His approach was largely historical. He read through piles of material about crises throughout history to identify common elements, and he published his results in a series of several books where he showed numerous examples of situations where financial markets clearly had been completely irrational, and where manias had been followed by deep depressions. He characterized the typical phases around a financial mania as:

- Speculation
- Financial distress
- Crises
- Panic
- Crash

One of Kindleberger's books, "The World in Depression, 1929–1939" from 1986 provided an analysis of the terrible events that he had experienced personally. He stated here that collapse in money supply could not explain the depression, since money supply fell more slowly than prices. This meant that the real purchasing power of money actually went up from 1929 to 1931. Secondly, he couldn't accept any theory that blamed the stock market crash and its negative wealth effect for the economic collapse — the collapse in production began before the stock market crashed. His main explanation was something different; it was financial instability.

> ***Kindleberger and Minksy — two approaches to the same problem***
>
> *Many authors refer to "Kindleberger/Minsky" when speaking of financial instability as a cause of economic instability. The reason is that Minsky mainly provided a number of theoretical models for financial instability and Kindleberger mainly provided comprehensive studies of historical episodes that seemed to confirm the relevance of some of Minsky's theories.*

MILTON FRIEDMAN AND THE UNIVERSITY OF CHICAGO

Another scientist who focused on monetary factors as a key source of instability was Milton Friedman. Friedman came from a poor Brooklyn family which had emigrated to the United States from part of Austria-Hungary.[1] He graduated from high school at the age of 15, went to Rutgers University just after his 16th birthday, and supported himself afterwards. As a college student, he decided to study mathematics to become an actuary, but when he saw the effects of the Great Depression, he became interested in economics. So when he received offers of two scholarships, he chose to study economics at the University of Chicago. One of his mentors there was Simon Kuznets, who would later supply the facts and figures for many of Friedman's analyses.

During World War II, Friedman worked in various state departments, where he developed a long-term skepticism about economic forecasts and about the efficiency of government intervention in the economy. In 1948 he joined NBER, where his task was to continue monetary research after Mitchell. Gradually, Friedman became known as the theorist among the staff at the Bureau. Then, in 1976, he received the Nobel Prize because he had been the leading figure in one of the most important developments in economic thinking of his century: the monetarist revolution.

The idea of fixing monetary growth rate had actually been orthodox at the University of Chicago since the 40s[2], but over the years, Friedman had become still more convinced of how the business cycle problem should be handled: *Society should manage the business cycle problem simply and only by ensuring a constant growth of money stock.* While proponents of active interventionism were getting in trouble with their ever more complicated simulation models, Friedman dug out Newcomb's old quantity equation of money:

$$MV = PQ$$

The left side of this equation was *M*oney multiplied with *V*elocity of money. The right side was *P*rice of goods multiplied with *Q*uantity of goods. Friedman's first point was that it was incredibly difficult to manage the economy through the use of active counter-cyclical measures. He shared the same suspicion as the chaos researchers: econometric models were not able to give satisfactory forecasts. Once you realized that the economy was diving, it would take too long before fiscal measures would take effect. And when such measures finally worked, it was quite likely that the upswing had already started, so that instability was increased; the "beer game effect", if you please. Besides, there were clear indications that government borrowing to finance additional spending crowded out private borrowing (the old "Treasury View"). The point was that inherent instability could be found in both sides of the equation. The left side (MV) was unstable because of inherent self-reinforcement caused by, for example, the initial drop in interest rates during monetary expansions, competition in the bank sector, etc. The right side (PQ) was unstable because of inventory effects, the accelerator, echoes, clusters of innovation, etc. And together they became even more unstable because of positive feed-back between monetary and real events. But in any equation you could of course stabilize the whole if you stabilized just one side. And the left side — the monetary part — was much easier to stabilize than the right side.

Friedman's postulate was backed by a growing bulk of research which indicated that a strong correlation existed between money supply and business cycles — the former leading the latter. In 1963 he published "A Monetary History of the United States", written with Anna J. Schwartz. Their research showed that *over the long term, money growth was wholly reflected in inflation, but not in growth*:

$$MV = \underline{P}Q$$

So much so, it seemed, that they declared and often repeated that inflation was "a purely monetary phenomenon". But the short term was different. *Over the short term, monetary fluctuations were responsible for business cycles*:

$$MV = PQ$$

Every severe business contraction in the United States since 1867 had been preceded by a large monetary contraction[3]. On average, monetary growth preceded economic peaks by about half a year and economic troughs by about a quarter of a year. The great depression in the 1930s had been accompanied by a large contraction in the money supply — a contraction which the Federal Reserve at any point could have halted — but never did. After the crash in 1929, American interest levels had fallen to very low levels, but money supply had fallen by a third anyway — something that most observers at the time had not been aware of. The Federal Reserve had generally assumed that raising interest rates during an expansion and lowering it during a recession was enough to stabilize the economy. But according to Friedman, an acceleration in the growth of money stock spurs spending, but once this spending has picked up, people become less cautious and start reducing their monetary reserves. Brokers at the stock exchange soon realize that this will lead to a growing inflation and so they mark down bond prices. This means that *money supply could keep expanding even as interest rates on bonds were rising*. Rising interest rates were in other words no guarantee that excessive money growth was being checked. And the opposite could also happen: *interest rates and money supply could fall together*. To solve this problem, you had to shift from the "I-regime" (management through interest rates) to the "M-regime" (management through money supply). Managing money supply would include, but not be limited to, manipulating interest rates.

THE CRITIQUE OF THE PHILLIPS CURVE

Like Jay Forrester, Friedman was critical of the Phillips curve theory but for different reasons. Both Friedman and Forrester accepted that there could be a limited, short-term relationship between unemployment and inflation within the time frame of the Kichin cycle, but while Forrester focused on the fact that it could be disturbed by phenomena characteristic

Stabilizing a system

Simon Newcomb's equation, MV= PQ can be used as a framework to describe the essentials of various proposals to solve the business cycle problem. Some examples of proposed solutions are highlighted in the table below:

Stabilize what?	*Simplified description*	*Early proponent*
MV	*Use central bank intervention tools to stabilize aggregate output*	*Henry Thornton*
P	*Adopt gold standard*	*David Ricardo*
P	*Re- or devaluate currency to stabilize inflation*	*Irwin Fisher*
Q	*Use fiscal policy to increase or reduce aggregate output*	*Maynard Keynes*
MV	*Use central bank management tools to ensure a stable, moderate growth in effective money supply; ignore fluctuations in aggregate output*	*Milton Friedman*

of the Kuznets- and Kondratieff cycles, Friedman suggested that the trade-off between inflation and unemployment was only temporary:

- Society has a natural unemployment level, which is dependent on structural characteristics of the labor and commodity markets, market imperfections, the cost of gathering information about job vacancies and labor availabilities, the cost of mobility, etc. When people have adjusted completely to any given inflation rate, then the equilibrium rate of unemployment is this "natural rate".
- The only way to force unemployment below this rate is to make money supply rise faster than anticipated inflation. This process will create inflation, however.

- Since people learn from what they see, anticipated inflation will trail after real inflation. Because of this, you have to force money supply further and further up, if you want to maintain it above anticipated inflation. As a consequence you end up with ever-accelerating inflation if you insist on maintaining unemployment below the natural rate …
- … until the economy collapses in hyperinflation or until (more likely) someone finally decides to pull the brakes. In both cases, you end up with huge unemployment as aggregate demand starts falling while anticipated inflation is very high.

So according to this "accelerationist" view, using inflation to create work was like peeing in your pants; at first it would feel warm, but would soon turn very cold. *The Phillips curve was only a short-run phenomenon*, just as had been demonstrated in France during the Mississippi bubble and in Germany after World War I.

Seeing the failure of the Phillips curve hypothesis (there was high inflation and unemployment simultaneously), and knowing the critique of fine-tuning policy, central bankers in the USA, England, Japan and Switzerland finally adopted monetarist policies by targeting annual growth ranges for monetary expansion during the late 1970s (The Japanese policy failed miserably in the 1990s, however).

THE THEORY OF "RATIONAL EXPECTATIONS"

During the early 1970s, the capitalist economies went into a very serious recession, partly triggered by the oil crisis. Several governments reacted (against some of the monetarists' advice) by increasing money supply to stimulate growth, but this time it didn't work at all. The result was not growth and low unemployment; it was inflation and continued unemployment.

This called for an explanation, and the most widely accepted theory was supplied by Robert E. Lucas, another economist from the University of Chicago. Lucas' explanation was simple. Assume it is widely published that money supply is going to accelerate. Government officials take the opportunity to announce that it is therefore safe for businesses to invest and employ more people, as new growth in output will follow the increase in money supply:

$$MV = P\underline{Q}$$

Three economists' critique of the Phillips curve theory

The Phillips curve describes a trade-off between inflation and unemployment. Some of the most important objections against this theory were given by Jay Forrester, Milton Friedman and Robert Lucas. A simplified version of their critique is given below.

Jay Forrester	*Fluctuations in unemployment may be largely explained as elements of Kitchin and Kondratieff cycles, and fluctuation in inflation as an element of the Kutnets cycle. If this is true, then there will not be a simple relationship between unemployment and inflation.*
Milton Friedman	*Experience shows that inflation does not reduce unemployment.* *Growth in the inflation rate does reduce it, but continuous growth in the inflation rate is obviously neither sustainable, nor desirable.*
Robert Lucas	*People tend to have rational expectations. If you attempt to stimulate the economy by injecting money, then people will anticipate inflation. Businesses will raise prices and unions will demand higher wages to compensate. The result will be "stagflation", which is increased inflation but no additional growth.*

People are smart, however. They have seen it all before and know that eventually the growth in money supply will lead to inflation. So companies raise their prices immediately, and unions respond by demanding higher salaries. So, alas, all you get is rising inflation, but no growth:

$$MV = \underline{P}Q$$

The suggestion that people will adapt to government stimuli in a way that may make them self-defeating was termed the theory of "rational expectations".[4] The events during the 1970s fitted much better with Friedman's and Lucas' models than with models assuming a long-term Phillips curve trade-off.

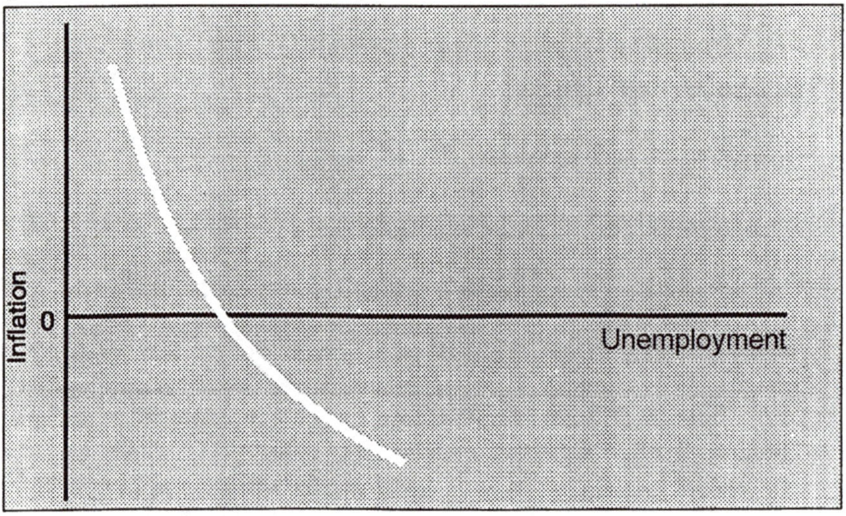

Figure 14.1: The Phillips curve.
This graph illustrates the Phillips curve as it was originally described. Friedman believed it was in fact vertical. Today, most economists subscribe to the "accelerationalist" hypothesis; that an accelerating inflation reduces unemployment, but only until the growth in inflation eventually stops. Then you get inflation *and* unemployment.

The political business cycle

W. Nordhaus and E.R. Tufte have both proposed a theory of a so-called "political business cycle". Nordhaus presented the idea in his article "The Political Business Cycle" from 1975, and Tufte followed with a book called "The Political Control of the Economy" from 1978. Both authors suggested that politicians regularly would stimulate the economy up to an election so that they would be more likely to be re-elected. This meant that you could expect politically stimulated booms before elections followed by recessions after.

But there was another variable in the equation. It was about the prices and trading volume of financial assets …

Business Cycles and Asset Prices

"It's easy to make money on Wall Street. All you have to do is — buy when the price is low. Then, as soon as the price goes up, sell and take your profit."

Mark Twain

15
Asset Prices and Liquidity

"We have nothing to fear but fear itself."
Franklin Roosevelt

Whenever the Federal Reserve Chairman of the United States makes a public speech there is always a possibility he says something that will shake the markets. You never know. This was also the case when Alan Greenspan entered the podium to make a speech for the American Enterprise Institute on the night of Thursday, December 5, 1996.

The speech was pretty much about the normal issues that you would expect a central banker to address. Nothing terribly interesting for the market until he suddenly raised a simple question:

> "How do we know when irrational exuberance has unduly escalated asset values, which then become subject to unexpected and prolonged contractions?"

It was only a question, of course, but it sounded as if he was genuinely concerned about the issue. So the journalists sensed the possibility of a sensation — and the quote went straight to the global wire services. The markets fell significantly the next day.

FINANCIAL LIQUIDITY

But why did the markets fall after Greenspan's remark? — why would anyone be concerned about the Federal Reserve Chairman's opinions about asset markets? It wasn't his job, was it? After all, the markets were, according to mainstream science "efficient", which meant that they shouldn't be "exuberant". And the chairman was supposed to deal with inflation, not asset prices, right? And anyway, even if the market were a little bit exuberant, how would a central banker be able to tell?

But the chairman knew that the development in asset prices could create complications for a central banker. One of the reasons related to a phenomenon called "financial liquidity". This phenomenon had been described by many authors, including Hamilton Bolton, the founder of the private research institute Bank Credit Analyst. In 1967 he published a book with the title "Money and Investment profits" where he pointed this issue out:

> "At any time, part of the money supply is store of value and part is medium of exchange, and these two parts are probably changing in relationship to each other. But the medium of exchange part is also, at any time, splintered into the part going into real new output and the part going into other real transactions — secondhand cars, or Corot paintings, or, for that matter, common stocks and bonds."

The implication was clear: You could have a situation where MV grew fast without having any effect on output (Q) and what is normally measured as inflation (P).

The monetary growth could be offset entirely by financial price inflation; growth in the value and turnover of bonds, stocks, paintings, real estate, etc.

The money circulating in financial markets was later often referred to as "financial liquidity". The distinction is illustrated on the next page, where sectors 1 and 3 are money sectors while sectors 2 and 4 represent what you get for money.

PULL AND PUSH BETWEEN SECTORS

Hamilton Bolton's point was that a good bull market is often preceded by an increase in financial liquidity (sector 3). Some of the early warnings can be growth in *time saving deposits, broker's cash accounts, broker's security loans* and *mutual funds' cash/asset ratio*. When these figures go up, it means that an increasing amount of money is ready for financial investment, but not yet put into circulation in these markets. Another indicator of increased financial liquidity is a fall in *velocity of money* (in sector 1). As long as sector 2 is "pulling" sector 1 upwards, liquidity in sector 1 will be forced and velocity will go up. But when that trend reverses, it means that the pull from sector 2 has stopped and that liquidity may flow to sector 3.

"Sector 1" Amount of "non-financial" money multiplied with turnover of that money		**"Sector 2"** Value of products and services multiplied with turnover of these products and services
plus	equals	plus
"Sector 3" Amount of "financial liquidity" multiplied with turnover of that liquidity		**"Sector 4"** Value (price) of stocks, bonds, real estate, art and other stores of value multiplied with the turnover of these assets

The *debit/loan ratio* (private and commercial bank deposits compared to total level of *short-term commercial loans*) is also an indicator of financial liquidity. In a market with a commercial pull environment, people and companies are confident and tend to try to raise money for new activities. Once that pull levels off, however, they get more concerned with paying back what they owe, or building cash positions (Keynes' "liquidity preference"). So a rise in debit/loan ratio indicates that sector 3 may get more liquidity. The same goes for *bank investments* (in securities) and *net free reserves* (excess reserves in the banking system). These indicators rise when the banking system sees less sound opportunities in, or demand from, sector 2.

Once the financial liquidity in sector 3 is put into circulation in sector 4, prices and trading go up. Interestingly the financial bull markets do not absorb liquidity; they create it. Whenever someone buys a financial asset, someone else has sold it, and as prices go up, more and more money is created in sector 3.

One of the processes that can accelerate booms in the financial markets is *buy-outs*, where companies are bought by individuals and consequently cancelled from stock market lists. Buy-outs reduce supply in sector 4, and it can be argued that the bank financing them is, at least partly, using money that would otherwise be classified in sector 1. Almost the opposite situation takes place when there are large waves of *new issues*. Stock and bond issues, including junk bonds, drain money from sector 3 to sector 1. New issues are therefore a bearish factor.

FRIEDMAN'S TRILEMMA AND THE WEALTH EFFECT

Financial liquidity was a complication to many economists, including Milton Friedman. But Friedman was aware of another complication, which he described as "the trilemma": It was impossible to achieve more than any two of the following three objectives at the same time:

- Control of exchange rates
- Control of the price level
- Freedom from exchange controls

Nobody wanted exchange controls anymore, because this would seriously hamper free trade. But given free forex trading, he pointed out, you couldn't achieve stable exchange rates and at the same time control the business fluctuations in every country. So it would not make sense to try to fix exchange rates.

Friedman's trilemma and the difficulty in separating commercial and financial liquidity were not the only problems

A third complication for central bankers was that changes in asset prices could have strong impact on the way that the rest of the economy behaved. After all, the bankers knew that stock prices for years had been one of the best of NBER's leading indicators of the economy. Some of them might also have noticed that Goldman Sachs' highly efficient "Financial Conditions Index" included not only included short-term interest rates and corporate-bond yields, but also the dollar's trade-weighted index and the stock market capitalization relative to GDP. Goldman Sacks included, in other words, asset prices in the measure of monetary stimulus.

Strengths and weaknesses of fiscal and monetary stabilization policies

Some of the strengths and weaknesses of Keynesian and monetarist approaches to the business cycle problem are:

	Keynesianism	*Monetarism*
Strengths	• *It is direct intervention. This means that you know for sure that there will be a primary effect* • *Potential psychological impact as Keynesian tools are easy to understand*	• *Can have immediate effect* • *Stable growth in money supply can instil confidence in currency and price stability, and this confidence leads to less speculation, higher savings rates and lower long-term interest rates*
Weaknesses	• *Too long time-lag between decision and effect* • *Tends to lead to continuous expansion of the public sector, and continuous growth of government debt* • *An expansive public sector and a rising government debt may "crowd out" private sector and lead to long-term stagnation and unemployment* • *Will often be abused for reelection purposes* • *May be defeated by rational expectations*	• *Difficult to measure effective money supply because of continuous development of new financial instruments, fluctuations in financial liquidity and because of changes of velocity of money* • *The "Pushing on a string" problem: Experience shows that markets in some cases will not respond to attempts to increase money supply* • *Risk of instability in foreign exchange markets*

How an increase in money supply affects asset prices

Increasing money supply can have different effects on asset markets depending on how the economy reacts to the increasing liquidity and on the timing:

	The velocity of money falls to offset the increased money supply	Excess is saved (increase in financial liquidity)	Excess is spent (on goods and services)
1 month	➢ No change in asset prices	➢ Bonds rise	➢ No effect
3 months	➢ No change in asset prices ➢ Bonds fall ➢ Equities rise	➢ Bonds rise ➢ Equities rise	➢ Economic activity rises
9 months	➢ No change in asset prices	➢ Bonds rise ➢ Equities rise	➢ Bonds fall ➢ Equities fall

Central bankers knew about at least four situations where asset prices could be relevant for their task:

- ➢ Increasing asset prices could generate a perception of wealth that leads people to spend more than what is sustainable in the longer term. This is called the "wealth effect".
- ➢ Strong rises in asset prices could lead to sharp reactions that were disorderly and which would require intervention from a "lender of last resort".
- ➢ Strong increases in asset prices could make it easier for companies to raise money (partly because assets could be used as collateral).
- ➢ Strong asset prices would enhance the perception of the economic future.

One of the people who understood this better than most was a Hungarian called George Soros …

16
Maelstroms and Master Minds

"The actual, private object of most skilled investment is to beat the gun, as the Americans so well express it, to outwit the crowd, and to pass the bad, or depreciating, half-crown to the other fellow."

John Maynard Keynes

He was born in Hungary in 1930, the son of a Jewish lawyer. During World War II his father had been able to obtain false identity papers for him, and maybe these saved his life. In 1947 he moved to London, where he graduated from the London School of Economics. After this graduation he struggled to get by, part of the time as a waiter, living off the leftovers from rich people's meals, and part of the time by selling ladies bags and jewelry in Blackpool, a blue collar holiday resort. He wasn't having a very good time.

During these years he also worked on a philosophical treatise entitled "The Burden of Consciousness". Once he had finished the treatise, he concluded that the title was the best part of it and started rewriting it, again and again, over three years. One day, when he read what he had written the day before, he found that he could not make head nor tail of it, and decided to give the project up completely. George Soros' career was all misery[1] until one day he had the idea to write to all stock brokerage houses in the city to apply for a job and was offered a position with Singer & Friedlander as arbitrage trader in stocks. Later he received an offer to work in New York, with F.M. Mayer, as a stock market analyst. After this job, he worked in several other stock broking companies until, in 1969, he founded the Quantum Fund with a partner. He was 39 years old at that time.

ECONOMIC MAELSTROMS

Quantum Fund employed leverage and used sophisticated instruments such as futures and options. George Soros believed that the financial markets and the economy were inter-locked in strong, positive feed-back processes[2] and felt that understanding of these processes was the single most important key to investment success[3].

In February 1970 he wrote a little analysis of a potential, self-reinforcing phenomenon involving real estate investment trusts. The report described how these trusts could generate apparent capital gains simply by selling additional shares at a premium over book value, which would make per share book value and earnings per share rise. As people noticed these deceptively rising figures, they would be willing to buy new shares issued at a premium, and the positive feed-back loop would create a bubble, until the system eventually collapsed.

Soros invested heavily in the new trusts. He didn't realize how popular his report was, however, until he received a telephone call from a bank in Cleveland asking for a new copy because theirs had been reproduced so often that it was no longer legible. When he heard that, he decided to take some profits. A few years later the same trusts ran into trouble as he had foreseen, and he decided to sell the group short more or less indiscriminately. As most of the mortgage trusts finally went broke, he reaped more than 100% profit on his short positions (which was possible because he had kept adding to his short positions on the way down). This was one of the early examples of the immense success of the Quantum Fund. From the year 1969 (where the fund was founded) to 1985 the net asset value per initial share in the fund grew from 41 to 6,760 USD, with only one year out of 16 yielding a net loss. An early investor would, in other words, by that time have 16,487 dollars for every 100 dollars initially invested!

SOFTWARE, HARDWARE, AND WETWARE

When somebody makes billions of dollars by forecasting economic and financial trends, it generates attention. Why could George Soros and other master dealers, none of whom pretended to be experts in the recognized economic theories, predict financial and economic events with higher accuracy than the numerous sophisticated, econometric computer models that the economists used? What did these speculators have, that Jan Tinbergen's successors and their computers didn't?

Artificial intuitions: Neural networks

"Neural networks" were computer scientists' first attempts to mimic the brain. A neural network was a software that was typically organized into layers, with one layer of input neurons, and a single output neuron. Between these two layers, there were many layers of "hidden neurons", which would scan the data to look for patterns and constantly communicate downstream to exchange information about patterns that could be used to develop complex rules. A neural network applied to financial markets would gradually get smarter and smarter, and in the end, if it worked, it would start submitting buy and sell orders at the right times. The funny thing was that unlike econometric models, you didn't know the theories behind the predictions of the system. It created its own financial/economic model, but you couldn't open the system up to see what was inside it. Maybe it took an electronic black-box to beat Milton Friedman's economic "black-box"!

During the late 1980s more and more trading houses installed these neural networks, as well as other computer trading systems, which were designed to outsmart the best traders by copying their thinking but beating their speed. As this happened, some brokers started to worry that these computer systems might increase volatility in the markets as they would behave identically. One early warning of this phenomenon came on a quiet Friday afternoon in New York, where very little was happening, and one broker in Wall Street was even seen doing a crossword. There was absolutely no warning before when, as if out of the blue, a flood of sell orders were suddenly issued by the silent army of computers throughout the country. Within 30 minutes the market fell 36 points, as a record 57 million shares changed hands. At the same time, security guards were sent to break up fist fights between desperate traders struggling to survive their battle against the computers in Chicago Mercantile Exchange.

One answer was that they had their intuition. Scientists had begun to focus more on the limitations of the computer hardware as compared to the human brain (or "wetware"), and what they were realizing was that the computer still in most senses was extremely inferior to the brain. The brain had a million billion synapses, or electrical connections, and while the internal communication in the computer was restrained by the number of legs in each chip, each neuron in the brain was typically connected directly to between 1,000 and 10,000 other neurons, and some with up to 200,000 others! In fact, the brain mostly consisted of these thin cell-extensions, or "wires", and the total length of these "wires" in a single brain was several hundred thousand kilometers. Because of this structure the computing capacity of the human brain was probably about 100 million times the number of processors in the largest existing computer. And not only was it much bigger: it worked in a smarter way. The structure of the brain allowed it to perform millions of transactions simultaneously, and scattered over a number of its regions, while the computer did one or a few things at a time. And finally it had been discovered that feelings, emotions and body states were necessary elements for judging complicated, intuitive problems. "Gut feelings", like pain in your back when you are moving into dangerous territory, were not unfortunate drawbacks for the mind — they were necessary to draw the attention to danger and opportunity[4]. Experiments had clearly demonstrated that people with a normal or high Intelligence Quotient but limited emotional capacity had very reduced intuition. Computers didn't have any of the sort. In a very messy, maybe even truly chaotic economic environment, this seemed to be important for the ability to predict.

A STRANGE DIARY

George Soros had eminent intuition and instincts, and as if to emphasize that, he would frequently tell people that he developed a pain in his back when one of his investments was getting dangerous. Indeed, he claimed that he hardly knew the models which would normally be used in a formal system[5]:

> "Existing theories about the behaviour of stock prices are remarkably inadequate. They are of so little value to the practitioner that I am not even fully familiar with them. The fact that I could get by without them speaks for itself."

He also doubted that you could ever write down a fixed recipe for beating the markets:

> "... by the time all participants have adjusted, the rules of the game will change again."

But he did have an overall theory of how things worked, and in 1985 he decided to put it to the test through what he called his "real time experiment". The method was to write down the hypothesis behind each of his investment decisions as it was made, and then validate these hypotheses simply by trying to make money on them. The experiment began on Sunday August 18, 1985. His resources were his intuition, his business network, his staff — and a pool of 647,000,000 USD.

The experiment started rather badly until, on September 28, he could enter into his diary:

> "I managed to hang on to my currency holdings with the skin of my teeth and after the meeting of the Group of Five last Sunday, I made the killing of a lifetime."

Predicting business cycles versus predicting financial markets

Both financial prices and aggregate economic output are factors in a complex non-linear and semi-chaotic system. It can be argued that there are two major, inherent barriers to forecasting: random noise and sensitivity to initial conditions.

Random noise is events that are unpredictable to the forecasters because it is impossible to capture information about them. They may involve personal decisions by important decision makers, weather, natural disasters, etc. They are a major factor in proportion to short-term movements, but are statistically almost evened out over longer horizons.

Sensitivity to initial conditions is caused by positive feed-back loops. As chaos theory has shown, this has little effect in the short term, but can make long-term forecasting impossible.

The window of time where prediction is easiest (given appropriate tools and competence) is a window between the short term (where random noise creates a barrier) and the long term (where feed-back loops create a barrier). An important element is to understand the feed-back processes and mode-locking interacting in the medium term, i.e. up to and including the next turning point. As interlocked feed-back loops are dissolved when a turning point is reached, the future visibility falls significantly after a turning point.

On October 22, 1986 he was on his way back from a trip to China and Japan, where he had watched his Japanese stock portfolio drop some 15% in price. He concluded:

> "I believe the current collapse in Japan will prove to be one of the landmarks of contemporary financial history. It resembles a classic crash more closely than anything we are likely to witness in our own market."

At this time he had built a considerable short position in the dollar. Three days later he increased this exposure even further:

> "I managed to sell 750 million USD worth of yen before it broke."

This principle of increasing the exposure as a trend progresses is called "pyramiding" by the traders and is often considered very dangerous. Soros had a reason for using it, however:

> "Pyramiding is a good way to sustain serious damage in margin speculation, since when the trend reverses, even temporarily, you risk being caught overexposed ... The reason I am nevertheless willing to increase my exposure is that I believe the scope for a reversal has diminished. One of the generalizations I established about freely floating exchange rates is that short term volatility is greatest at turning points and diminishes as a trend becomes established."

What Soros was describing here was in essence a mode-locking phenomenon, although he didn't use that word.

In the beginning of November his short position peaked at 1.46 billion dollars, but he had many other exposures, as the entry in the diary from November 1 indicates:

> "... by Tuesday afternoon I had covered half my stock index short and swung around from being short USD 500 million in government bonds to an 800 million USD long position. But the 7-year action did not go well — I must have been the biggest buyer — and then by Tuesday I was losing on all fronts. Then came two unexpected developments: the dismissal of Sheik Yamani as Saudi oil minister and the indication that the Japanese discount rate will be lowered. Suddenly, my position looked much brighter. I used the opportunity to reduce my holdings in

> the U.S. government bonds to 1200 million USD. I also increased my cross position — long DM, short yen — to 1 billion USD. I have bought an additional 250 million USD worth of DM, giving me a modest net short position in the dollar."

When he finished the experiment on November 8, 1986, his net gain for the 14 months period was 113.7%. Within little more than a year he had more than doubled the value of the pool.

THE ALCHEMY

He described the experiment in a manuscript entitled "The Alchemy of Finance". The core theme of the book was his theory of "Reflexivity", the essence of which was that the perceptions of the investors changed trends in the financial markets, and that these trends in turn changed the economic events. Some of his generalizations were that the general bias of the forecasters followed the prices (people got more bullish as prices moved up; more bearish as they moved down), and that once prices were locked in a trend, this would automatically get more and more robust (because of the inherent feed-back loops) until eventually it had run its course. The success of his real time experiment reinforced his thesis that the financial markets and the economy were interlocked in positive feed-back loops.

Soros concluded that you should focus mainly on identifying the likely feed-back processes and be ready to abort your positions as soon as the mode-locking in a trend was dissolved. He also described the peculiar behavior of the markets, when two theses with contradictory implications could be made: The prices would not seek a balanced middle position; they would rather discount only one of the alternatives until, at some point, it suddenly chose to discount the other instead. He never used any of the terminology of the chaos researchers, but this description of multiple, alternative scenarios sounded very much like the concept of attractors and bifurcations.

In the beginning of 1987 he submitted "The Alchemy of Finance" to Simon & Shuster for publication. Little could he then know that he would that year witness some of the most dramatic financial events of the century …

17
War Games

"I can calculate the motions of heavenly bodies, but not the madness of people."

Isaac Newton

The year was 1987, and art was in. Since 1985 the prices and trading volume of most art categories had risen steeply, and Christie's, Sotheby's and thousands of galleries and dealers were thriving.

Many felt that this golden era had begun with the sale of the "*Jay Gould Collection*". Before his death, Jay Gould had invested some of the money from his famous railway and gold speculations in art, but in April 1985, 175 pictures from this collection were auctioned on behalf of his heirs by Sotheby's in New York. At that time there were perhaps some 400,000 active art collectors world-wide (people spending at least USD 10,000 a year on art), and maybe 250–350 "very big" collectors (people with collections worth millions of dollars). But the audience at the auctions had always been very narrow, and the large majority of the people who could afford expensive art had never set foot in an auction house.

Sotheby's director wanted to change that, and the Jay Gould Collection sale was ideal for the purpose. Ideal because these pictures were by well known artists, there was no discussion of their authenticity, they came from a famous collection, and even because most of them were second class, which meant that they would be reasonably affordable. So they had been sent on an inspection tour to London, Tokyo, Lausanne and around the United States before going on auction (one commentator wrote that there had been "five months of intense partying" prior to the auction)[1]. The auction house itself had been reasonably successful, but it had in particular been interesting to see the many new faces in the auction hall: the art audience was beginning to expand. (The best example of this was perhaps when Andy Warhol's collection went on auction. It consisted of 10,000 objects, almost all of which was pure junk and kitsch, like plastic plates, sauce boats and cookie jars. Thousands of people flocked to attend the auction and the collection fetched a ridiculous USD 34 million. This was two years after the Jay Gould sale).

It was not only the audience that grew, however. It was also the amount of money that the buyers had at their disposal. Buyers at Sotheby's auctions could now borrow the purchase sum for 12 months, and the sellers could receive some of the expected sales sum in advance. Similar arrangements appeared in Japan, where customers could deposit art in a department store and borrow 80% against its agreed value.

Another important factor was the Japanese "bubble economy" and the appreciation of the yen, which made international art appear less expensive from a Japanese perspective. Almost every Western economist would agree with George Soros that the Japanese credit inflation couldn't last much longer. A single family house in Tokyo could cost 30 or 40 million dollars, and a golf club membership 300,000. It was even estimated that the value (or price, rather) of all real estate in Tokyo was about to exceed the price of all real estate in USA. As dealers in Western trading floors were beginning to refer to Japan as "The Land of Rising Sums", the bubble was still growing, and one of the sectors that would feel the strongest effect was art.

SALES OF A VAN GOGH

In January 1987 Christie's proudly announced that it would sell van Gogh's "Sunflowers" on his birthday, March 30. When the auction house first received the painting, they estimated its value at GBP 5–6 million. On second thoughts they raised it to almost double that figure.

Then, a few weeks before the auction was due to take place, the British government bought "Stratford Mill" by John Constable for GBP 10 million. This made the staff at Christie's think again. If that picture could sell for that price, what would museums be willing to pay for "Sunflowers"? This thought was at the same time encouraging and scary. Encouraging because it confirmed a very strong market. But scary because due to tax regulations, "Sunflowers" had to fetch 15–18 million pounds at an auction in order to give the seller the same after-tax revenue as a sale to a museum for 10 million. So either the picture had to reach that level, or people might say that the sellers had been ill advised not to try to sell it to a museum instead. A few weeks before the auction, Christie's estimate was expressed at "GBP 10 million, maybe more — and maybe a lot more."[2]

On the night of the auction the rooms were absolutely packed, and the atmosphere tense. Would this van Gogh set a new record?

Charles Allsopp opened the bidding at GBP 5 million, close to the first estimates. The next bid came quickly after. It was 5.5 million. Then 6 million. Then 6.5. The price was now over the initial estimate, and there were many bidders, some in the main hall, some in the side room, and some giving their bids via telephone.

The next bid was 7 million pounds.
Then 7.5
Then 8
Then 8.5
Then 9
Then 9.5....

APPLAUSE

Spontaneous applause broke out when 20 million pounds was bid for the painting. Twenty million, and there were still two bidders! The bids from these two anonymous investors were received via telephone by two of Christie's employees. Finally, as the price reached 22.5 million pounds, one bidder gave up, and the picture was sold at the highest price ever paid for a piece of art: 22.5 million pounds plus 10% commission, or 24.75 million pounds in total. A few days later it was disclosed that the buyer was Yasuda Fire and Marine Insurance, Japan. The other bidder had been Alan Bond, the Australian tycoon.

The successful sales of "Sunflowers" had a strong effect on the market. Three months later a less famous van Gogh was sold for GBP 12.6 million, again with Alan Bond as the underbidder. And people were already beginning to wonder which picture would set the next record.

A candidate appeared during the summer when Christie's announced that they would sell van Gogh's "Irises", a picture that most people would rate higher than "Sunflowers". The sale would take place in November 1987, and if all went well, this would perhaps take the new world record.

NOVEMBER 1987

However, as November came, there were many people that had developed a strange feeling. They were beginning to doubt the basic soundness of the stock markets.

To those who trade on the stock exchange, there is no worse feeling than such a doubt. This feeling does not normally evolve as a consequence of a single event; it is rather because of a number of incidents that somehow do not fit with the big picture you happened to believe in. As each of these incidents occur, a small seed of doubt is sown in your subconscious, and as days pass, it grows until it becomes more and more dominant. And then, without any ready explanation, it finally breaks out of hiding and you realize that you have been walking on the thinnest ice that may break any moment. Almost panicky, you feel that you must reverse your actions instantly.

It was exactly that feeling that many stock-traders experienced on Friday, the 16th of October, 1987.

THE STOCK MARKETS AND THE BUSINESS CYCLE

Most larger portfolio managers and speculators in the world were probably quite aware of the existence of the typical business cycle sequence that Roger Babson had described in 1911. Babson had concluded:

> "Industry, as a whole, generally follows several months behind stock prices. The prices of commodities generally stop rising at about the time business reaches its heights."

One of Babson's conclusions was that it was easier to forecast economic movements through studies of the stock market than to forecast the stock market through economic studies. This general tendency for stocks to forecast economic trends had since been widely used as a forecasting tool by, among others, the National Bureau of Economic Research.

But bonds had turned out to be even better. As mentioned before, and as even Thornton had observed, interest rates tended to rise as the upswing matured. In a paper published by the National Bureau of Economic Research in 1966, "Changes in the Cyclical Behavior of Interest Rates", Phillip Cagan concluded for the interest rates:

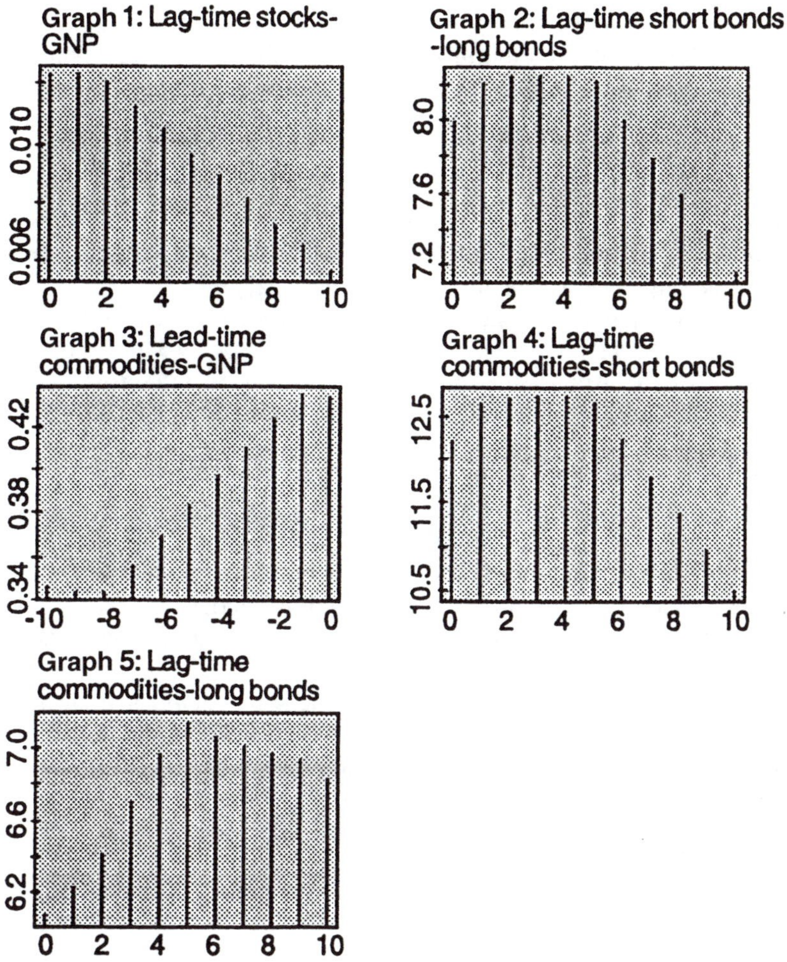

Figure 16.1: Financial sequences around the business cycle.
The graphs illustrate cross-covariance analysis in between the movements of short bonds, long bonds, the stock market, GNP, and commodity prices in the USA for the years 1900–1983. The statistics used are based on quarterly figures, and each diagram illustrates the covariance between two time series. A lag is detected if covariance peaks after one or more quarters. The first illustrates that GNP turns on average at the same time or one month after the stock market: There is a high correlation, but a short lag-time. The second illustrates the clear four-quarter time-lag from short bonds to long bonds. The third illustrates a one-quarter lag from GNP to commodity prices. The fourth illustrates a two to four-quarter lag from commodities to short bonds. The last illustrates a five-quarter lag from commodities to long bonds. Together the graphs illustrate the traditional short bond — long bond — stock market — GNP — commodities cycle sequence. Source: C.P. Klock: Business Cycle Theory, Master Thesis, (unpublished), Copenhagen Business School, 1992.

> "… The evidence therefore supports the following generalizations: (1) Interest rates maintain a sequence, with the active open-market rates usually turning first and the rates of negotiated and inactive markets usually turning last. (2) All long rates used to but no longer lag far behind short rates …"

As Cagan mentioned, the lag between short and long rates seemed to have narrowed by 1966, but before the global equity boom started in 1982 the sequence was again perfectly classical.

Another financial characteristic of business cycles was that of credit quality. In 1955 the business cycle specialist Geoffrey Moore[3] had held a speech for the American Finance Association, in which he described financial conditions that could precede a depression:

- A rapid increase in the volume of credit and debt
- A rapid, speculative increase in the prices of investment goods such as real estate, common stocks, and commodity inventories
- Vigorous competition among lenders for new business
- Relaxation of credit terms and lending standards
- Reduction of the risk premiums sought or obtained by lenders.

During such conditions, he had explained, the quality of new credit would worsen progressively. Moore had reviewed some studies of the credit expansion during the 1920s, examining foreign-government bonds, domestic corporate bonds, urban mortgage loans on dwellings and business properties, and farm mortgage loans:

> "All but the last of these types of credit underwent a marked expansion in volume during the twenties. All but the last showed marked deterioration in quality; that is, the proportion of funds advanced that later went into default or foreclosure (mostly after 1929) was much greater for advances made in the second half than in the first half of the decade."

Another economist, George W. Edwards, expressed it in this way[4]:

> "The history of business cycles shows that the stage of prosperity in general is marked by an ever-increasing inefficiency. In the field of security investment, the buying public, swayed by over optimism, seeks more and more after securities of higher yield, and investment

Friction in different markets

Carl von Klausewich used the term "friction" in his "Von Kriege" to describe the complications of executing the generals' plans in the field.

Friction is also present in business, but to very different degrees. One end of the spectrum is financial markets, where dealers and brokers experience very little friction. If you have the necessary trading lines, then you may execute a trade of perhaps USD 100 million in less than one minute. But other markets have much more friction. When a retailer order his goods, it will usually take days or weeks before they are delivered. Reselling them may take longer. Buying real estate can take months, and selling it in a bad market can take years. Getting capital goods delivered may take years. The differences in friction have an effect on how different markets relate to the business cycle. Having virtually no friction, the financial markets forecast it. Capital goods markets, on the other hand, tend to lag aggregate output.

bankers, under the stress of competition, issue securities of higher yield, greater risk and poorer quality."

BULLISH CONSENSUS AND FINANCIAL LIQUIDITY

To the best traders it was no secret that a lot of these signals for a reversal were present now. First of all, there had been a rapid credit expansion during the preceding years, which had now turned, however. As the dealers could read in newsletters from Bank Credit Analyst and other analysts, the financial liquidity had been falling since the beginning of the year. Secondly the American interest rates had started to rise in August, 1986. That in itself had been okay because everyone knew that money rates could rise for a year or more before the stock market was damaged[5]. But now the trend had been going on for 14 months, and during the summer, it accelerated.

The next development had been in the Treasury bonds. They had been able to stay firm for a long time after the money rates had started rising. Eventually, however, T-bonds had been dragged down, as they almost always were. That was in April 1987, and when they fell, they fell dramatically.

Another warning was the market sentiment[6]. Every dealer worth his salt knows that the time to sell is when everybody else seems most bullish. The problem is to find out exactly when this point is reached. Now it looked more and more as if it actually happened in August. That was the month when *Business Week* published a 25-page "Mid-year Investment Outlook" full of stock market investment recommendations. It was also the month when "Hadady Bullish Indicator" had rung the alarm. This weekly indicator, produced by a Californian research company, contained a weighted index of the published investment recommendations for more than a hundred leading American banks, brokers

BCA FINANCIAL LIQUIDITY INDEX

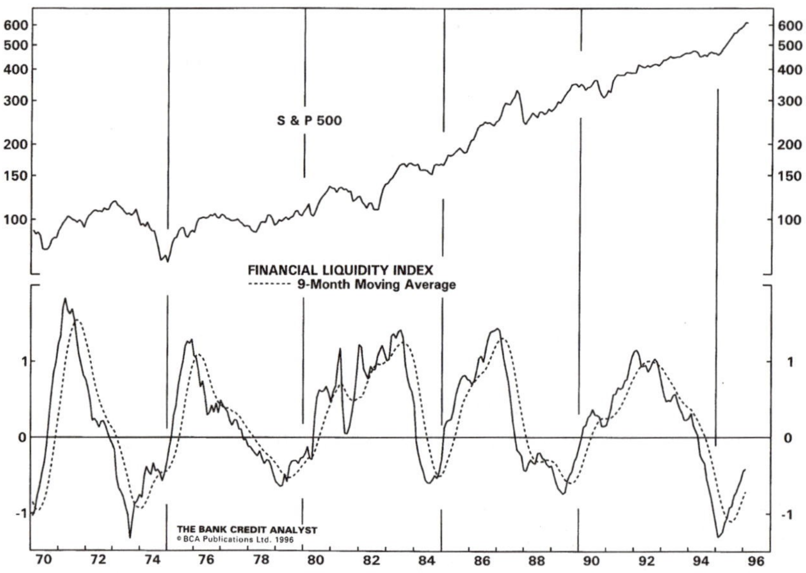

Figure 16.2: Bank Credit Analyst Financial Liquidity Index, 1970–1996.
This is an indicator of the trend in American financial liquidity compared to the performance of the Standard & Poors 500 index (500 American stocks). The market is obviously influenced by a range of other factors, including earnings and book values, the dollar exchange rate, and financial liquidity in other countries. The graph nevertheless shows that financial liquidity has been a valuable indicator for the stock market. The apparent collapse in liquidity in 1995 is partly attributed to increased use of new financial instruments that are not reflected by the index. Source: Bank Credit Analyst, Tel. +15144999706.

and investment advisors. The rule of thumb in Hadady's indicator was, simply stated, that you should sell if more than 70% of the advisors recommended to buy. That figure had been reached in August, just the day before the market peaked. Since then, prices had been falling gradually.

The last detail was by far the worst, however: on Friday, October 16, Dow Jones Industrials had fallen with an enormous volume by no less than 108.35 points, the worst nominal fall ever. As most traders knew, David Ricardo's old rule about cutting losses and letting profits run wasn't silly. Now many investors had substantial losses — was it time to bail out? Dealers met in local bars all over the world to discuss the latest events. Why had Dow Jones fallen so far? It was scary. It had fallen after a sustained bull-market, stimulated by an enormorous credit expansion. Sentiment had peaked, and interest rates were steadily rising. And it was only five days until the 58th anniversary of the 1929 crash. In 1929, the initial fall had also been under heavy trading volume, an unpleasant resemblance. And ooops! 58 years, you said? Wasn't there something about a "Kondratieff-cycle"? Better have another beer!

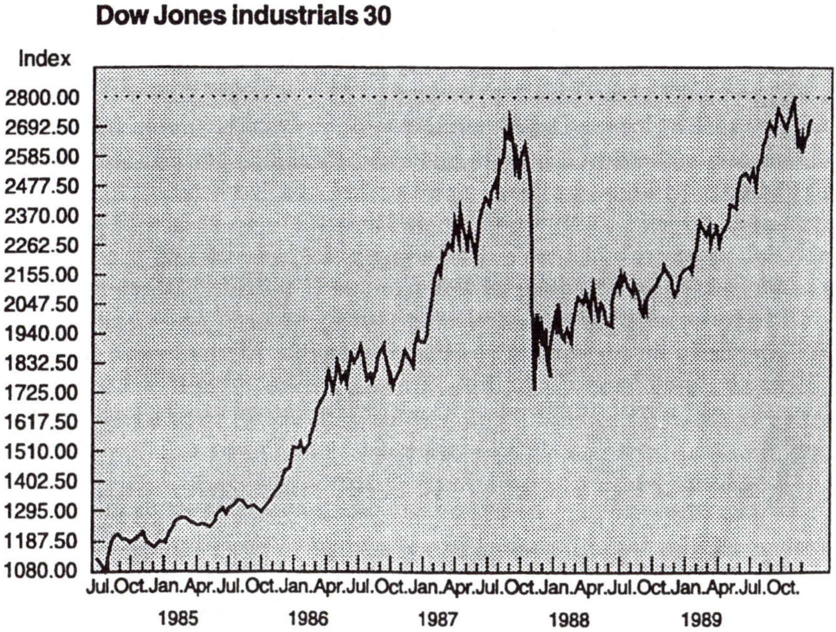

Figure 16.3: Dow Jones Industrial Index, 1985–1989.

STORMY MONDAY

Peter Lynch, the famous manager of the mighty Fidelity Magellan Fund, had left the USA the day before the disastrous Friday[7]. Now, as he was playing on the Irish Killarney golf course, he was worrying whether he should really be on holiday at all. His putting was just disastrous, and when the game was over, he couldn't remember his score — his mind was elsewhere. Peter Lynch was afraid his shareholders would lose money. A lot of money.

The day had started as an all-out disaster. In Tokyo, the index dropped by a modest 2.5%, but in Hong Kong it fell 11%, after which trading was suspended. When the European market opened, London and Zurich dropped 11%, Frankfurt 7%, and Paris 6%.

Jean-Luc Lepine, the director of Banque Demachy, went to a business dinner at one of Paris's elegant restaurants that night[8]. When the meal started, he knew the Dow Jones had already collapsed; it had beaten Friday's record and was down by an incredible 180 points. But by the time dessert arrived, the Dow Jones was down 300 points. As he was preparing to leave the restaurant, somebody told him it was down by 500, which Lepine thought was a joke. Measured in percentages, such a fall would be worse than ever seen before, despite presidential assassinations, riots, the Great Depression, Vietnam, Korea and two World Wars. This time there was nothing, absolutely nothing, to explain such a collapse, or even the terrible drop of the Friday before this weekend. But it was happening. People were selling in panic.

IMPLOSION IN FINANCIAL LIQUIDITY

Actually it wasn't only people that wanted to sell. About 25% of the sales orders were generated by the silent army of computers. But the rest of the sellers were people, and one of them was George Soros. Expecting a crash in Japan, Soros had shorted Japanese stocks while remaining long on Wall Street. Now he was heading for shelter, and in what an American trader described as "the worst sales he had ever seen", the Quantum Fund started offering S&P futures contracts in lots of a thousand through Shearson[9]. The brokerage house asked 230 to begin with, but as the other traders circled around his lots like vultures, the price plummeted to between 195 and 210. As soon as his orders had been cleared, the prices started to recover, however, and they closed at 244.50. It was later estimated that the Quantum Fund had sold its contracts at a discount to the underlying shares of 250 million USD. At the same time, Soros had sold individual shares at prices, that were sometimes the lowest of the day.

The Dow Jones Index ended the day 506 points down. It had lost 23% of its value in seven hours and was down some 40% since its peak in August. Peter Lynch's Magellan Fund had lost two billion dollars. The American break had taken the whole world with it, wiping out paper values around the globe of 2,400,000 million dollars in one single, terrifying blow.

AUCTION AT CHRISTIE'S

If professionals in the art business had been nervous before, they were scared stiff now. Would art markets crash as well, or would their much smaller audience simply ignore the crash Monday and keep bidding? The first clue came Wednesday, when Christie's held a jewelry auction which, to most people's surprise, went well. This was followed by a book sale Friday, where a Gutenberg Bible went for USD 5.9 million — the highest price ever paid for a printed book. So when van Gogh's "Irises" went on sale on November 1, there was fear, but also hope. Maybe it would break the record after all?

There were more than 2,000 people present for the auction. Christie's had employed tall, elegant women to show serious bidders to their seats, and there were "barkers" stationed by each pillar. The "barkers" were supposed to spot bids and shout them out so that no bid would be ignored. There were some 100 items on the list, and "Irises" was about a third down the list.

Although everyone expected it to be something special, one could almost sense the collective gasp as the opening bid was given: "15 million dollars." From this level, which was about twice as much as ever paid for a picture before "Sunflowers", the price jumped one million dollars at a time. No one in the hall could know that the reserve (the set minimum price) was as high as 34 million dollars, well above the world record. But the bidding soon passed this level, went to 40 million and kept rising until the last bidder pulled out at 49 million dollars. Again, as at the sales of "Sunflowers", the hall exploded in a massive applause. After the auction Peter Watson, the well-known art journalist, was walking down the stairs when he bumped into Billy Keating, an American living in London[10]. Peter had dined with Billy and his associate Angela the night before, so he asked "Where is Angela, Billy, upstairs?". Billy looked coy, so Peter assumed that Angela had been bidding from one of Sotherby's private rooms above the main floor. He didn't think much of the incident at the time, but later it dawned to him that these two people were known to assist Alan Bond. It was later confirmed that Bond had bought the picture.

TWO REMARKABLE MONTHS

It was November 1989, almost exactly two years since the sale of "Irises". Sotheby's was holding an auction, and lot sixteen was Willem de Kooning's "Interchange", which was estimated at USD 4–6 million dollars[11]. The bidding was supposed to be in units of USD 200,000. As it reached 1.7 million, however, a voice suddenly cried out:

"Six million dollars!"

The auctioneer frowned for a second before resuming on his task. The next bid was supposed to be 6.2 million, but again the system was broken as a new bid was given via phone:

"Seven million"

After that, the bidding continued with the regular 200,000 dollar jumps, edging up to 15.8 million. The two bidders were Mr. Alveryd, a Swede, and Mr. Kamayama from Japan. The next bid broke the order again:

"17 million"

This was a mistake, however — Mr. Kamayama had not been concentrating. The auctioneer recognized this and accepted the bid as 16 million. But at 16.8 million it jumped again:

"18 million"

Mr. Kamayama had apparently lost his concentration again, so the bid was corrected to 17 million. Finally the Swede gave up and Mr. Kamayama got the picture for USD 20.9 million dollars, including commissions.

This episode was symptomatic of the events in the markets during November and December 1989. These two months were perhaps the most remarkable in the history of art trading. During November alone, Picassos worth 3,777 million dollars shifted hands. More than 300 pictures were sold at prices exceeding 1 million dollars, and 58 at prices above 5 million dollars. The art index was up about 580% since the beginning of 1985. What a market! What a trend!

18
Trends, Turbo-Chargers and Turning Points

"The poet only asks to get his head into the heavens. It is the logician who seeks to get the heavens into his head. And it is his head that splits."

G.K. Chesterton

Trends in asset markets are fascinating. Take for instance equities. When the price of equities starts to rise, the reasons may not appear very obvious. Most bull markets start when news is still bad and the press still mocking the markets. One of the explanations for the first advances is that skilled speculators are forecasting better times and taking a gamble. Another is that short sellers are meeting their targets and want to lock in their profits, so they can "square out" their positions. But as prices have risen for a while, a series of positive feed-back loops set in:

- The press needs to explain what happens, so they call some traders who invent some post factum rationalizations. Potential investors read this, and as the price movements and the published explanations are well in line, they change their attitudes and decide to buy.
- The remaining bears can now see that their financial liquidity is eroding as their short positions generate losses. As they get tired of meeting daily margin calls, they execute their stop loss buy-orders.
- The bulls, in contrast, gain more financial liquidity with each price rise. This not only confirms their view, but also increases their ability to put money where their mouth is.
- Bull markets create higher turnover, and this encourages stock brokers to employ more people who can call more potential customers to persuade them to buy as well.

- As the surge has continued for some time, it becomes easier to raise money through junk bonds and new share issues, and this enhances the commercial value of the shares, and thus their price, and thus the financial liquidity controlled by their shareholders.

So the initial, fragile bull market is gradually reinforced by an increasing number of inter-connected turbo-chargers that attract new investors, generate financial liquidity, force out the skeptics, and create the commercial value that closes the loop. Similar processes take place when the economy is in a rising trend: profits go up, confidence rises, inventory and capacity fall behind and lead to compensatory investments, etc., etc. But each feed-back has its own mechanics, and some will work fast while others are slow. Stop-loss orders in stock markets kick in fast, for instance, while increased sales effort and increased issuance of new shares come later. This raises a question: How will different inherent properties of each feed-back process influence the whole? How different can the processes be before they are no longer able to create mode-locking phenomena? In late 1989, Erik Mosekilde, Jesper Thomsen and John D. Sterman decided to investigate that issue by analyzing the Kondratieff sub-model of M.I.T.'s system dynamics model of the economy[1].

BUTTERFLY EFFECTS AND FEIGENBAUM CASCADES

One of the things they wanted to investigate was whether it was likely or not that mode-locking could lead to major depressions. The M.I.T. model had been improved gradually over the years to resemble real economic phenomena as well as possible. One alteration was that consumer demand was now an external figure. The most interesting phenomenon was actually centered around this element. Consider this: if there were several, cyclical phenomena, then you couldn't just consider the total output to be the sum of the individual oscillatory movements as suggested in Schumpeter's drawing from 1935 (Figure 10.2). The likely outcome was much more complicated, because each cyclic phenomenon would interact with the others. They decided to test this hypothesis by subjecting the Kondratieff model to Kithin's and Kuznets' oscillations, respectively.

The hypothesis was confirmed: there was a strong tendency to mode-locking, so that the Kondratieff cycle changed its frequency considerably when the model was exposed to the two other oscillatory impulses. It

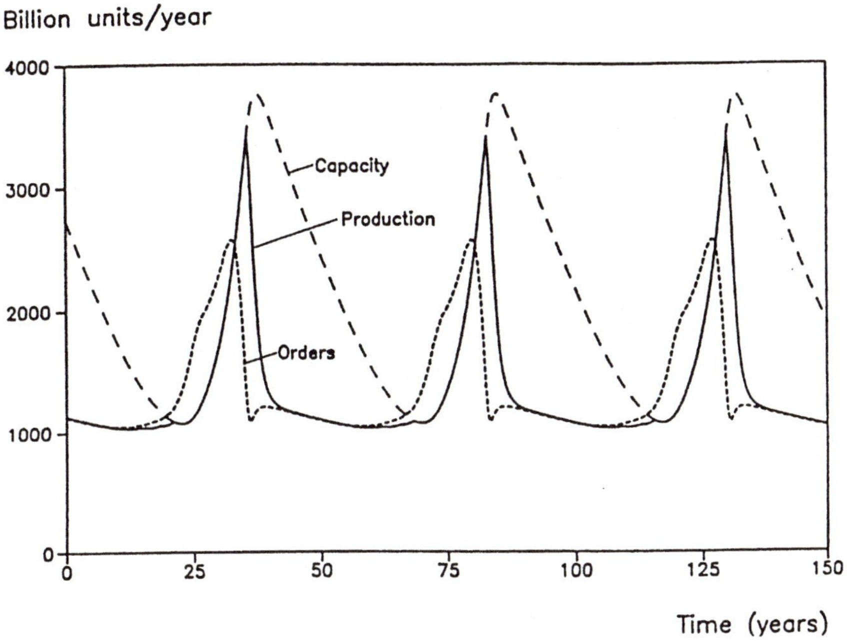

Figure 17.1: A Kondratieff cycle simulation.
This is a simulation of the Kondratieff cycle based on a modified version of The System Dynamics National Model from the Sloan School of Management. The three curves illustrate capacity, production, and orders. The system is inherently unstable, as it is driven by self-ordering in the capital sector (ordering of capital for production of capital, but with a time-lag). The cycle period is 47 years. Source: Mosekilde, Larsen, Thomsen and Sterman, 1992.

was particularly remarkable that the Kondratieff frequency was extended by 40% when subjected to a Kuznets oscillation (Figure 17.3).

The next experiment was to test this economic model for the inherent property most often associated with chaos: the butterfly effect. Although the M.I.T. model was by no means made with the objective to simulate chaos, Jesper Thomsen's tests showed that it was indeed highly chaotic.

The third experiment with the model was to analyze the transition phase between chaotic and orderly modes. Again he found one of the classical, chaotic phenomena: the transition had the shape of a Feigenbaum cascade.

Erik Mosekilde spent hours looking at the prints — and thinking. Assume that the model was reasonably accurate. Where in the phase space

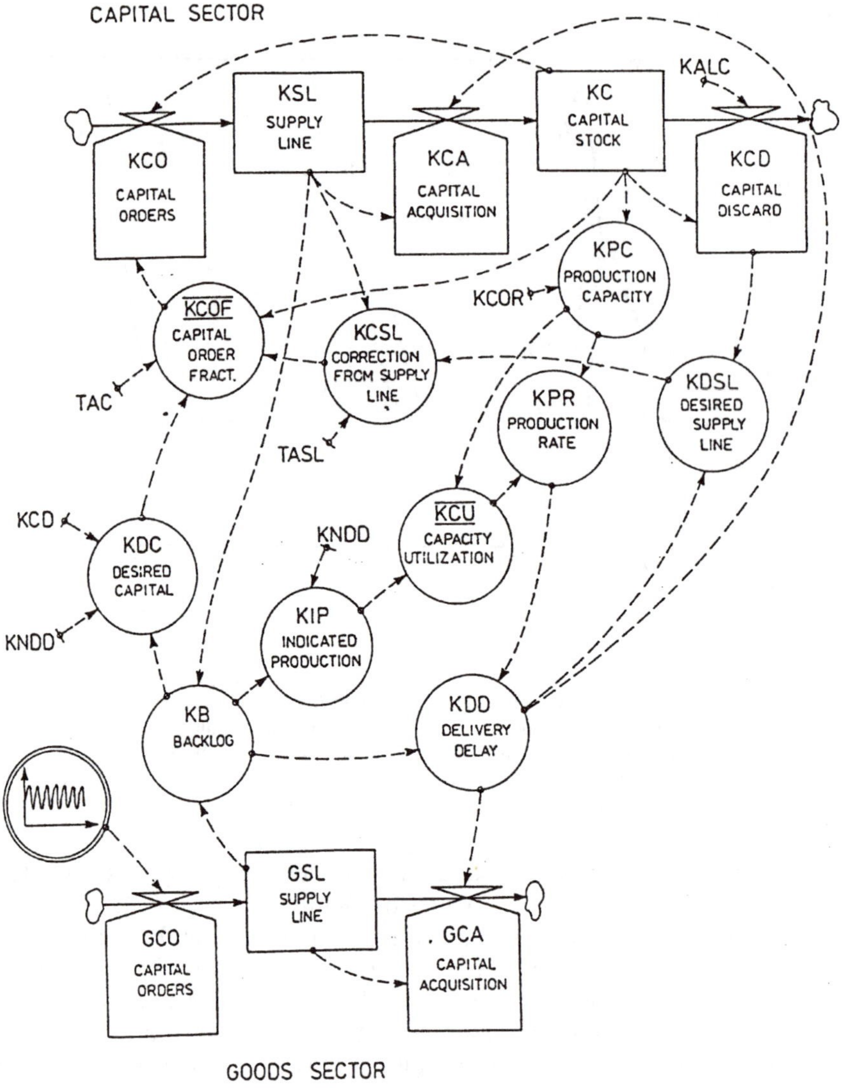

Figure 17.2: A graphical presentation of the Kondratieff simulation model.
This model was used by Jesper Thomsen to test chaos effects on a multi-cycle system. A traditional use of such a model would be to insert best estimates for the parameter values and then test the model's ability to simulate real events. If it didn't do that well, you would typically modify the equations. The system dynamics approach, in contrast, was essentially to keep the equations unaltered while repeating the simulations again and again, each time modifying the parameter values slightly. By doing so, you would get insight into the dynamic properties of the system.

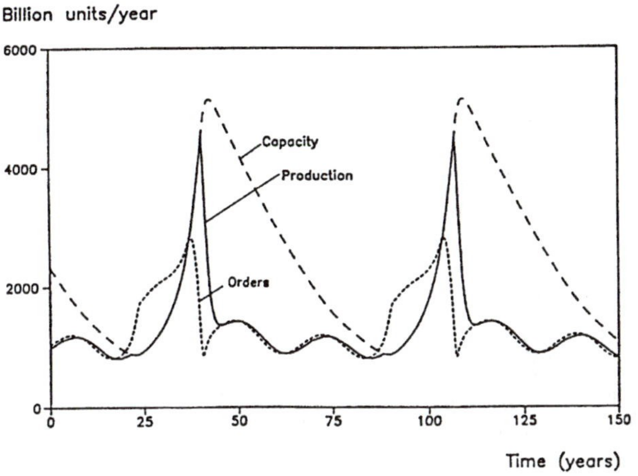

Figure 17.3: Simulation of a Kondratieff-Kuznets scenario.
This simulation was conducted by subjecting the Kondratieff model mentioned in Figure 17.2 with an external sinusoidal oscillation given a period of 22.2 years, corresponding to a typical Kuznets cycle. The result of this modified Kondratieff simulation was mode-locking, where the average Kondratieff cycle length increased by 40% to accommodate precisely three periods of the external (Kuznets) signal.

would the real economies actually be? The system dynamics simulations did little to suggest where the actual economy fitted in. If in reality it was situated in a stable area, were butterfly effects anything but theory? But perhaps he didn't need a computer to figure out at least part of the answer. There had been stable economies in the socialist states, but this hadn't worked well. Other countries were in complete chaos. But wasn't it most likely that the developed capitalist countries were situated somewhere in a border area where there would sometimes be periods of stability, most of the time mild fluctuations, and occasionally very big booms including madness and crazes followed by dramatic turning points and then busts?

Virtually all major bull markets feature particular crazes. The stock markets that Mosekilde could study had seen obsessions with "growth stocks", "new issues", "concept stocks", "conglomerates", "biotechnology", etc., etc.

LOCAL LOOPS

It was the same with the art markets of the late 1980s, which had appeared increasingly obsessed with van Gogh and Picasso. So

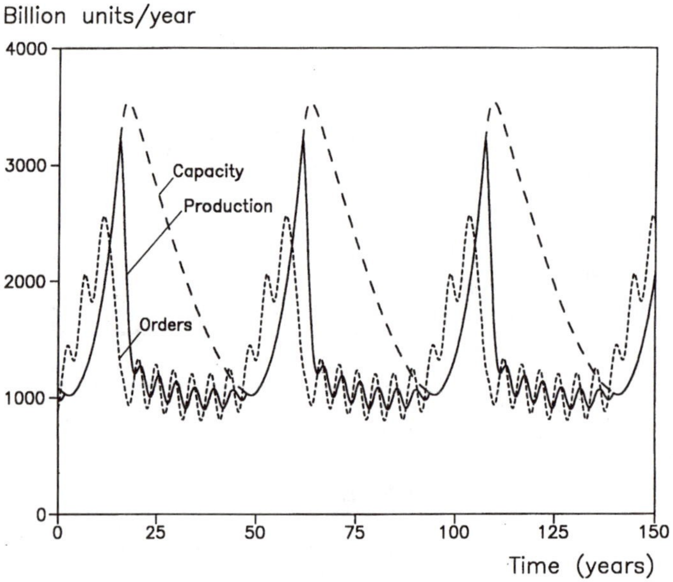

Figure 17.4: Simulation of a Kondratieff-Kitchin scenario.
When subjected to external sinusoidal oscillations with a 4.6-year period, the Kondratieff model (Figure 17.2) mode-locked to form an overall oscillation, where one Kondratieff matched 10 Kitchins over 46 years. This 1:10 relationship was maintained for Kitchin periods between 4.47 and 4.7 years. When the Kitchin cycle length was changed beyond these borders, the mode-locking grew more complicated, for instance 2:19 and 2:21. The mode-locking process proved sensitive to the amplitude of the forced signal. By refining the calculations with small amplitudes of the forced signal, self-similar structure could be detected.

Chistopher Burge, the Chief Executive Officer of Christie's in the United States, had reasons to be satisfied when he packed for the Christmas holiday at the end of 1989 (just after the tests of the M.I.T. model), because he carried with him a draft press release about the sales of another van Gogh[2]. And this one might very well set the third world record in four years. It was the famous "Portrait of Dr. Gachet".

Christie's had estimated the sales price at USD 40–50 million, and the sellers had set the secret "reserve" at USD 35 million. There were perhaps 10–20 people in the world that might be interested and able to pay that sort of amount. Five in USA, three in London, but none of them English, three in Switzerland, one in Germany, and five to ten in Japan. Alan Bond, the Australian, was no longer in the game. After he bought "Irises" it had been revealed that part of the purchasing amount had been financed by Sotheby's. This was in fact not a good sign for the market, and especially

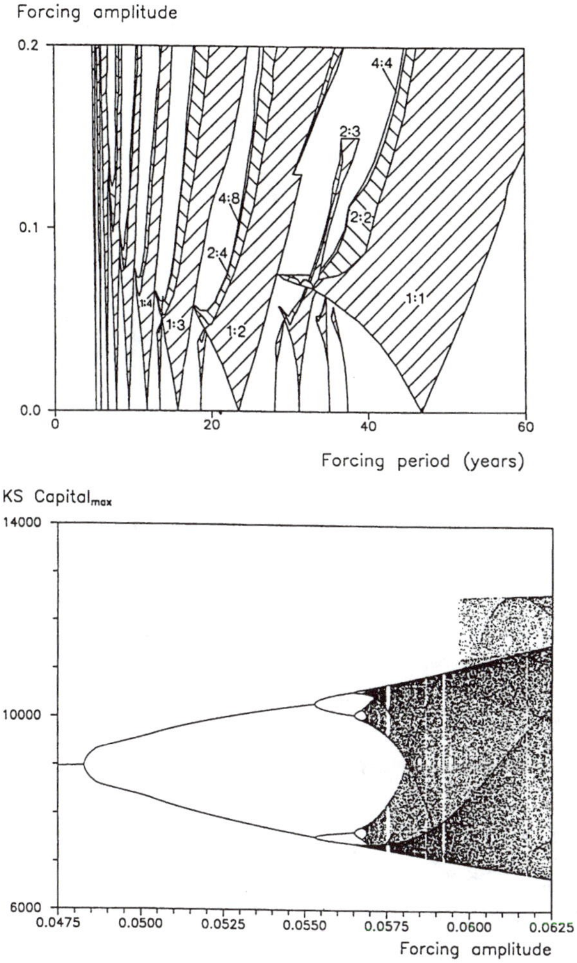

Figure 17.5: Mode-locking phenomena.

The upper graph shows a diagram illustrating mode-locking phenomena in the Sloan School of Management business cycle model (see Figures 17.1–17.4). The horizontal axis is alternative frequencies for external cycles imposed on the Kondratieff system, and the vertical is the amplitudes of these external cycles. As could be expected, the mode-locking between the Kondratieff and the external cycles is limited to narrow frequency bands, if the external cycles are weak (have small amplitudes). Resonance (mode-locking) is more prevalent at large amplitudes, as can be seen from the highlighted areas. Between these areas there is either quasi-chaotic behavior (strange attractors) or chaos.

The lower graph shows the transition from mode-locking to chaos between the two cycles, when the frequency of the external cycle was 19.6 years and its amplitude was gradually increased from 0.0475 to 0.0625. The transition is a Feigenbaum cascade.

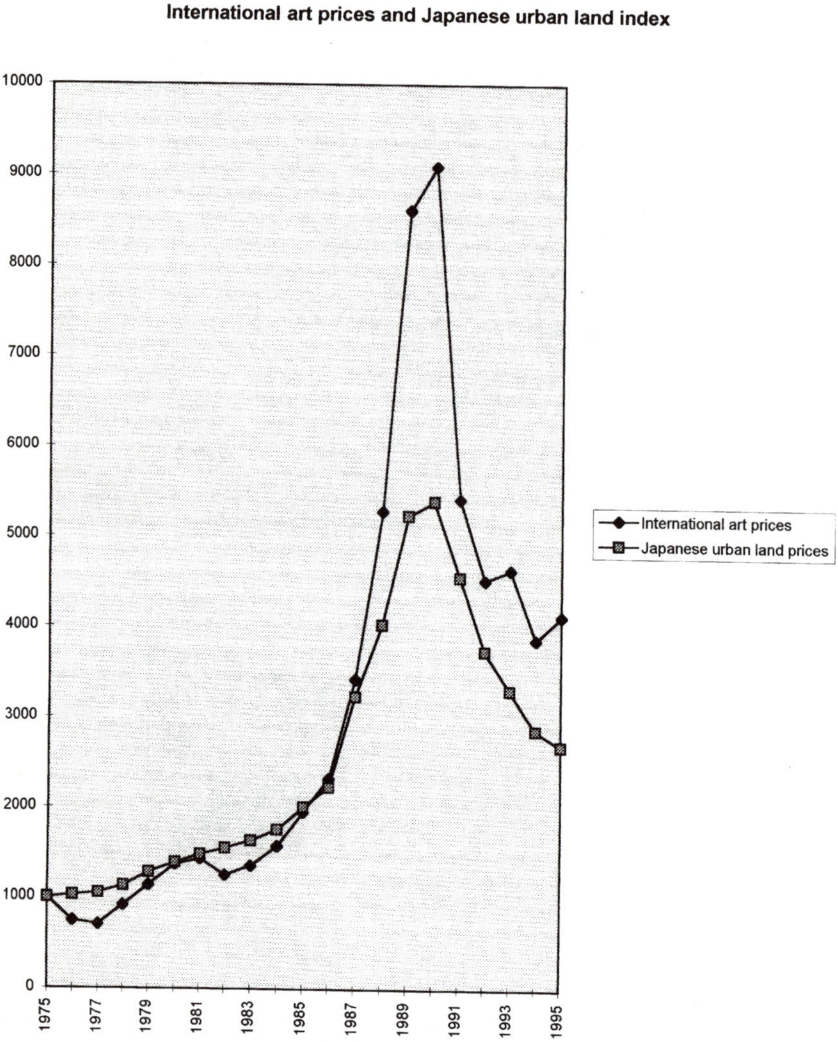

Figure 17.6: Japanese Urban Land Price Index and The Daily Telegraph Art Index 1975–1995 (1975 = 1,000).

The first index illustrates average prices for art sold in the years 1975–1995. It is calculated by Art Market Research, tel: +44 171 24 98071. The unit is dollars. The second is an index of urban land price in Japan, calculated in yen (figures supplied by Bank Credit Analyst). The correlation is striking, but will be even stronger if both indexes are calculated in the same currency.

since he had not been able to raise the remaining amount either, so that the picture had been re-sold to a museum for an "undisclosed" amount. Undisclosed indicated that it had been lower. Another negative factor was that the Japanese stock market had peaked just after Christmas and was now falling rapidly: the bubble was finally bursting. And finally: several European auctions in the first months of 1990 had failed miserably.

THIN AIR

The sale had been prepared like never before. Electronic systems had been checked again and again, an emergency team had been flown in from Canada to repair a computer, and a dress rehearsal had been held. And Barbara Strongin and her team had worked intensively with one of the most important parts of the preparations: the seating. The serious bidders had to get the best places, and ideally there should be no bidding from the side rooms. The team knew most big players personally, but in case they were in doubt, they could check on their computers how much a client had bought at Christie's within the last few years. The rough cut-off point for a seat in the main hall this night was USD 300,000 of purchases within the last few years. All seats had now been allocated, but there were still 100 names on the waiting list for the main hall. Finally the shutters went down and everybody left the halls to dress.

At six-thirty the audience began to arrive. Before the doors closed, 1,700 people had been let in and shown to their places. There were 20 lots before "Dr. Gachet" on the list, and these sold reasonably well. Finally, when lot 21 was next, the television lights were turned on. Now was the time!

The auctioneer opened the bidding at a cool 20 million dollars, and thereafter it started climbing rapidly with one million dollar jumps. As it reached 35 million, the reserve price, the auctioneer pushed back his spectacles: the sale was at least secured now. The price kept rising, however, until at 40 million there was a pause. A bidder had apparently dropped out, so was this it?

It wasn't. Suddenly a Japanese dealer in the back of the hall raised his hand. The next bid came from Maria Reinshagen, an employee of Christie's, Zurich, who was on the phone with a client. Applause broke out as the price reached 50 million dollars. But the battle continued as the price rose steadily to 60 million, then 70, 71, 72, and then 73 million dollars. It was Maria's turn now, and she whispered for a long time on the phone. Then she raised her arm.

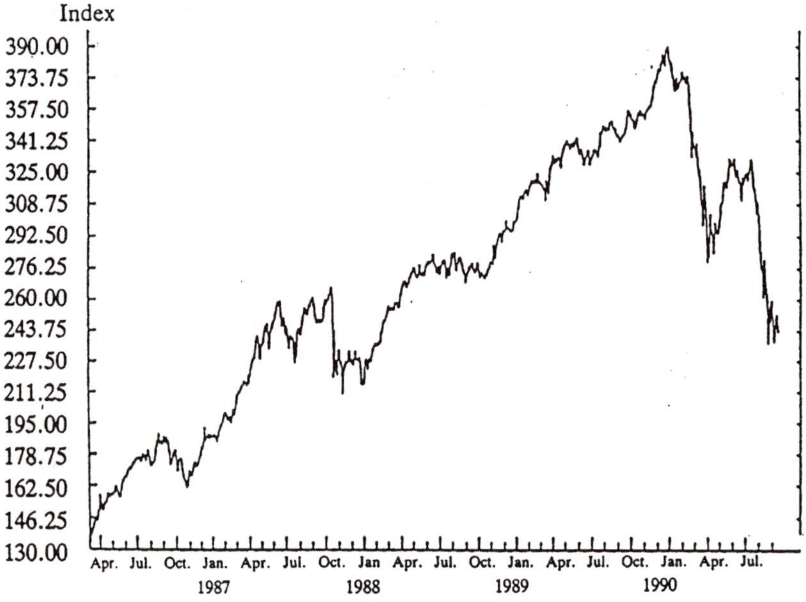

Figure 17.7: Tokyo New Stock Index, 1987–1990.

"74 million dollars."

But Kobayashi wasn't quite finished. As he bid 75 million, the audience could see that Maria was listening more than talking on the phone, and finally she looked up and shook her head. The bidder, whoever it was, had had enough, and the picture went to Mr. Kobayashi for 75 million plus commissions, or 82.5 million in total. Only two days later he bought Renoir's "Au Moulent de la Galette" for 71 million dollars plus commission.

INCREASING STRAIN

That was the peak. Prices and trading volume in the art markets started to contract soon after, and within the next two years the art price index dropped by about 50%. The Japanese stock market was down even more, however, and it was now clear that the international economic and financial system was headed towards severe strain. Following the crash in 1987, massive amounts of liquidity had been injected into the system by central banks to avoid total disaster, but while many asset markets had boomed, the real sector had not responded well. Many things indicated that this could perhaps be one of the rare times where Kitchin, Kuznets and Kondratieff downswings coincide, and there had now been a number of financial collapses, including massive waves of real estate defaults as well as the savings and loan scandals. The recession appeared simultaneously in the USA, Japan, and Europe, and authorities in USA and Japan reacted promptly and aggressively to stimulate credit growth.

But the response in Europe was completely different. Because of the fall of the Berlin Wall, Germany suffered, as the only OECD country, from rising inflation. The Bundesbank was consequently *raising* German interest rates, and to protect their currencies, the member ERM countries had to maintain even higher interest rates, in spite of post-war record unemployment.

One of the countries where the high interest rates hurt most was the UK, and the criticism of the UK's exchange rate policy mounted. This was an example of Milton Friedman's "trilemma" — the problems of trying to control exchange rates and inflation levels while at the same time avoiding exchange controls. As the time passed and the pain grew, criticism of the UK's exchange rate policy mounted, and traders began selling the pound short.

In August 1992, Norman Lamont, the British chancellor of the exchequer, declared that "We are not going to devalue the pound." "... if, as some suggest, we cut loose from the EMR and slash interest rates, things would worsen. The pound would dive and inflation explode." But in spite of his defence of the fixed exchange rate policy, speculation against the pound was clearly growing. On August 28, he appeared before television cameras in front of the Treasury. Speaking quickly and firmly, he reiterated that there would be no question of devaluating the pound. As he spoke, the Bank of England started buying up no less than 300 million pounds in a show of strength. But when experts on body language and psychology played back the tapes afterwards, they noticed that he breathed too heavily and spoke too fast for somebody who was convinced of his own words[3]. The most revealing detail was how often he blinked, however. A person speaking what he believes to be the truth will typically blink perhaps six to eight times per minute. But Lamont blinked 64 times in 45 seconds ...

He didn't give up, however. On September 3 he announced that the government planned to borrow the equivalent of GBP 7.5 billion in foreign currency to support the pound. Three days later John Major gave a speech to the Confederation of British Industry in Glasgow where he denied "categorically" that the British government would devaluate the pound. On the same day Mr. Lamont repeated that surprise, there, would be no devaluation.

Traders all over the world were following these events closely. Among those who were most interested were two gentlemen in New York who had gradually become quite sure that Mr. Lamont and Mr. Major would eventually lose their battle[4]. One day, one of them suggested to the other that they should make a bet against the pound. A big bet. Perhaps of three, or perhaps four billion dollars. The other agreed that they should make the bet. But he didn't agree on the amount. He wanted to bet more

What triggers turning points?

Negative feed-back, echoes and lags are important elements when the economy peaks:

1. Negative feed-back loops
   - *bottlenecks*
   - *business expenditures and profitability*
   - *critical lengthening of investment periods*
2. Echoes
   - *re-investment echoes*
3. Lags
   - *accelerator phenomena*
   - *cobweb phenomena*
   - *lagged inventory adjustments*

As regards equities, the friction is much smaller, so lags have less if any importance. Distribution from strong hands to larger numbers of weaker investors plays a role, however:

1. Negative feed-back loops
   - *valuations fall behind actual price*
   - *rising cost of money*
   - *drain of liquidity to the real sector*
   - *new issues*
2. Echoes
   - *waves of profit-taking*
3. Cascades

19
Milton Friedman's "Trilemma"

"In industrial fluctuation we are up against a problem very deep-seated in the nature of capitalist industry — perhaps of all industry whether capitalist or not — perhaps of man himself. I do not believe we can solve it."

Dennis Robertson

George Soros and Stanley Druckenmiller had become extremely confident in this particular deal. The chances that the pound would be devaluated were very high. And even if for whatever reason it didn't happen, there would be so little to lose; in that unfortunate case they would probably be able to get out of a short position in pounds with just a minor loss. So when Druckenmiller, George Soros' crown prince, suggested to him that they should bet 3–4 billion dollars, Soros didn't agree on the amount. This would be like shooting fish in a barrel, so why not make a real big bet. Real big. Like 15 billion dollars?

This was one of the things Druckenmiller admired about Soros. He knew when to bail out of a deal turning sour, but he also knew when to strike big. They started by selling short USD 7 billion. As a part of their strategy, they also bought British stock and French and German bonds — markets that were likely to benefit from a devaluation of the pound.

On Tuesday September 15, 1992, the currency started falling rapidly, and although the Bank of England responded by buying 3 billion pounds to support the exchange rate, the market ended the day very weak. During the evening Mr. Lamont had a dinner with the American ambassador but, perhaps a bit impolitely, he tried every 10 minutes to reach the officials in the Bundesbank, hoping to convince them to lower German money rates. When he finally reached them, however, he found no willingness to help. After the dinner he met with officials from the Bank of England to make a game-plan for the next day. They agreed to start with intervention from early in the morning, perhaps followed by an increase in the interest rates later.

WAKE-UP CALL

The next morning at 7:30 the traders of the Bank of England started as agreed, by buying up USD 2 billion worth of pounds. One hour later, Mr. Lamont called the Bank of England and John Major to discuss the situation. At 10:30 Lamont called Mr. Major again to suggest an increase in interest rates of 2%. Major agreed, but the pound kept falling anyway. Although the Bank of England ended up spending 15 billion pounds during the day, the battle was clearly lost.

It was 7:00 a.m. New York time when Stanley Druckenmiller called George Soros to break the news:

> "George, you've just made 958 million dollars!"

Within the following 10 months Spain devalued three times, Portugal twice, and Ireland once. New tensions started in the ERM system in the spring and summer of 1993 as the recession deepened. It became more and more obvious that the recession-marred countries remaining in the ERM system couldn't defy Friedman's trilemma much further. The price of controlling exchange rates and maintaining freedom from exchange controls was that no monetary steps could be taken to avert the recession which was threatening to evolve into a depression.

On Monday, July 26, 1993, George Soros published an article in *Le Figaro*, where he criticized the interest rate policy of the Bundesbank but added that he would not sell the franc short because he didn't want to be accused of derailing the ERM system. On Thursday the *Financial Times* contained an article by six economists[1], that concluded:

> "Governments have done little but seek a variety of excuses for the loss of jobs. It looks as if the 1930s are being re-enacted. Then, it was felt imperative to hang on to gold at any price: today the feeling is to hang on to the D-mark."

But as the Bundesbank and other central banks chose to ignore the advice of George Soros and the six prestigious economists the next day, Soros dashed off a brief statement that he would now feel free "to resume trading in the French franc", adding:

> "It is futile to attempt to protect the European Monetary System by abstaining from trading in currencies when the anchor of the system, the Bundesbank, acts without regard to the interest of the other members."

As the European markets closed Friday night, the French franc was under heavy pressure, and it was clear that something had to be done. The Bundesbank called in a meeting on the Sunday[2]. Before the meeting commenced at 12 noon, the British chancellor Kenneth Clark infuriated everyone by telling the journalists that "we told you so."

The first participant to address the plenary session was the German finance minister Theo Waigel, and the atmosphere turned rather frosty as he claimed that Germany had done everything in its power to avert the crisis. A number of options were soon proposed, but none seemed attractive to the participants. Mineral water and French bread were served.

During the next 10 hours one solution after the other was discussed, but no-one seemed to be able to agree on anything. As beer was served at 10 o'clock that evening, the drafting began on press notices stating that the ERM would be swept away completely.

At 22:40 p.m. (7:40 a.m. Tokyo time) the first quotes from the Japanese money markets put the franc at 3.4550 against the mark — well below its ERM band limit. At 23:30 p.m. the plenary was reconvened in a last, desperate attempt to find a solution, which could preserve the ERM. A 10% band was proposed, and then a band of +/– 15%, which became the solution. At 23:30 p.m., 15 minutes before the opening of official trading in Tokyo, the participants left to meet the press. The first to break the news was spokesman Karlheinz von den Driesch from the German finance ministry, who was pushing his way through the wall of television cameras and frantic reporters when he spotted a familiar journalist to whom he whispered:

> "Wide fluctuation bands for everyone."

After this victory George Soros gave an interview to Gary Weiss of *Markets and Investments*, who asked about his opinion of the European currency crisis[3].

> "It's all very reminiscent of what happened during the interwar period, between World War I and World War II, and it's really amazing how

> people haven't learned from the past experience. It's as if Keynes had never lived. Some of the same mistakes: overvalued currencies, sticking to monetary discipline in a time of recession, you know, very high interest rates. It's a tragic situation."

But then, Soros had really contributed to change it, and the interest rates were now dropping rapidly throughout Europe. Once again he had forcefully demonstrated what he had written in his book six years before:

> "... there can be no assurance that fundamental forces will correct speculative excesses. It is just as possible that speculation will alter the supposedly fundamental conditions of supply and demand."

Rational expectations and government policy

When Denmark and Ireland made drastic budget cuts in the early 1980s, the markets responded by marking up bond prices, holding back on salary demands, and investing in new businesses. Perversely, fiscal contraction appeared to stimulate the economies. This was interpreted as examples of rational expectations working beneficially.

The theory of rational expectations has had a large influence on governments and central banks. The theory is now often incorporated into the econometric models used by government and central banks so that, for instance, it is assumed that people expect the same inflation in the future as the system (through iterations) calculates. If the society has rational expectations about the long-term effect of public economic measures, then it pays to make these measures clear, predictable and sound for the long term. Elements in that may be to announce inflation targets, budget deficit targets, or fixed exchange rates. The balancing act is to announce policies and targets that can be achieved, however. The currency crises in the 1990s were blows to some policies made for the long term that turned out to be unsustainable for unique reasons.

A DIFFERENT KIND OF INFLATION

There are many ways of looking at increasing asset prices. A private investor may see it as increasing wealth that can justify a purchase of a new car. A fund manager might talk about it as a bull market. But a central banker might view it in a completely different way — as an alarming case of "asset inflation".

These issues of asset inflation were in fact so important to central bankers that the Bank of International Settlements in Basle, Switzerland decided to arrange a meeting about it two years later. The bank invited several leading bankers and scientists to present their views on the subject during two days in October 1997.

One of the most interesting presentations came from Shuichi Uemura and Takeshi Kimura from Japan. Their presentation was very focused on the relationships between land prices, stock prices and economic activity, which they claimed had been key to the meltdown in the early 1990s. As they stated:

> "Rising land prices made a considerable contribution to the increase in corporate net asset values during the late eighties, and it is likely that the unrealized profits on land, which contained a bubble, were translated directly into share price formation. This is consistent with the phenomenon seen in the nineties, when share prices have been slumping as land prices dropped."

They continued their analysis by observing that:

> "… we can assume that a mechanism then took root in which share prices valued in terms of rising land prices further boosted the value of the shares issued by companies that had extensive stock portfolios because of cross-holding relationships".

Interestingly, by studying the exact movements of the two markets they concluded that share prices were leading land prices.

Their speech was interesting not only because they had analyzed a great crash that had taken place a few years before, but also since a similar event was unfolding as they spoke. It was the great crash in Asia/Pacific …

Growing Up

"Philosophy begins in wonder. And, at the end, when philosophic thought has done its best, the wonder remains."

A.N. Whitehead

20
Booms and Bubbles of the Nineties

"It is essentially meaningless to talk about complex adaptive systems being in equilibrium: the system can never get there. In fact, if the system ever does reach equilibrium it isn't just stable. It's dead. And by the same token, there is no point in imagining that agents in the system can ever "optimize" their fitness, or their utility, or whatever. The space of possibilities is simply too vast; they have no practical way of finding the optimum."

John Holland

Ability to understand the conditions that create crashes is one of the qualities that a hedge fund manager is supposed to have. He is, for instance, suppose to be able to see whether the present economic scenario contains economic bubbles which are likely to burst soon. And he is, in such a situation, supposed to have mastered the timing and have the guts to sell what will fall in price when the collapse sets in. If he takes big positions, or if there are many people like him, then it will bring the collapse forward. But it will also limit the extent of the inevitable crash because it sets in earlier than it otherwise would have, and the earlier the return to reality starts, the less dramatic it needs to be.

George Soros and his people thought they had spotted such a bubble in the beginning of 1997. It was in a small country far away, but the signs were pretty clear: Thailand was headed for trouble.

Thailand's basic problem was actually not that difficult to detect; the symptoms kind of covered the skyline of the country's capital. Anyone who visited Bangkok could see it — a forest of cranes involved in new construction work in spite of the scary number of already completed buildings that were only half filled if not completely empty. This phenomenon indicated overinvestment — the problem that von Mises and many other economists had described so well. The suspicion of severe overinvestment would be confirmed if you studied the statistical numbers: they showed that the country had very high debt levels. Interest rates had been kept too low for too long, and bank lending had not been controlled well enough. This had created credit inflation, Irwin Fisher style. Now, the practical question was this: assuming that a number of companies and funds started selling the Thailand baht — would the central bank then be able to resist the pressure?

The statistics indicated that it wouldn't. The country's accumulated foreign debt was considerably larger than its currency reserves — even short-term debts seemed to exceed the reserves. So assume that many of the local companies with loans denominated in foreign currency hadn't hedged their risk yet, and assume that they suddenly got very scared and wanted to hedge their foreign exchange exposure. The amount of baht for sale would easily exceed the reserves of the central bank. The currency would be devalued.

TWO KINDS OF GROWTH

There exist two kinds of economic growth. One is sustainable, none-inflationary growth created by productivity; which means growth through education, innovation and rationalization. The other is growth created by credit inflation, low wage costs, and large public sector projects.

Asia-Pacific (except Japan) had been the darling of investors and visionaries for years because of its healthy growth. The sustainable part of the growth in Asia/Pacific was created because families invested in their children's education, because entrepreneurs developed new products and services and because people worked hard. The area had extremely impressive and consistent growth rates, high savings rates, low taxes, and focus on the export sectors. Instead of public welfare spending you had a tradition of family solidarity. Technological know-how was built up through innovation, licensing, acquisition, import and joint ventures. The area's share of global exports grew steadily. So how did the problems occur in Thailand?

The problem was created by a normal phenomenon. As people got used to the comfort of continued growth and wealth creation, they tended to get careless, and that created the conditions that can lead to corrections, recessions, depressions — and crashes, just as Clement Juglar described it as early as in 1862. A well-structured economy will of course have built-in controlling mechanisms, or negative feed-back processes, and these controlling mechanisms will limit the potential excess and thus limit the basis for any crash. They will have shareholders controlling boards, boards controlling managers, managers controlling employees, banks controlling their creditors, and governments controlling banks and everybody controlling governments. They will also have mechanisms that make it possible to clear sick businesses out of the system before they absorb too many resources that could have been put to better use, and before their continued presence creates too much insecurity among the people and entities they transact with. And finally they will have a separation between the government and the central bank, so that the central bank can counter some of the potential distortions created by any government aiming for unsustainable growth.

Some of the Asian/Pacific countries lacked many of these inhibitors against excess during the 1990s. The typical problems were insufficient financial control functions and lack of regulations to handle financial crisis situations, too many cozy relationships between business partners, banks and bureaucrats, at times naiveté regarding the motives of foreign investors, and, in some cases, lack of clear separation between government and central bank. The combination of these problems allowed some of the countries in the region to continue the expansion phase of their business cycles until their economies contained significant speculation bubbles.

THE SYMPTOMS

Economic bubbles create a number of symptoms even before the financial collapse begins. This was also the case in Asia/Pacific, where many of the bubble symptoms in themselves were not sufficient cause for alarm, but where their combination created a very dangerous picture. The most important symptoms (although they were not all available in all countries) were:

- *Overinvestments.* Almost all countries suffered from overinvestments. Firstly their investment levels were even higher than their impressive domestic savings levels. This meant that they had to import capital in order to sustain their growth rates. This is not a problem if the money is invested well. But that was too often not the case. A number of their investments were not sufficiently profitable to be justified — and in particular to be justified from the perspective of foreign investors. In fact, many investments

Structural disinhibitors in the Asia/Pacific economies in the 1990s

One of the reasons for the magnitude of the crash in Asia-Pacific in the 1990s was that many of the countries had too few controlling mechanisms to prevent excess. Some of these problems were:

- Insufficient financial control functions. *Some of the Asian countries had very inadequate financial regulations. They might, for instance, allow people without a reasonable minimum of capital and professional training to set up stock brokerage/banking operations. Or the financial supervisory functions of banks might be insufficient, meaning that banks were not forced to close down or merge at the time when their capital base became insufficient. Such lack of controls allowed the financial sector to continue to lend far beyond the sustainable level.*
- "Crony capitalism". *Crony capitalism is a term that describes economies where business is largely done between networks of friends who exchange benefits. It might be networks of "friendly" companies investing in each other or buying assets or products from each other, bankers lending to their associates, or business executives exchanging favors with bureaucrats from the public sector. This way of doing business has several major advantages, as the people who transact might know and respect each other's personalities, so that they are able to substitute comprehensive contracts with personal trust. However, the risk is that they make decisions that favor the individual, but not the organizations that they represent or the economy as a whole. An example is the case when two entities decide to buy assets from each other at inflated prices. By doing so they can increase their respective perceived asset position and profits, even although no real asset appreciation has taken place. It can also be the case when investment projects are allowed to go ahead even if their underlying economics are dubious.*
- Insufficient regulation to handle financial crisis situations. *A typical problem was that laws did not allow a smooth clearing in case of financial collapse. Some countries did not have*

well-developed bankruptcy laws, which meant that companies could continue to operate a long time after they had become insolvent and had defaulted on some of their payments. Furthermore, once they did collapse, there was no clear protection of their creditors. As for the banking world, it was not always clear who would be protected and who would not if a bank collapsed. This meant that depositors would be very quick to remove their money from banks that they thought were in trouble.

- Naiveté regarding the motives of foreign investors. *Most of the countries were partly dependent on private foreign investors to supply credit and capital investments for their growth. Private investors invest to make money. They will only invest far away from their home country if they think they can obtain higher returns there than through their investments at home. However, if the higher returns are created only through asset inflation, and not through the return capital from the underlying businesses, then it is only a matter of time before the foreign investors will get cold feet and pull out. Some of the governments in the region failed to realize that it is not enough to allow foreign investors to get in. If you want access to foreign capital over the long term, then you must also allow the foreign investors to make a healthy return on their investments and to take their money back out whenever they want to.*
- Government interference in monetary policy. *Some countries allowed their government to manipulate monetary policy. This resulted in continued excessive monetary stimulation through too low interest rates and too lax borrowing to banks.*

were directed into construction of new real estate for which there was no demand. These investments generated zero productivity gains and, as it turned out, negative returns.

- *Overvaluations of currencies.* Currencies were often pegged to currencies of countries with lower inflation rates. This meant that effective exchange rates (exchange rates adjusted for inflation differences) rose from year to year. The peg system encouraged corporations to lend in other currencies, like dollars, without hedging the exchange rate risks. This became a time-bomb as many of these companies would be unable to honor their debts if their currencies devalued. The result of the overvaluation combined with overinvestment was current account deficits.

- *Low interest rates* as compared to monetary growth rates. A number of the countries had a high rate of monetary growth, which was not checked by sufficiently high interest rates. This stimulated the economies excessively and let corporations in some countries accumulate large debts denominated in local currency. The stimulation contributed to development of over-capacity and over-extension (Examples were the fact that there were more than 230 banks in Indonesia, or that some leading Korean Chaebols leveraged more than 400%).
- *Beginning budget deficits.* You would normally expect a budget surplus in booming economies. Revenues from the booming activity should enable the governments to save for a rainy day. However, in Asia/Pacific there were cases of budget deficits even in the midst of a boom. This meant those governments were stimulating where they should have put on the brakes.

Economies with such a combination of symptoms are time-bombs. The dominoes can fall in different sequences, but here is an example of how the crash may begin in a time-bomb economy:

- An economic event scares a few investors who start pulling their money out of the country. "Pulling out" means that they sell their assets in the bubble economy and exchange the cash proceeds for another currency — dollars, for instance.
- Enough of this selling will put the local currency under some pressure …
- … and this will now scare local companies that have borrowed in foreign currency. They start hedging their risk by selling local currency against the currency they have borrowed in.
- The central bank will now raise money rates to protect the currency …
- … but the rising interest rates will put pressure on domestic activity, and corporate/private spending and investment will be pulled back.

> **An indicator of overinvestment**
>
> *One way to measure potential overinvestment is the ratio between growth of investment/capital and GDP. A high rate of growth in investment/capital combined with a more limited growth in GDP may indicate that the investments are inefficient and excessive. However, this indicator will only work with a delay. Assume, for instance, that all growth in a given economy comes from the excessive construction of office buildings. Each new building contributes to GDP as well as to the accumulated investment/capital as it is being constructed. However, since it isn't taken into productive use after its construction, it will only contribute to GDP once. Assume that another economy invests in production capacity that is being used as a means of increasing productivity and GDP. The investment/capital expansion will here lead to sustained increase in GDP.*

- The resulting sudden fall in economic activity scares everybody even more, and renewed selling pressure on the currency builds up …
- … until the central bank gives up its defenses after having sold significant amounts of foreign currency in vain.
- The currency goes into a free fall, and in order to protect the companies that are still exposed through financing in foreign currency, the central bank raises interest rates again …
- … which further dampens local economic activity, and thus reduces government tax revenues.

Of all the countries in Asia/Pacific it was Thailand that at the end of 1997 was at the biggest risk of being put through such a process of collapse.

Breakdown

The table below provides an overview over the economic situation in a number of countries in Asia/Pacific at the end of 1997.

Table 20.1: Financial problems in Asia/Pacific by the end of 1997

	Overinvestment	Domestic Indebtedness	Foreign Indebtedness	Comments
Thailand	XXX	XXX	XXX	Thailand's foreign debts were 62% of GDP, and its forex reserves equaled 90% of its short-term foreign debts by the end of 1997. Its domestic debts were 167% of GDP. 40% of the loans were property loans, and there was clear overinvestment in property and other sectors.
Philippines	X	X	XXX	The Philippines' foreign debts were 55% of GDP and its foreign reserves only 90% of its short-term foreign debts. Its domestic debts stood at a modest 73% of GDP (and only 18% of loans were in property).
Malaysia	XXX	XXX	XX	Malaysia's foreign debts were 42% of GDP, and its forex reserves equaled 150% of its short-term foreign debts by the end of 1997. However, its domestic debts were 155% of GDP. 30% of the loans were property loans. Malaysian stock market capitalization was a bubbly 3 times GDP in 1994. Malaysia had 5.5% of GDP currency account deficit in 1997.
Indonesia		X	XXX	Indonesia's foreign debts were 65% of GDP, and its forex reserves equaled an alarmingly low 40% of its short-term foreign debts by the end of 1997. Its domestic debts were a modest 61% of GDP. 45% of the loans were property loans.

Singapore		XX		Singapore had very low foreign debts and very large reserves. However, it did have somewhat high domestic debt levels, standing at 113% of GDP.
Hong Kong	XX	XX		Hong Kong had high levels of currency reserves and relatively low levels of foreign debts. However, its domestic lending was 153% of GDP and it had a clear property bubble.
Taiwan		XX		Taiwan's foreign debts were only 12% of GDP, and its forex reserves equaled a healthy 380% of its short-term foreign debts by the end of 1997. However, its domestic debts were 142% of GDP.
South Korea	XXX	XXX	XX	South Korea's foreign debts were 36% of GDP, and its forex reserves equaled only 40% of its short-term foreign debts by the end of 1997. Its domestic debts were a record 178% of GDP. Many of its largest companies were extremely leveraged and produced poor returns on investment.

XXX = Highly exposed
XX = Somewhat exposed
X = Exposed, but not in itself enough to cause a crash

One of the forewarnings of the crash had come in May 1996, when it was revealed that Bangkok Bank of Commerce had 47% of its assets as bad loans. A second blow came in September 1996, when Moody's Investor Service downgraded Thailand's short-term dept issues. Its parliament was dissolved two months later, in November 1996, and it had become even more clear how deep the problems were when it was disclosed that approx. 14% of all corporate loans were non-performing by the end of the year. The next crack in the surface appeared in February 1997, when Moody's announced a review of the country's long-term foreign currency rating for possible downgrading. And the sense of urgency grew even further in March when the stock exchange shot down trading in banks and finance stocks. And then, finally, the main attack on the currency set in May 1997.

George Soros' Quantum Fund was among the sellers, but the first wave of capital flight met heavy resistance as the Bank of Thailand increased overnight money rates to several thousand percent. The initial defense was in fact so successful that Stanley Druckenmiller from the Soros Fund Management was quoted in Bloomberg for saying that:

> "They kicked our butts and they've taken a lot of profits we might have had. They did a masterful job of squeezing us out."

This was only a temporary victory for the bank, however. On July 2, 1997 at 8:30 in the morning currency traders all over the world could read on their dealer screens that the Bank of Thailand announced that they would no longer defend the peg system of the baht. Just like that. No new target, no gradual devaluation plans. They would just let it drop. And so it did drop — by 15% within the same day.

While the Thai baht could not by any means be descried as a major currency, there was still something extremely alarming about its collapse. Thailand might be small, but it was an ASEAN country, a member of one of the Asian community of super-growth tiger economies. If their currency could collapse, could this then happen to the currencies of other ASEAN members? People began to raise questions about the Asian economies. The regional collapse had begun, and the next currencies to fall were:

- The Philippines: Peg abandoned July 11
- Malaysia: Peg abandoned July 14th
- Indonesia: dollar-rupiah trading band increased on July 11th, then suspended altogether August 28th
- Korea: Peg abandoned November 17th after significant falls
- Taiwan: Peg abandoned October 18th.

The currency devaluation was followed with the onset of more general crises, as stock markets melted down, tens of thousands of companies went into bankruptcy, millions of people lost their jobs, and several countries had severe riots. Within a year the economies of Thailand, The Philippines, Malaysia, Indonesia, and South Korea had contracted more than an astonishing 50% when measured in American dollars. The Russian stock exchange fell by more than 95% as more than half its workers went unpaid. Japan, which had struggled with the overhang of problems from its bubble economy in the 1980s, was dragged back into

> ***Self-reinforcing effects of the crashes***
>
> *It could be argued that the currency devaluation created the basis for new competitiveness and thus for the end of the crisis, but the first effects were in fact negative. Central banks reacted to the falling currencies by maintaining interest levels considerably higher than pre-crash levels in order to limit the devaluation. As they struggled to save the leveraged companies, the banks, the property investment companies and the economy in general they realized that you can't meet all goals if you have played all cards off your hands before the crisis even starts.*

renewed recession as several of its largest financial institutions failed. The business cycle was back.

Boom in the West

The crash in Asia-Pacific didn't leave much of an impact in the Western economies, however, as they were in the middle of their own boom. It was called the "Internet Boom" (or by some: "the Internet Bubble"). The boom was driven by a combination of factors, but the most important of these were related to a massive wave of new innovations.

It was about microelectronics — about the continued development of Charles Babbage's old idea. Two phenomena were key to the events:

- Moore's Law, which stipulated that chip capacity would double every 18 months while its price fell by half
- Gilder's Law, which said that the total bandwidth of telecommunications would triple every 12 months.

Both of these two laws described sustained processes in the computing/telecommunications worlds. Processes that were *exponential.*

The second key factor behind the events during the 1990s was the increasing endorsement of so-called "open standards" in high tech markets. Open standards meant convergence, and this again meant that applications were able to run on larger and larger numbers of different systems provided by different vendors. So open standards created economies of scale and benefits for the end-users.

The third independent driver of the growth of the Internet was a new, global trend towards de-regulation of telecommunications markets, which led to the formation of many start-up telcos and a rush among new and old operators to launch innovative and competitive services. The Internet turned out to be one of the main instruments in their new competitive battle, and an important effect was steadily falling prices.

The combination of core innovations (leading to new applications), open standards (leading to technical convergence) and de-regulation (leading to falling prices) enabled the exponential growth in the number

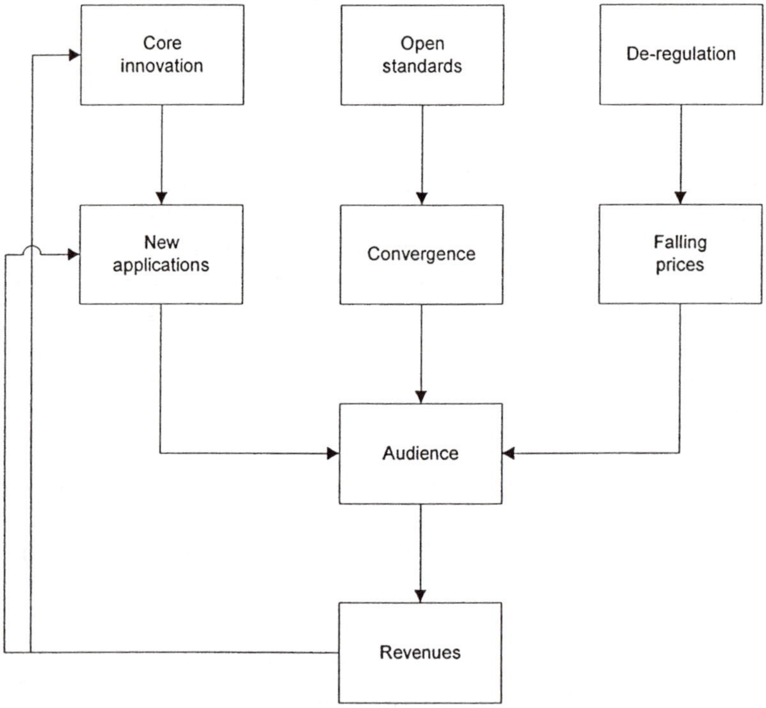

Figure 20.1: Growth drivers of the Internet.

of Internet users and in revenues. This revenue stimulated again the frantic development of new core technologies and new applications — positive feed-back loops created sustained growth.

THE NETWORK EFFECT

These positive feed-back processes were not the only factors in play. One of the changes that created sustained growth was a phenomenon called the "network effect". The network effect described the situation where the value for a given user of being connected to a given network rose in exponential proportion to the number of other people connected to the same network. The Internet created a very powerful network effect, since the value of being connected rose — at least within some parameter intervals — in exponential proportion to the number of users. A network with one million users had a value to each user that was far higher than the combined value of two separate networks that had half a million users each. This phenomenon was called Metcalfe's Law.

The number of people connected to the Internet grew at an exponential rate, and the value of being connected to each individual grew at an exponential rate. The result was that Internet data traffic doubled every 3–4 months.

INCREASING RETURNS

Another interesting phenomenon in the so-called "digital economy" was the possibility of increasing return. Conventional economic theory assumed that corporations had decreasing returns on investment (lower return on each new dollar that they invested). However, companies that supplied digital output such as software and Internet services could experience a different return structure; they might find that their return on each new dollar invested was actually *larger* than the return on the previous dollar invested in the same concept. The main reasons were:

- The Network Effect (Metcalfe's Law).
- Minimal marginal costs of replicating their software or accepting additional network users.
- The possibility for large players to become de facto standard providers.

So *supply stimulated supply* (increasing return) and *demand stimulated demand* (network effect) — a truly explosive dynamic structure. And there was more to it.

MARKET CLEARING TECHNOLOGIES

Most economic simulation models assumed that people had perfect information, and that money, goods, services and people could flow freely. Everyone knew that this wasn't true, but they also knew that every new innovation in communication and transportation technology brought the economy one bit further towards those assumptions. The canals, the railways, the cars, the telegraph, the telephone etc. Each of those innovations had made it easier for people to exchange money and to move money, goods, services and people to the place where they could be most efficiently used. The Internet was in this connection a giant step forwards towards free and efficient markets:

- The Internet created transparent markets, which intensified price competition.
- The Internet enhanced productivity by enabling disintermediation of middlemen, stimulating collaborative work approaches and accelerating the exchange of software (and thereby its own continued development).
- The Internet enabled e-commerce whereby you could buy virtually anything from anywhere and have it shipped to wherever you were.
- The Internet made it possible to find jobs anywhere.
- The Internet made it possible to trade assets and transfer money from a desk-top to any company anywhere.

All of this meant productivity gains and low inflation, and low inflation meant low interest rates and high equity prices. This, combined with a demographic boom of middle-aged people saving for their pension meant access to an abundance of capital available for new Internet projects. And this, in turn, created the basis for the economic boom.

BUBBLEBATH

The boom was massive, and with any massive boom come the bubbles. New Internet companies were founded every day, and while some had clear plans and revenue models there were many others that didn't have a clue. The scary part was that they all seemed to be able to attract money and this created a series of so-called "Internet bubbles" — companies with public valuations that weren't justified even if the most optimistic forecasts were fulfilled.

And there appeared to be a good reason for it. In particular if you were in the venture capital business. It had seemed, at least for a time, that no one investing at early stages in Internet companies could possibly lose. Either the companies succeeded to the point of making it to an IPO (Initial Public Offering) — in which case the venture capitalists could sell out based on billion-dollar market capitalizations. Or the company didn't really make it, in which case you could always sell it for a few hundred million dollars to someone who needed the people and the infrastructure. There was virtually no way to lose, at least not if you had a broad portfolio of investment!

The transition from a great bull-market to outright bubble was difficult to pinpoint but many professionals in the business saw the initial public offering of Theglobe.com as the trigger point. When this company went public in November 1998, the shares were offered at nine dollars apiece. However, they soared to no less than 97 dollars during the first trading day and settled at USD 63.50 a share, a gain of more than 600 percent. This was rather remarkable since the company during the nine months prior to its IPO had booked total revenues of just USD $2.7 million. It had no proprietary technology, no patents and was not a leading website by any measures. And yet, the market valued it at around one billion dollars on that magic day. As ZDNet asked Bill Bass, an analyst at Forrester Research Inc. to give a comment, he responded:

> "I cease to amazed at what happens with Internet stocks. I'm 'amazed' fatigued."

Bill Bass was not the only analyst to be alarmed. One of the best articulated warnings of the state of the market was given in the book "*The Internet Bubble: Inside the Overvalued World of High-Tech Stocks — And What You Need to Know to Avoid the Coming Shakeout*". The authors of the book (Anthony B. Perkins and Michael B. Perkins) had identified an index of Internet companies that they tracked. In February 2000 they wrote an article in *San Jose Mercury News* where they summarized some of their concerns:

> "The 315 Internet companies we (the authors of *The Internet Bubble*) track would have to grow at a compounded annual rate of 96 percent over the next five years to justify their current stock market valuation. This is almost twice the historical growth rate of Microsoft (53 percent). The total market capitalization of these companies is more than $1.2 trillion, but based on only $29 billion in revenue in 1999"

Valuations had gone up and up, until the point where the market cap of Yahoo! exceeded the combined valuations of Boeing, Caterpillar, and Philip Morris, despite the fact that these companies had 339 times as much revenues and 159 times the earnings.

The Internet/technology crash evolved gradually over the spring of 2000. It was global — hammering high tech and Internet stock indexes from Paris, to Bombay, Seoul, Tokyo and the US exchanges. While indexes fell dramatically, the behaviour of individual shares was even wilder. In Japan, Softbank and Hikari Tsushin fell so quickly that they hit downward trading limits almost daily when the panic reached its crescendo. And numerous shares fell more than 95% percent from their peaks. And by the way, you could buy the shares in Theglobe.com for around one dollar apiece by August 2000. It was almost 90% down from its initial offering price less than two years before, and close to 99% down from its peak.

A COMBINATION OF FACTORS

The booms in Asia and the West had many things in common. Innovations and productivity gains had in each created the first and fundamental stimulus. There was an element of "real business cycle" in both markets. But both had become "bubbly" and both had displayed a number of factors described by different business cycle schools. What they illustrated more than anything was that business cycles involve a number of different factors that interact in complex patterns.

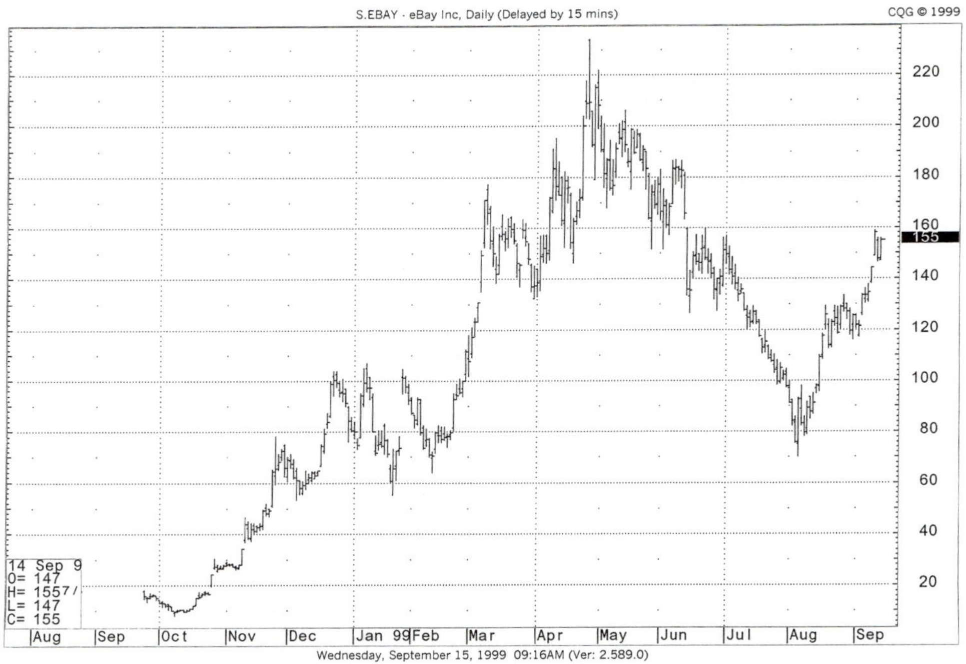

Figure 20.2.: Irrational exuberance?
The Internet company Ebay went public in September 1998 and took off like a rocket from the first day of trading. The month after, it reached a share price corresponding to a market capitalization of USD 3.2 billion, corresponding to 100 times its revenues and 2,800 times its earnings. At the end of January 1999 it reported a quarterly profit of USD 2.8 million. Investors reacted by adding USD 3.5 billion to its market capitalization — within one trading day. This market valuation increase was equivalent to 1,250 times the quarterly revenues. However, it was only a few months until the company again had doubled its value before falling 70% over the summer.

21
The Puzzle-Solvers

"As far as the laws of mathematics refer to reality they are not certain; and as far as they are certain they do not refer to reality."

Albert Einstein

The Boston area is generally considered a very nice place to live. Located not too far north of New York, it has a beautiful bay, nice beaches, a well-kept old city center, lots of green surroundings, and a lively night-life. It is also known for having the largest concentration of academic institutions on earth.

During the end of the 20th century there were three of these institutions that evolved as centers for a new approach to business cycle theory. These three institutions were Cambridge, Harvard and M.I.T.

FROM SCHOOL TO SCHOOL

The background for their new approach was a long history of different schools of thought and different analytical approaches; a history where it seemed that business cycle theory starting with Juglar had pretty much gone full circle.

It had all started with the classical approaches assuming that business cycles mainly were caused by endogenous factors within the economic system, as Juglar had suggested. The classical economists had generally assumed that there wasn't too much to do about it, and that the economies in any case would return to normality if left pretty much alone during crises. Some had gone further and stated that business cycles in fact were a key driver of economic growth and renewal.

The next big wave had started as the depression during the 1930s that had convinced many that the economy was prone to fall into lasting crises and that it wouldn't necessarily be able to readjust itself. That assumption had been the beginning of Keynesianism, which focused on inherent instability created by fluctuations in profits, investment, credit and other variables. Keynesianism described how markets could fail and how government could intervene to correct those errors. Keynes' approach dominated completely during the 1950s, as it was taught at Cambridge, Massachusetts, as well as at Harvard and M.I.T. One of the most influential advocates of this school was Samuelson from M.I.T, whose best-selling book "Economics" from 1948 became mandatory reading for thousands of students across the globe. Samuelson was not only a leading textbook writer, scientist and teacher — he even became advisor to President Kennedy and received the Nobel prize together with Robert Solow.

Cross-currents

Samuelson's fame had grown even further as the magazine *Newsweek* had the brilliant idea to let him and his main opponent, Milton Friedman, write dueling columns where they could argue for their conflicting views — Friedman of course representing monetarism as the next hot school on the arena. Friedman was in many ways seen as the emerging winner of the battle as events during the 1970s indicated that the assumption of an inflation/unemployment trade-off was misguided, and his camp had been further enforced when Lucas (one of Samuelson's former students) published his famous article about rational expectations. It was then no longer just a Samuelson/Friedman battle, but rather a battle of Samuelson/Solow against Friedman/Lucas.

The battle was not clear-cut, though. While Samuelson continued to offer typical Keynesian explanations of macroeconomic phenomena, he would at the same time teach his students how to use mathematical microeconomic models featuring the rational behavior that Lucas advocated. And Lucas himself had not claimed that people in reality were *completely* rational or that government should do *absolutely* nothing. He agreed with the other camp that government actually should play at least a limited role. This was the beginning of an era where more economists accepted some views from Keynes as well as from Friedman, and where Keynesianism gradually became re-defined as "New Keynesian Economics" and where monetarism evolved into "New Monetary Economics".

The new monetary approach was more focused on new development on the micro-level. The scientists would, for instance, study new monetary innovations that would change the effective money supply or velocity of money. Many of these changes might not show up in the official money supply statistics but could be important anyway.

The New Keynesian Economics school, which evolved during the 1970s, emphasized a number of problems:

- That competition could be imperfect because of monopolies, regulations, etc.
- That wages sometimes could be fixed at levels that were too high to clear (because of unions)
- That markets could be too thin to clear
- That markets at times didn't clear because of irrational fear or greed ("animal spirits")
- That market behavior could become irrational because of sunspots (mainly the financial markets)
- That some sectors of the economy (in particular in high tech industries) could have increasing returns on investment, which would inhibit competition.

New Keynesian Economics was grounded in Lucas' rational expectations models derived from individual utility and profit maximization, not from aggregates. It was, in other words, based on micro-economic assumptions, and its models assumed that an economy that was below full employment could be brought to full employment through several channels:

- Inherent market dynamics would drive down salaries to a level where more companies would employ more people and where prices of produced goods would fall, which would enable people to buy more units (a typical classical assumption).
- Intervention, either through public expenditure or through monetary expansion, would create full employment.

The New Keynesian Economics did not claim that one of these outcomes always was more efficient than the other; it all depended on the flexibility of the labor markets in the given situation.

However, the change in Keynesianism as well as in monetarism became symptomatic for a new main distinction in analytical approaches. Keynes and Friedman had mainly examined the economy "top-down", but Lucas, the new New Keynesian Economics school and the New Monetary Economics had taken more of a bottom-up approach.

The macro-versus-micro battle

Top-down means macro. The macro economists tried to focus on the large things that really mattered while pretty much ignoring the rest. The approach was based on assumptions about overall phenomena. The other camp were the so-called "micro economists", who focused on how individuals behaved and then aggregated this behavior into larger-scale models. This camp was called "neoclassical". Many of the neoclassical micro economists used a special language where many sentences started with the words: "Let…". These sentences would typically introduce a list of simplifications that could be rather unrealistic, if not outrageous. They might, for instance, include that:

- There was perfect competition.
- Everyone had perfect knowledge.
- There was perfect labor mobility.
- There was a market for any desire.
- There were no derived benefits or damages from economic action (such as pollution).
- There were no changes in tastes.
- There were no changes in technology.

The difference between the two analytical camps was not only in the choice of methodologies. It was also in the focus: the macroeconomists would typically describe broad examples of phenomena that caused the economy to malfunction. They would focus their efforts on identifying the essential problems. The neoclassical camp, on the other hand, would typically describe how the economy was able to find its own balance. This difference in focus was not because one camp consisted of pessimists and the other of optimists. It evolved because of an issue that was inherent to the analytical approaches:

- The macroeconomists used models that didn't necessarily assume any inherent equilibrium.
- The micro economists, on the other hand, used general equilibrium models (which assumed rational expectations and inherent equilibrium). These models were often much more elegant and flexible than the macroeconomist's models. However, the necessary underlying assumptions would be so limiting that the final result of the models could have little practical relevance.

The two camps didn't remain separated, however. More and more economists from one camp started to pick good elements from the other. More and more traditional macroeconomists would, for instance, change their style so that they still focused on inaccuracies in the economy, but began to use microeconomic modeling to simulate it. And the micro economists would start to accept that human beings are not entirely rational, and they would start to build positive feed-back into their models to create less stable but more realistic results.

A specter of theories

The economists at the leading academic institutions in Boston (and other places) had witnessed the continuous change in focus from one school to the next and then the next, and they had seen how supporters of some schools had adapted some of the best analytical approaches from competing camps. And they had also witnessed how the range of reasonably credible business cycle models had continued to grow and grow.

What they were facing at the end of the millenium was a landscape where business cycle models could be divided according to four main dimensions:

- *Endogenous models* assumed that the instability was caused by non-linearity in the economic system.
- *Exogenous models* assumed the instability came from external shocks.
- *Deterministic models* assumed that economic behavior was relatively predictable and orderly.
- *Stochastic models* assumed the behavior was relatively complex and unpredictable.

> **Rational expectations in business cycle simulations**
>
> *Robert E. Lucas published in 1981 his book "Studies in Business Cycle Theory" in which he proposed that the expectations used should be rational. This assumption of rationality and equilibrium is really an extension of the core principles proposed by Adam Smith. One of the reasons that so many economists have endorsed it is that it makes theoretical modeling very easy. A typical economic model based on the assumption that everybody is rational and is trying to optimize their own situation will have a stable equilibrium. Such models are today known as "neoclassical economics" (it was Karl Marx who introduced the term "classical" to Adam Smith and his immediate successors).*
>
> *Almost all modern business cycle models contain equations that include expectations. The concept of rational expectations is introduced by letting the theoretical "agents" have the same expectations about the future as the expectations of the model itself.*

All of the models had drifted towards a few common assumptions:

- Focus more on aggregate supply, its determinants and effects.
- Assume that markets are fully competitive and that markets clear.
- Assume rational expectations.

There had also been a shift of focus from internal instability to external shocks. There had been several reasons for this. One was simply mathematical convenience: modeling inherent instability meant use of non-linear functions, while a model that is based on external shocks can be linear, which means that it is easier to work with. Another reason was a growing belief that the capitalist economy had come closer to a structure where it had a stable balance.

However, each of the categories of models had their advantages and disadvantages. *The endogenous, deterministic* models were attractive because they could generate un-damped cyclical solutions, asymmetries, irreversibility and discontinuities — which meant that they generated something that looked like the real world. Furthermore, they could be based on relatively realistic assumptions about permanent structures in the economy. However, the problem with this category of models was

Table 21.1 Overview over different approaches to business cycle modelling at the end of the millenium.

	Endogenous models ***(Assuming that the instability is caused by non-linearity in the economic system)***	**Exogenous models** ***(Assuming that instability comes from external shocks)***
Deterministic models ***(Assuming that economic behavior is relatively predictable)***	These models described economic systems with inherent non-linearity that created fluctuations. Some models produced regular fluctuations, (which was unrealistic), other produced chaotic movements, and some were somewhere in the middle. Most classical and neo-classical models would fall into this category.	This group of models assumed that the economy received external shocks with a somewhat predictable pattern, and that these shocks were responsible for business cycles. Jevons' sunspot theory, which postulated that regular changes in an external factor (sunspots) could drive the economy, was the first model in this category. Political cycles might also fall in this category.
Stochastic models ***(Assuming that economic behavior is relatively complex and unpredictable)***	This group included models that assumed rational expectations and equilibrium. However, they assumed that there was more than one possible equilibrium and that it could be difficult or impossible to predict which of its several potential equilibria the economy would find. Furthermore, the models assumed that the move from one equilibrium to another could be triggered by a random event. Such an event could trigger changes in general (rational) expectations and thus become self-fulfilling (like Jevons' sunspots). These theories tended to focus on financial instability as a major cause of business cycles.	Models focusing on external shocks and unpredictability dominated in the 1980s. They assumed an intrinsically stable equilibrium (neoclassical approach) and that the business cycles only would occur if the economy was continuously exposed to external shocks (the "rocking-chair-and-stick" view). These "real business cycle" models would typically suggest a dynamic behavior where the amplitude of fluctuations was determined mainly by the size and frequency of the shocks, and where the length and sequence of cyclical events was determined by the inherent nature of the propagation mechanism. The shocks could either be random or serially correlated (like war, manias, habits, technology, policy changes), but they would not be regular.

that they often produced a behavior that could only be predicted in the relatively short term. Butterfly effects would obscure the longer-term behavior.

The *stochastic, endogenous* models had some of the same advantages and disadvantages. They described some of the phenomena that Keynes had seen when he talked about the economy falling into traps and that George Soros and other hedge fund managers would recognize from financial markets. Ormerod referred to these models in his "The Death of Economics" from 1997:

> "The realization that there might be many craters so deep that, once having got into them at once, our imaginary player can never get out has been of great concern to economic theorists in the past decade or so. The implication of such a situation is that there is not just one but many possible solutions to the equations which describe a competitive economy. In other words, there is not just one equilibrium in the economy, but many equilibria."

And later:

> "If there is a unique solution to the equations which describe a competitive economy, large changes can be analyzed within this framework, since the economy by definition always ends up at the unique equilibrium position. But with many solutions it is possible to make statements only about the consequences of small changes in the locality of any particular solution. Otherwise the economy might not slide back into its original crater, but be shifted to a position in the field which goes into a different crater altogether. But again: they did not deliver a solution to long term predictability."

The *deterministic, exogenous* models were the most problematic of them all. There were virtually no economists that believed that this category of models described anything but very marginal phenomena.

And finally, the *stochastic, exogenous* models were elegant since they managed to maintain equilibrium. However, they were not widely accepted since they did not appear very realistic (it should be mentioned, though, that few, if any, proponents of real business cycle models actually claimed that technology shocks accounted for all fluctuations. Prescott, for instance, claimed that they accounted for "more than half the fluctuations in the postwar period, with a best point estimate near 75 percent").

Premature death

People have always made fun of economists, but they were now themselves beginning to express more and more frustration.

One problem was that models were remote from reality. It was, for instance, well known that Sir John Hicks, who had received his Nobel prize for his work in general equilibrium theory, had later on abandoned the concept simply because he didn't find it realistic. Many if not most of the authors that had contributed during the post World War II era had mainly been concerned with the theoretical possibilities rather than with what actually causes business cycles. There had generally been little regard for how the pieces fit each other and how they matched events in the real world — if at all. Each model had often dealt with a few phenomena that were treated in isolation, which made it impossible to assess whether they were realistic or not. Scientists who were largely interested in mathematical beauty have thus forgotten the classical notion that business cycles could not be explained by single causes, and the result has been an abundance of partial theories and little focus on the context of these theories. Wassily Leontief complained, for instance, that over 50% of the articles in American Economic Review during the 1970s comprised mathematical models with no data. Furthermore, he noted that when data were used, it was in order to confirm the theory. He thought it should be the other way around (Leontief in Alfred Fichner (ed).: Why Economics is not a Science, Macmillan, London, 1983):

> "Not having been subjected from the outset to the harsh discipline of systematic fact finding, traditionally imposed on and accepted by their colleagues in the natural and historical sciences, economists developed a nearly irresistible predilection for deductive reasoning. As a matter of fact, many entered the field after specializing in pure or applied mathematics. Page after page of professional economic journals are filled with mathematical formulas leading the reader from sets of more or less plausible but entirely arbitrary assumptions to precisely stated but irrelevant theoretical conclusions."

There was of course a clear exemption: the simulators who created unified mathematical models. But their problem was that they were beginning to appear as software developers who have problems understanding and explaining the hairball they have developed.

A third category of economists seemed to be occupied in a major industry of interpreting what famous economists "really meant"; a subject that seemed more reminiscent of evangelism than of interesting and relevant science.

Paul Ormerod reflected the gloom in his somewhat premature declaration of "The Death of Economics" when he declared that:

> "The research agenda of the theoretical economics in recent years has contained an important item. Namely, to try to rescue the model of competitive equilibrium from the fundamental problems raised for it, not by mere sociologists, or by applied economists and economic historians who sully their hands with facts and evidence, but by members of the Imperial Guard itself — mathematical economic theorists. And the attempt has failed."

TOWARDS A PRAGMATIC APPROACH

It was in this somewhat gloomy environment that a new breed of economists from Boston developed a more pragmatic approach to economic thinking and business cycle theory. Some of these economists were Larry Summers, Martin Feldstein and Paul Krugman.

Larry Summers was a true star among economists. Born in 1954 and graduated from Harvard in 1982, he had received the prestigious John Bates Clark Prize as "the best economist under 40", had been the youngest professor in the history of Harvard University, and was finally appointed Treasury Secretary of The United States in 1999. Summers, who wasn't known for being a diplomat (or for dressing like one), was more than anything a pragmatic economist. He believed in free market economies and free trade, but also in the need for government to intervene from time to time. He was, for instance, a strong advocate for the bailouts of the Mexican economy in 1995.

Martin Feldstein was an Oxford PhD who joined Harvard in 1967. He was here investigating how government taxes and spending change people's behavior — a consideration that contributed to the Reagan revolution. In 1977 he was named president of NBER, which at the time had become a somewhat sleepy place that was best known as the passive arbiter of when recessions started and stopped. Feldstein moved the institute from New York to the more scientific environment in Cambridge, where he managed to attract leading economic thinkers such as Fischer and Dornbush to the organization. NBER started again to produce leading edge research, and many of the most powerful economists in the world have since worked there.

Paul Krugman, who finished at Yale in 1974 and received his doctorate from MIT in 1977, achieved luminary status in less than a decade as an economist. Krugman was generally concerned about government interference in markets, but he would also frequently demonstrate examples of situations where active government could be useful. Krugman participated in an economic summit in Little Rock in 1992 and found there that much of what was said was pure nonsense. He decided thereafter to cut back on his basic research activities and instead focus on educating a wider audience in what were the most fundamental issues in economic policy. This led him to focus a number of contemporary phenomena and their economic consequences. He defined four basic rules for himself:

- Listen to the Gentiles.
- Question the question.
- Dare to be silly.
- Simplify, simplify.

"Listen to the Gentiles" meant listen to what people working in the industry that you study actually have to say about the subject — also when they don't use an economist's language at all. "Question the question" meant don't try to build a very complex model if the question is only about a simpler issue. Deal only with the core of the issue. "Dare to be silly" was about simplicity. Krugman made a little note on his website where he described what economists often did for a living:

> "If you want to publish a paper in economic theory, there is a safe approach: make a conceptually minor but mathematically difficult extension to some familiar model. Because the basic assumptions of the model are already familiar, people will not regard them as strange; because you have done something technically difficult, you will be respected for your demonstration of firepower. Unfortunately, you will not have added much to human knowledge."

Krugman's approach was different. He preferred to focus on new issues where the assumptions were new and the models were simple and easy to understand. And that tied in with his last rule, which was to "simplify, simplify." He described it in this way:

> "The injunction to dare to be silly is not a license to be undisciplined. In fact, doing really innovative theory requires much more intellectual discipline than working in a well-established literature. What is really

> hard is to stay on course: since the terrain is unfamiliar, it is all too easy to find yourself going around in circles. Somewhere or other Keynes wrote that "it is astonishing what foolish things a man thinking alone can come temporarily to believe". And it is also crucial to express your ideas in a way that other people, who have not spent the last few years wrestling with your problems and are not eager to spend the next few years wrestling with your answers, can understand without too much effort.
>
> Fortunately, there is a strategy that does double duty: it both helps you keep control of your own insights, and makes those insights accessible to others. The strategy is: always try to express your ideas in the simplest possible model. The act of stripping down to this minimalist model will force you to get to the essence of what you are trying to say (and will also make obvious to you those situations in which you actually have nothing to say). And this minimalist model will then be easy to explain to other economists as well."

Krugman wrote a series of articles and research papers that described economic issues that were relevant for the current debate. He dealt with general equilibrium (there are several competing equilibria), the trade deficit with Japan (not important since it is very small compared to US GDP), jobs and wages lost to cheap Third World labor (far more jobs are lost because of a shift towards a high-tech economy), and the notion that economic war has replaced the cold war (nonsense, trade creates wealth for both parties, war doesn't).

The new approach of Summers, Feldstein and Krugman reflected changed perceptions of the essential nature of economic systems. They tended to view the economy more as eco-systems than as mechanical systems, and they talked more about probable patterns than about predictable prices and quantities. The new approach was about studying specific situations, thinking about which of a multitude of economic models seemed most relevant, and then making qualified guesses about what should be done and what the consequences would be. It was a departure from the age of grand "schools" and a move away from big intellectual systems towards a more pragmatic puzzle-solver approach. They were, like John Law, not focused on discovering the Great and Indisputable Model of Everything, but on understanding the real world and its complex problems.

Economics was perhaps finally growing up.

The Beat of the Heart

"Give us this last man, oh Zarathustra! Turn us into these last men!"

Friederich Nietzsche

I had been outside for about 10 seconds earlier in the morning, so I knew that it was cold. Now I was back inside, sitting comfortably by the fireplace, eating my breakfast and reading the newspaper.

I put the paper down and looked out of the windows to enjoy the sight of millions of ice crystals blinking like tiny blitz lights in the air. Suddenly I noticed two round bears coming up from the garden. A big black one, and a very small white one. Whenever they had taken a few steps forward, the small one would stop to investigate something in the snow, and the big one would then turn around and wait patiently. Finally they appeared under the balcony, right in front of the windows.

The big one opened the terrace door, letting frosty air into the room. It was my wife Itziar, dressed in her long, black coat. Little Sophie was with her and ran over to my chair so that I could take off her white coat and tiny boots. Both of them had red chins and I saw that their eyes were shining.

"You seem to be enjoying yourself", Itziar said. "...You have been eating breakfast for four hours now, do you know that?"

Sure. I could eat breakfast the whole day.

"Let me guess", she said, "You have been reading the newspapers or books about business cycles?" "Both."

"So what have you found out — I mean about business cycles?"

"No cure. But interesting. You can modify the fluctuations, but it is impossible to avoid them completely. If you try that, then they will just get worse."

She poured up some coffee and looked at Sophie, who was now playing with an apple on the floor. I looked out of the window. Small ripples rolled very slowly towards the lake shore. Maybe the water would start to freeze over along the coast this week? Itziar was looking out the windows as well. She was thinking. Then she pulled a crumpled note in my hand-writing of her pocket.

"I have been looking for this...," I said. "... where did you find it?"

"Down in the garden house", she answered. "Now I know why you bothered to write it down." And then she read it aloud:

> "Cycles are not like tonsils, separable things that might be treated by themselves, but are, like the beat of the heart, of the essence of the organ that displays them."
>
> Joseph Schumpeter, 1939

APPENDIX 1
List of Important Events in Business Cycle Theory

Year	Event
1705	John Law publishes *Money and Trade with a Proposal for Supplying the Nation with Money*, where he calls for the establishment of a land-bank.
1716	Law & Company is founded.
1734	Cantillon dies and leaves behind him the manuscript for *Essai sur la nature du commerce en general*. The manuscript includes an analysis of the effects of velocity of money.
1759	Adam Smith publishes *Theory of Moral Sentiments*.
1764	Adam Smith sails to France, where he meets Quesnay.
1773	Adam Smith publishes *The Wealth of Nations*, which includes the concept of the "Invisible Hand".
1788	Jean Babtiste Say reads *The Wealth of Nations*.
1797	The British House of Commons invites Henry Thornton to testify about the courses of a panic.
1799	David Ricardo reads *The Wealth of Nations*.
1802	Henry Thornton publishes *Paper Credit of Great Britain*, which is a detailed account of how monetary policy works. He proposes stabilization through active monetary policy.
1803	Jean Babtiste Say publishes *Traite d'economie Politique*, which includes "Say's Law", suggesting that supply creates its own demand.
1808	James Mill meets David Ricardo and starts to persuade him to write about economics.
1809	David Ricardo publishes *The High Price of Bullion, a Proof of the Depreciation of Bank Notes*.
1816	David Ricardo publishes *Proposals for an Economical and Secure Currency*. He suggests that use of paper money that is convertible with gold will stabilize the economy.

1819 James Mill's son John Stuart Mill publishes *Elements of Political Economy* at the age of 13.

1822 Charles Babbage publishes *Observations on the Application of Machinery to the Computation of Mathematical Tables.*

1826 John Stuart Mill introduces the concept of Competitive Investment in his *Paper Currency and Commercial Distress.*

1845 John Stuart Mill publishes *Principles of Political Economy*, where he relates velocity of money to economic upswings and speculation and emphasizes the importance of confidence.

1857 Karl Marx writes the first draft texts for *Das Kapital*, which contain descriptions of business cycles.

1862 Clement Juglar publishes *Les Crises commerciales et leur retour périodique en France, en Angleterre et aux Etats Unis*; the first clear description of business cycles as caused by inherent instability phenomena.

1867 First volume of Karl Marx's *Das Kapital* is published.

1871 William Stanley Jevons publishes *The Theory of Political Economy*, which contains the first formal description of "Rational Man".

1873 Walther Bagehot (the editor of the *Economist*) publishes *Lombard Street: A Description of the Money Market*, which describes the roles and main economic consequences of banking.

1875–1882 William Stanley Jevons writes a series of articles about business cycles, which he tries to explain as the consequence of sunspots, or of expectations of sunspots.

1885 Simon Newcomb introduces what is later called the "Quantity Theory of Money" in his *Principles of Political Economy.*

1889 Leon Walras publishes *Elements of Pure Economics*, where he attempts to describe the economy in mathematical terms.

1890 Marshall publishes *Principles of Economics*, where he describes positive feed-back processes in the economy.

1896 Irwin Fisher distinguishes between natural and real interest rates in his *Appreciation and Interest.*

1907 Knut Wicksell publishes *The influence of the Rate of Interest on Prices*, where he introduces the concept of real rate and natural rate.

1910 Rodger Ward Babson publishes *Business Barometers used in the Accumulation of Money*. The book describes how money rates, stocks, bonds, commodity prices and real estate fluctuate in relation to business cycles.

1910 Nikolai Kondratieff describes a long-term cycle in *Archief fur Sozialwissenshaft*.

1911 Irwin Fisher publishes *The Purchasing Power of Money*. The main theme is the destabilizing effects of inflation and fluctuations in money supply.

1912 Joseph Schumpeter publishes *The Theory of Economic Development*, where he introduces the theory that innovations arrive in clusters and that these can explain the business cycles.

1913 Ralph George Hawtrey publishes *Good and Bad Trade*, which focuses on monetary instability and an explanation of business cycles.

1913 Wesley Mitchell publishes *Business Cycles*.

1915 Dennis Holme Robertson publishes *A Study in Industrial Fluctuation*, which emphasizes fluctuating capital investments as a key driver behind business cycles.

1920 Irwin Fisher publishes *Stabilizing the Dollar*, where he suggests initiatives to stabilize inflation and money supply.

1920 Wesley Mitchell co-founds the National Bureau of Economic Research (NBER).

1923 Joseph Kitchin publishes *Cycles and Trends in Economic Factors*, where he describes a short-term business cycle phenomenon.

1926 Irwin Fisher publishes *A Statistical Relationship between Unemployment and Price Changes*. This describes what is later known as the "Philips Curve".

1927 Pigou publishes *Industrial Fluctuations*.

1929 Babson predicts a stock market crash, Fisher disagrees.

1930 Kuznets publishes *Secular Movements in Production and Prices*, where he describes a medium-term cycle.

1930 Ragnar Frish founds "The Econometric Society" together with Joseph Schumpeter, Irwin Fisher and others.

1931 R.F. Kahn introduces the concept of the Multiplier in *The Relation of Home Investment to Unemployment.*

1933 Hayek publishes *Monetary Theory and the Trade Cycle*. He suggests that the monetary system in itself is unstable and that monetary inflation can go on for some years without leading to inflation.

1933 Ragnar Frish publishes *Propagation Problems and Impulse Problems in Dynamic Economies*, where he shows how random shocks can generate cyclical fluctuations in the economy.

1934	Joseph Schumpeter introduces in *The Theory of Economic Development* the concept of "creative Destruction".
1933	Joseph Schumpeter starts to write a book about business cycles.
1935	Robert Bryce visits the USA and gives a speech about John Maynard Keynes' new ideas.
1936	Maynard Keynes publishes *The General Theory of Employment, Interest and Money* in which he suggests that the state should use fiscal policy to stabilize the economy. The book also describes "Propensity to Consume" and "Propensity to Save", "Liquidity Preference" and the "Multiplier".
1936	Jan Tinbergen develops a 24-equation model of the American economy.
1937	Von Haberler publishes *Prosperity and Depression* on the initiative of The League of Nations. The book examines all the existing business cycle theories.
1937	The first issue of *Econometrica* is published.
1938	Einarsen publishes *Reinvestment Cycles*, a book that describes some "echoes" in investments in the Norwegian shipping industry.
1938	Ezekiel publishes *The Cobweb Theorem.*
1939	Jan Tinbergen publishes two articles where he tests the theories in Haberler's book. One of his conclusions is that fluctuations in aggregate profit are by far the most important explanation of fluctuations in aggregate investment.
1939	Paul Samuelson publishes an article where he examines the combined effect of the accelerator and the multiplier. He finds a complicated pattern where several completely different effects are possible, depending on parameter values.
1939	Joseph Schumpeter publishes *Business Cycles*, where he suggests that there are three dominant fluctuations; "Kitchin", "Juglar" and "Kondratieff", and that depressions can be the result of synchronized downturns.
1941	Lloyd Appleton Metzler publishes *The Nature and Stability of Inventory Cycles*, which explains how fluctuations in inventory can generate short-term business cycles.
1943	A.C. Pigou publishes *The Classical Stationary State*, where he suggests that deflation under a recession increases the purchasing power of the circulating cash, which is a negative feed-back loop. This is later called the "Pigou Effect".

1946 ENIAC, the world's first computer is formally introduced to the public.

1946 Jay Forrester gets approval for his Whirlwind project.

1948 Milton Friedman joins the NBER.

1950 H.E. Hurst publishes *Long Term Storage Capacity of Reservoirs*, where he introduces the Hurst Exponent.

1953 Mises publishes his *Theory of Money and Credit.*

1954 Kenneth Arrow and Gerard Debreu publish *Existence of an Equilibrium for a Competitive Economy*, which provides a mathematical demonstration of how an economy may become inherently stable.

1956 Jay Forrester joins the Sloan School of Management, where he later introduces the concept "System Dynamics".

1957 Hyman Minsky publishes *Central Banking and Money Markets*, which is the first of a series of publications where he describes instability in capital markets as key aspects of business fluctuations.

1958 The Philips curve is re-discovered by Philips, who publishes *The Relationship between Unemployment and the Rate of Change of Money Wages in the United Kingdom, 1861–1957*.

1961 Edward Lorenz discovers the butterfly effect in a simulation of a weather system.

1961 Muth publishes *Rational Expectations and the Theory of Price Movements*. This is the fore-runner of the "Rational Expectations" hypothesis.

1963 Milton Friedman publishes *A Monetary History of the United States* with Anna J. Schwartz. They conclude that over the short term, money growth is reflected in inflation, and over the longer term it is reflected in business cycles.

1967 Hamilton Bolton publishes *Money and Investment Profits* where he describes the effects of financial liquidity.

1969 Ragnar Frisch and Jan Tinbergen receive the Nobel Prize for "having developed and applied dynamic models for the analysis of economic processes".

1970 Paul A. Samuelson receives the Nobel Prize for "the scientific work through which he has developed static and dynamic economic theory and actively contributed to raising the level of economic analysis in economic science".

1971 Simon Kuznets receives the Nobel Prize for "his empirically founded interpretation of economic growth which has led to new and deepened insight into the economic and social structure and process of development".

1971 Robert May discovers Feigenbaum Cascades in the simulation of a fish population.

1971 Friedrich A. von Hayek and Gunnan Nyrdal receive the Nobel Prize for "their pioneering work in the theory of money and economic fluctuations and for their penetrating analysis of the interdependence of economic, social and institutional phenomena".

1975 James York publishes *Period Three Implies Chaos*, which introduces the term "Deterministic Chaos".

1976 Jay Forrester publish *Business Structure, Economic Cycles and National Policy.*

1976 Milton Friedman receives the Nobel Prize for "his achievements in the fields of consumption analysis, monetary history and theory and for his demonstration of the complexity of stabilization policy".

1979 Edward Lorenz publishes *Predictability: Does the Flap of a Butterfly's Wings in Brazil Set Off a Tornado in Texas?*

1980 Lawrence R. Klein receives the Nobel Prize for "the creation of econometric models and the application to the analysis of economic fluctuations and economic policies".

1981 Lucas and Sargent publish *Rational Expectations and Economic Practice*, where they apply the rational expectations hypothesis to econometric models.

1982 Finn Kydland and Edward Prescott publish *Time to Build and Aggregate Fluctuations*, which introduces the modern concept of "real business cycles".

1986 Mosekilde and Aracil receive the Jay Forrester Award for their System Dynamics research.

1989 Sterman publishes *Deterministic Chaos in an Experimental Economic System.*

1990 Sterman, Mosekilde and partners study the M.I.T. System Dynamics National Model and find hyperchaos in it.

1991 Edgar Peters publishes *Chaos and Order in Capital Markets* where he demonstrates the presence of Fat Tails (indications of positive feed-back) in a number of markets.

1995 Robert E. Lucas Jr. receives the Nobel Prize for "having developed and applied the hyphothesis of rational expectations".

APPENDIX 2
List of the Largest Financial Crises in History

Year	Country	Speculation in:	Peak	Acute crisis
1557	France, Austria, Spain (Habsburg Empire)	Bonds	1557	1557
1636	Holland	Primarily tulips	Summer 1636	November 1636
1720	France	Compagnie d'Occident Banque General, Banque Royale	December 1719	May 1720
1720	England	South Sea Company	July 1720	September 1720
1763	Holland	Commodities, based on kite flying	January 1763	September 1763
1773	England	Real estate, canals, roads	June 1772	January 1773
1773	Holland	East India Company	June 1772	January 1793
1793	England	Canals	November 1792	February 1793

1797	England	Securities, canals	1796	Feb.–June 1797
1799	Germany	Commodities, financed by kite flying	1799	Aug.–Nov. 1799
1811	England	Export projects	1809	January 1811
1815	England	Exports, commodities	1815	1816
1819	USA	Production enterprises generally	August 1818	November 1818
1825	England	Latin American bonds, mines, wool	Beginning of 1825	December 1825
1836	England	Wool, railways	April 1836	December 1836
1837	USA	Wool, land		September 1837
1838	France	Wool, building sites	November 1836	June 1837
1847	England	Railways, wheat	January 1847	October 1847
1848	European continent	Railways, wheat, real estate		March 1848
1857	USA	Railways, land	End 1856	August 1857
1857	England	Railways, wheat	End 1856	October 1857
1857	European continent	Railways, heavy industry	March 1857	October 1857

1864	France	Wool, shipping, new enterprises	1863	January 1864
1866	England, Italy	Wool, shipping, new enterprises	July 1865	May 1866
1873	Germany, Austria	Building sites, railway, stocks, commodities	Fall 1872	May 1873
1873	USA	Railway		March 1873–September 1873
1882	France	Bank stock		December 1881–January 1882
1890	England	Argentinean stock, stock flotation	August 1890	November 1890
1893	USA	Silver and gold	December 1892	May 1893
1895	England, Continental Europe	South African and Rhodesian gold mine stock	Summer 1895	End of 1895
1907	USA	Coffee, Union Pacific	Beginning of October 1907	1907
1921	USA	Stocks, ships, commodities, inventories	Summer 1920	Spring 1921
1921	USA	Stocks, ships, commodities, inventories	Summer 1920	Spring 1921
1921	USA	Stocks	September 1929	October 1929

1931	Austria, Germany, England, Japan	Miscellaneous	1929	May–Dec. 1931
1974	International	Stocks, office buildings, tankers, aircraft	1969	1974–75
1980	International	Gold, silver, platinum	January–February 1980	March–April 1980
1985	International	Dollars	February–March 1985	February–March 1985
1987	International	Stock	August 1987	October 1987
1990	Japan	Stock, real estate	December 1989	February 1990
1990	International	Art	March 1990	1991
1997	Asia/Pacific	Real estate; general overinvestment	1996	June–October 1997
1997	Russia	General overinvestment; undercapitalized banks	1996	August 1997
1999	Brazil	Government spending	1998	January 1999
2000	International	Internet and technology shares	2000	June 2000

APPENDIX 3
List of American Leading, Coincident and Lagging Indicators

Leading, coincident and lagging indicators for the American economy were generated by NBER until 1995, where the task was transferred to The Conference Board, which is a private not-for-profit organization.

The Conference Board publishes "Leading, Coincident and Lagging Indicators" (jointly referred to as "LEI", or Leading Economic Indicators") as well as the "Business Cycle Indicators" database with more than 250 economic series (called "BCI", or "Business Cycle Indicators"). The BCI includes and highlights the LEI data, but contains additional time series. The following is an overview over the elements of the LEI time series as described by The Conference Board.

1. LEADING INDEX COMPONENTS

- *Average weekly hours, manufacturing.* The average hours worked per week by production workers in manufacturing industries tend to lead the business cycle because employers usually adjust work hours before increasing or decreasing their workforce.
- *Average weekly initial claims for unemployment insurance.* The number of new claims filed for unemployment insurance are typically more sensitive than either total employment or unemployment to overall business conditions, and this series tends to lead the business cycle. It is inverted when included in the leading index; the signs of the month-to-month changes are reversed, because initial claims increase when employment conditions worsen (i.e., layoffs rise and new hirings fall).

- *Manufacturers' new orders, consumer goods and materials (in 1992 $).* These goods are primarily used by consumers. The inflation-adjusted value of new orders leads actual production because new orders directly affect the level of both unfilled orders and inventories that firms monitor when making production decisions. The Conference Board deflates the current dollar orders data using price indexes constructed from various sources at the industry level and a chain-weighted aggregate price index formula.
- *Vendor performance, slower deliveries diffusion index.* This index measures the relative speed at which industrial companies receive deliveries from their suppliers. Slowdowns in deliveries increase this series and are most often associated with increases in demand for manufacturing supplies (as opposed to a negative shock to supplies) and, therefore, tend to lead the business cycle. Vendor performance is based on a monthly survey conducted by the National Association of Purchasing Management (NAPM) that asks purchasing managers whether their suppliers' deliveries have been faster, slower, or the same as the previous month. The slower-deliveries diffusion index counts the proportion of respondents reporting slower deliveries, plus one-half of the proportion reporting no change in delivery speed.
- *Manufacturers' new orders, nondefense capital goods (in 1992 $).* New orders received by manufacturers in nondefense capital goods industries (in inflation-adjusted dollars) are the producers' counterpart to BCI-08.
- *Building permits, new private housing unit.* The number of residential building permits issued is an indicator of construction activity, which typically leads most other types of economic production.
- *Stock prices, 500 common stocks.* The Standard & Poor's 500 stock index reflects the price movements of a broad selection of common stocks traded on the New York Stock Exchange. Increases (decreases) of the stock index can reflect both the general sentiments of investors and the movements of interest rates, which is usually another good indicator for future economic activity.
- *Money supply (in 1992 $).* In inflation-adjusted dollars, this is the M2 version of the money supply. When the money supply does not keep pace with inflation, bank lending may fall in real terms, making it more difficult for the economy to expand. M2 includes currency, demand deposits, other checkable deposits, travelers checks, savings deposits, small denomination time deposits, and balances in money market mutual funds. The inflation adjustment is based on the implicit deflator for personal consumption expenditures.

- *Interest rate spread, 10-year Treasury bonds less federal funds.* The spread or difference between long and short rates is often called the yield curve. This series is constructed using the 10-year Treasury bond rate and the federal funds rate, an overnight interbank borrowing rate. It is felt to be an indicator of the stance of monetary policy and general financial conditions because it rises (falls) when short rates are relatively low (high). When it becomes negative (i.e., short rates are higher than long rates and the yield curve inverts) its record as an indicator of recessions is particularly strong.
- *Index of consumer expectations.* This index reflects changes in consumer attitudes concerning future economic conditions and, therefore, is the only indicator in the leading index that is completely expectations-based. Data are collected in a monthly survey conducted by the University of Michigan's Survey Research Center. Responses to the questions concerning various economic conditions are classified as positive, negative, or unchanged. The expectations series is derived from the responses to three questions relating to: (1) economic prospects for the respondent's family over the next 12 months; (2) the economic prospects for the Nation over the next 12 months; and (3) the economic prospects for the Nation over the next five years.

2. COINCIDENT INDEX COMPONENTS

- *Employees on nonagricultural payrolls.* This series from the Bureau of Labor Statistics is often referred to as "payroll employment." It includes full-time and part-time workers and does not distinguish between permanent and temporary employees. Because the changes in this series reflect the actual net hiring and firing of all but agricultural establishments, government agencies, and the smallest businesses in the nation, it is one of the most closely watched series for gauging the health of the economy.
- *Personal income less transfer payments (in 1992 $).*The value of the income received from all sources is stated in inflation-adjusted dollars to measure the real salaries and other earnings of all persons. This series excludes government transfers such as Social Security payments and includes an adjustment for wage accruals less disbursements (WALD) that smooth bonus payments (to more accurately reflect the level of income that wage earners would use to base their consumption decisions upon). Income levels are important because they help determine both aggregate spending and the general health of the economy.

- *Index of industrial production.* This index is based on value-added concepts and covers the physical output of all stages of production in the manufacturing, mining, and gas and electric utility industries. It is constructed from numerous sources that measure physical product counts, values of shipments, and employment levels. Although the value-added of the industrial sector is only a fraction of the total economy, this index has historically captured a majority of the fluctuations in total output.
- *Manufacturing and trade sales (in 1992 $).* Sales at the manufacturing, wholesale, and retail levels are invariably procyclical. This series is inflation-adjusted to represent real total spending. The data for this series are collected as part of the National Income and Product Account calculations, and the level of aggregate sales is always larger than GDP when annualized because some products and services are counted more than once (e.g. as intermediate goods or temporary additions to wholesale inventories and a retail sale).

3. LAGGING INDEX COMPONENTS

- *Average duration of unemployment.* This series measures the average duration (in weeks) that individuals counted as unemployed have been out of work. Because this series tends to be higher during recessions and lower during expansions, it is inverted when it is included in the lagging index (i.e., the signs of the month-to-month changes are reversed). Decreases in the average duration of unemployment invariably occur after an expansion gains strength and the sharpest increases tend to occur after a recession has begun.
- *Ratio, manufacturing and trade inventories to sales (in 1992 $).* The ratio of inventories to sales is a popular gauge of business conditions for individual firms, entire industries, and the whole economy. This series is calculated by the Bureau of Economic Analysis using inventory and sales data for manufacturing, wholesale, and retail businesses (in inflation- and seasonally-adjusted form) based on data collected by the Bureau of the Census. Because inventories tend to increase when the economy slows and sales fail to meet projections, the ratio typically reaches its cyclical peaks in the middle of a recession. It also tends to decline at the beginning of an expansion as firms meet their sales demand from excess inventories.

- *Change in labor cost per unit of output, manufacturing.* This series measures the rate of change in an index that rises when labor costs for manufacturing firms rise faster than their production (and vice versa). The index is constructed by The Conference Board from various components, including seasonally adjusted data on employee compensation in manufacturing (wages and salaries plus supplements) from the BEA, and seasonally adjusted data on industrial production in manufacturing from the Board of Governors of the Federal Reserve System. Because monthly percent changes in this series are extremely erratic, percent changes in labor costs are calculated over a six-month span. Cyclical peaks in the six-month annualized rate of change typically occur during recessions, as output declines faster than labor costs despite layoffs of production workers. Troughs in the series are much more difficult to determine and characterize.
- *Average prime rate charged by banks.* Although the prime rate is considered the benchmark that banks use to establish their interest rates for different types of loans, changes tend to lag behind the movements of general economic activities. The monthly data are compiled by the Board of Governors of the Federal Reserve System.
- *Commercial and industrial loans outstanding (in 1992 $).* This series measures the volume of business loans held by banks and commercial paper issued by nonfinancial companies. The underlying data are compiled by the Board of Governors of the Federal Reserve System. The Conference Board makes price level adjustments using the same deflator (based on Personal Consumption Expenditures data) used to deflate the money supply series in the leading index. The series tends to peak after an expansion peaks because declining profits usually increase the demand for loans. Troughs are typically seen more than a year after the recession ends. (Users should note that there is a major discontinuity in January 1998, due to a change in the source data; the composite index calculations are adjusted for this fact.)
- *Ratio, consumer installment credit outstanding to personal income.* This series measures the relationship between consumer debt and income. Consumer installment credit outstanding is compiled by the Board of Governors of the Federal Reserve System and personal income data is from the Bureau of Economic Analysis. Because consumers tend to hold off personal borrowing until months after a recession ends, this ratio typically shows a trough after personal income has risen for a year or longer. Lags between peaks in the ratio and peaks in the general economy are much more variable.

➢ *Change in Consumer Price Index for services.* This series is compiled by the Bureau of Labor Statistics, and it measures the rates of change in the services component of the Consumer Price Index. It is probable that because of recognition lags and other market rigidities, service sector inflation tends to increase in the initial months of a recession and to decrease in the initial months of an expansion.

APPENDIX 4
Typical Sequence of Events of a Business Cycle

The following is a description of the typical sequence of events within the economy, financial liquidity, the media, bonds, stocks, commodities and gold over the four phases of the business cycle.

1. Slump

The economy is poor, investments low, and unemployment is rising. The property market is depressed. Earnings are bad, bankers are scared, and nobody is in a position to help anybody.

Financial liquidity is good and rising. Time saving deposits and brokers' cash accounts are high. Short-term interest rates are falling. (Financial liquidity is the liquidity available for stock and bond investments.)

The media focus is primarily on the negative elements of the economy, even though first bonds and then stocks have already started to climb.

Bonds are in a clear rising trend, after the drop in short interest rates.

Stocks have started to rise some time after bonds. In the start phase-consumption-oriented paper such as building stocks, retail chains and manufacturers of short-term consumables in particular are rising strongly. Financial institutions providing consumer credit facilities are also among the good securities. In bottom position are mining stocks and manufacturers of capital goods. Stock rises provoke astonishment as earnings are still falling.

Commodities are falling strongly, and the same applies to *Gold* which peaked some time before the actual slump

2. Economic Expansion

The first upturn in the *economy* is due to an increase in consumer demand. Newbuilds and purchases of consumer goods soar and demand for consumer credit increases. Industry and retail links start with relatively high stocks, which are gradually reduced. In the mature phase of the upturn industry seriously starts to register a rising order intake. Money supply exceeds targets and the prime rate may be raised for the first time, after earlier reductions. Inflation has reached bottom. Property prices for private homes rise, while the professional property market stagnates.

Financial liquidity has stopped rising. Time saving deposits and brokers' cash accounts are falling and mutual funds are increasingly tied up in investments. Brokers' security loans are accelerating. Short interest rates begin to nudge upwards. Leveraged buy-outs contribute to increasing the liquidity impact.

At the start of the upturn *the media* are still pessimistic, only turning to optimism after midway in the upturn. Adverts for new mutual funds are still few and far between.

Bonds have been rising for a long period. Some months after short interest rates began to climb bonds go into a culmination phase.

Stocks have also been rising for some time, possibly 6–9 months, before the economic upturn began. In the upturn phase industrial stocks in particular are rising strongly. Considerable takeover activity contributes to the rises.

Commodities have bottomed at a low level, and there is no indication of increases in the first phases of the upturn. Later on more and more commodities start to rise.

Gold enters a bottom formation after falling over a long period.

3. Boom

The economy is booming and industry's capacity utilization is high, but there are more and more bottlenecks. Inflation and short-term interest rates are rising. Industry has started to expand capacity, and demand for labor, capital and commodities is rising. More and more enterprises start to sell out bond portfolios to raise liquidity for this capacity expansion.

Financial liquidity has long been falling and "liquidity reserves" are now low. (Liquidity reserves could be likened to a charging battery.) The primary source of liquidity expansion is equity price increases, converted to security capital as positions are traded. There are many new issues and accelerating rises in money market rates.

The media are positive and a lot of column inches are devoted to stock investments. There are a multitude of advertisements for investment offers, some for borrowed funds. New mutual funds appear and more or less "blind" issues are not unusual.

Bonds go into a falling trend after breaking out from a large top formation.

Stocks start to drop some months before the climax in the economy. The drop starts with consumer stocks, hitting them hardest, and affects commodities, mining, chemical and drug industries last. Internationally the drop will probably start in leading markets such as the UK, the USA and West Germany, and last in commodity producers such as Australia, Canada and South Africa. This tendency is amplified because many institutional investors, instead of abandoning the stock markets altogether, will move into defensive, commodity-related stocks.

Commodities are now in a clear rising trend, also including Dry Cargo Freight Futures.

Gold breaks up from its bottom formation and starts a rising trend.

4. Economic Decline

The economy is now marked by drastic reductions in private consumption. Industry faces rising excess capacity, partly due to recent ill-timed investments. Inflation rises for a period, but peaks in the middle of the decline. In this period many interest-rate sensitive sectors are hit by bankruptcies and enforce sales are common on the property market.

Financial liquidity stabilizes and liquidity reserves gradually start to rise. However, owing to price drops many market operators face margin calls, as paper liquidity quickly shrinks. Compulsory liquidations are frequent.

The media are pessimistic. Higher interest rates are prophesied and capital intensive industries are caught in credit squeezes. There are more and more adverts for investments in precious metals and stones. Silver is bought up for smelting.

Bonds reach bottom before the end of the economic decline. Because of margin calls, many of the last sales are forced.

Stocks also fall, reversing later than bonds.

Commodities peak before inflation and have now started to drop.

Gold is beginning to fall simultaneously with, or shortly after, commodities. Gold price drops start six to nine months before inflation peaks.

An Important Reservation

It should be said that the above scenarios are naturally simplifications. Events never kept strictly to the model, for three reasons:

1. In small economies with a large international sphere of contact, the pattern is disturbed by exogenous factors. The model is increasingly accurate the larger the subjects described. It is most easily interpreted globally.
2. Sometimes isolated political or technological events will seriously distort the pattern ("stochastic exogenous disturbances").
3. If stocks crash instead of undergoing a gradual bull-trend reversal, the system can be disturbed by the shock waves, promoting strong federal bank intervention. In this instance, the federal bank's activities can be so extreme that the markets are no longer a barometer, but rather a major cause of economic movements.

Having said this, the markets should always be considered on the basis of this model.

Structure of Subordinate Markets

The aforementioned model concerned overall phase shifts between key markets, but there is also an internal market rotation for bond and stock markets.

As to interest rates, the short rates fluctuate the most. When short rates are close to peaking the shortest will often be considerably higher than the slightly longer rates. However, short-term bond prices do not fall most, due solely to the purely mathematical/technical factor that short securities are less sensitive to interest rates than long ones. For long-term bonds there is a different market rotation. Junk bonds are the market leader. A bear market for long bonds thus begins in the least secure papers. But the most interesting leaders/laggers phenomenon is shown by stocks. The sequence through the three phases of a bull market is as follows:

First Phase: In the bull market's first hesitant phase, the greatest increase is in stocks related to households' consumption and investments:

- utilities
- small loan institutes
- consumer goods, drugs
- food chains
- foodstuffs
- packaging materials
- finance companies
- retail stores
- banks
- insurance

Second Phase: In the middle of the upturn many companies' and stores' inventories are being pressed far down due to rising demand. New industrial orders rise even more significantly than consumption and this makes *industrials* the best shares in this phase. Often this phase is where the market begins to develop a penchant for companies with less financial clout but more innovative ideas. Sometimes the number of mutual trusts will increase strongly and bubbles — more or less blind issues — will begin to appear. Industrial peak about the same time or shortly after the total index. Important industrials can include:

- energy
- firms of contractors
- paper
- textiles
- consumer durables (e.g. automobiles)

Third Phase: While consumer stocks function as leaders and industrial stocks generally peak simultaneously with the total index, stocks related to *fixed investments* and *commodities* are typical laggers. Examples are:

- machine plants
- chemicals
- transport stock (including aviation)

- metalworking
- mines

The reason is that in the final phase of the boom the industry will suffer a dearth of capacity so (inadvisable) investments are made in new capital.

Stocks which are very sensitive to economic trends are described, not surprisingly, as "cyclicals". The most business-cycle sensitive sectors among those mentioned are automobiles (and tyre manufacturers), chemicals, airlines and metalworking. The easiest way to get an overview of leaders/laggers' performance is to study the stocks subindex. In the USA the utilities index is a slight leader, the industrials index a weak lagger and the transportation index a definite lagger. In a number of other countries similar leading and lagging sub-indices are computed, e.g. F.T. Stores in the UK (leader) or Metals and Mining in Australia (lagger).

Notes

CHAPTER 1

1. The major source for this chapter is Mackay, 1980 (first published in 1841).
2. Scotland was an independent country at that time.
3. Paper money was a Chinese invention from the early part of the eleventh century. John Law's scheme is generally believed to be the first use of paper money in Europe.
4. Mackay, 1980.
5. Law & Company is often described as the first European central bank. But goverment-sponsored banks with more limited responsibilities had been founded earlier in Sweden (1668), England (1694), and Scotland (1695).
6. "Junk bonds" is a modern expression for bonds that carry a considerable risk.
7. These figures are based on Mackay and do not pretend to be accurate.
8. "Debt-for-equity swap" is a modern expression. Such swaps were widely used to solve the Latin American debt problems in the 1980s.
9. "Payment at sight" means that your paper money can be changed to more tangible values — like gold.

CHAPTER 2

1. Daily stock prices can be found in the tables in "Banqueroute de Law" by Edgar Faure, which is available in Biblioteque de L'Arsenal in Paris.
2. Thomas, 1995.

CHAPTER 3

1. Adam Smith's life is described in Scott, 1937; Staley, 1989; Schumpeter, 1954; and Spiegel, 1983.
2. Sperling, 1962; Tvede, 1990.
3. Ashton, 1959.
4. He was Master of the Mint until 1727, see Staley, 1989.
5. The phenomenon is called "sweating". See Friedman, 1992.
6. Schumpeter, 1954.

7. Willis, 1979.
8. Thornton's life is described in Hetzel, 1987; Peak, 1978; Schumpeter, 1954; Spiegel, 1983; Staley, 1989; and Thornton, 1939 (reprint). Ashton, 1959, contains a description of an event, where the old East India Company in the year 1700 tried to force the Bank of England into bankruptcy.
9. Trevelyan, 1960.
10. Ashton, 1959.
11. Thornton, 1939.
12. The speech is reprinted in Thornton, 1939.
13. There are life sketches in Schumpeter, 1954; Spiegel, 1983; and Staley, 1989.
14. Ricardo.

CHAPTER 4

1. Jevons, 1876.
2. There are descriptions of his life in Schumpeter, 1954; Spiegel, 1983; and Staley, 1989.
3. Kindleberger, 1978.
4. Bechmann, 1988.
5. The gold speculation is described in Bechmann, 1988; Klein, 1986; O'Conner, 1962; and Sharp, 1989. The daily close prices for gold in the relevant period as they appear in the stock lists do not always correspond exactly to the prices quoted by the authors, but this may be due to very large intra-day price moves, which are not recorded in the stock lists.
6. Sharp, 1989.

CHAPTER 5

1. There is a short description of Babbage's life in Slater, 1987.
2. Juglar's life is described in Beauregard, 1909.
3. Marshall is often considered the last of the Classical Economists.
4. Schumpeter, 1954.

CHAPTER 6

1. Schumpeter, 1954.
2. Schumpeter, 1954.
3. Burns and Mitchell, 1946.
4. There is an excellent record on his life and work in Burns and Allen, 1991.
5. Mitchell's analysis of the business cycle was based on a method in which he first determined for each cycle the beginning and end of nine phases by marking troughs and peaks in the aggregate indicators. He then expressed the value of any time series

of a given phase as percentage of its value through all the 9 phases. In this way, he reduced the effect of the long-term trend, so that he could isolate the deviations around it. Having done this, he calculated average fluctuations of a large number of cycles to identify a prototype of the development through a cycle. Mitchell lived to see that his indicators were successful but not to see whether they would work in other countries. That test was not initiated until NBER many years later — in 1973 — decided to try to develop an international economic indicator system (called "IEI"). The Americans cooperated with scientists from leading OECD countries to duplicate, as far as possible, Mitchell's warning system in these other countries. Again the indicators worked, confirming Juglar's old notion that business cycles are indeed an independent phenomenon.

6. Out of the six lagging indicators presently used for the United States by NBER, five represent increased costs. These are:

Indicator	*Effect*
Labor cost per unit of output	High production costs
Commercial and industrial loans outstanding	High financial expenditures
Inventories in manufacturing and trade	High financial expenditures; need to lower purchases
Ratio of consumer installment	High personal financial debt to personal income costs
Average prime rate charged by banks	High financial costs in all sectors

Lagging indicators are clearly "trouble indicators". This is why inverted lagging indicators are reliable leading indicators, and why a rise in leading indicators is much more reliable when accompanied with a strong fall or low level in lagging indicators.

7. There is a chapter on Kuznets' life in Spiegel and Samuels, 1984.
8. Kondratieff's life and work is described in Mager, 1987.
9. It is often debated whether a Kondratieff phenomenon might be restricted to the capital sector only, with little influence on aggregate output. See Forrester, 1976 and 1976b and Sirkin, 1976.
10. There is wide disagreement regarding the timing, see Mager, 1987.
11. Both Edgar Peters and Erik Mosekilde have told me that it is necessary to observe some nine cycles before the existence can be judged with reasonable, statistical assurance. That will, in the case of Kondratieff, mean some 450 years of observation!
12. Mager, 1987.
13. Mager, 1987.

CHAPTER 7

1. There is an excellent description of his life and work in Fisher, 1956.
2. There are descriptions of the German hyperinflation in Bechman, 1988 and Kindleberger and Laffargue, 1982.

CHAPTER 8

1. About Mises' life and work, see Mises, 1981.
2. Patinkin and Leith, 1977.
3. Patinkin, 1978.
4. Patinkin, 1978.
5. There are descriptions of his life and work in Schumpeter, 1951; Robinson, 1972; Spiegel, 1983; and Staley, 1989.
6. Chua and Woodward, 1983.
7. Patterson, 1956.

CHAPTER 9

1. Lefevre, 1964; Thomas and Witts, 1979.
2. Patterson, 1956.
3. Thomas and Witts, 1979.
4. Allen, 1991.
5. Grant, 1992.
6. Grant, 1992.
7. This is not a standard expression.
8. Galbraith, 1971.
9. The literature about this book is overwhelming. Some references from my own list are: Bernstein, 1985; Burket, 1987; Garrison, 1984; Nenties, 1988; O'Donnel, 1990; Patinkin, 1976, 1977, 1978; Pesaran, 1985; Staley, 1989; and Sylos-labini, 1984.
10. The multiplier was not Keynes' theory, but Kahn's. Keynes popularized it, however. See Patinkin, 1978.
11. Patinkin, 1978.

CHAPTER 10

1. Robert Bryce later became Deputy Minister of Finance in Canada.
2. Allen, 1991, is an excellent source to Schumpeter's life and work. Another good source is Spiegel, 1983.
3. Somary, 1963.
4. Equilibrium theory is based on a method in which you let all parameters in a simulation flow, until they fall to rest at some level.

CHAPTER 11

1. Zeitschrift für Nationalökonomi, Wien, 1,5, 1930.
2. About Tinbergen, see Spiegel and Samuels, 1984 and Van den Linden, 1988.

3. Keynes was often called "the winning economist, but the losing gentleman". But in his debate with Tinbergen, there has since been large agreement, that he was also the losing economist; it is difficult to imagine the subsequent development of economic theory without the use of econometrics. Since Tinbergen's pioneering work, enormous amounts of money have been poured into ever-larger econometric models. One such example was Lawrence Klein's giant model of the American economy (later "Klein-Golberger") in the early 1980s, which contained over 1,000 equations, and which was combined via "Project Link" with other national models to form a several-thousand-equation multinational model. The critique of Keynes is described in Hansen and Clemence, 1959.
4. "Computers" as we know them didn't exist. The term referred to simple calculators or even to people who did manual calculations.
5. "Business cycles in the U.S.A.", 1919–1937, printed 1938 and "A method and its Application to Investment Activity", 1939.
6. See Hansen and Clemence, 1959.
7. Reprinted in "The American Economic Association", 1944.
8. This is my own distinction.
9. The expression is taken from Eachus, 1988.

CHAPTER 12

1. Slater, 1987.
2. Beer could only flow from the brewery down the chain; orders could only flow up the chain. So the point was to minimize your inventory and backlogs. Each player could place new orders if desired, but had to receive what he had ordered, and ship what had been ordered from him. Unfilled orders were listed as backlog (with the two-dollar penalty) until they could be filled.
3. Sterman, 1989.

CHAPTER 13

1. Science has known the phenomenon at least since 1897, where Pareto discovered it in income distribution. It is called "Pareto" or "Pareto-Levy".
2. Hurst, 1965.
3. The IBM Thomas J. Watson Research Center, N.Y.
4. Gleich, 1987.
5. Mandelbrot, 1971.
6. Gleich, 1987.
7. One area where such a phenomenon seemed to have surfaced was climatology. When you let a computer simulate weather development day in and day out, hundreds or even thousands of years into the future, then it could suddenly, completely unprovoked, swing into a global ice-age, stay there for many years, and then swing back again. There seemed to be two equilibria in the simulation system, much as there might be in the real climate.

8. Brownian noise is external disturbances.
9. Andersen, 1988.
10. What I mean is, that he didn't use it to measure the occurrence of circuit breakers. He only used it to measure the Hurst effect. I believe it was Mandelbrot who rediscovered the Rescaled Range technique, see Mandelbrot, 1968, 1969, and 1972. There is a good explanation of the phenomenon in Feder, 1988.
11. Lucas, 1981.

CHAPTER 14

1. There is an excellent record on Friedman's life and work in Frazer, 1988.
2. Interesting literature about money supply and velocity of money includes Fisher, 1923; Friedman and Schwartz, 1963; 1963b; Friedman, 1986, 1992; Garrison, 1984; Gordon, 1952; Haberler, 1960; Hayek, 1933; Holtrop, 1929; Humprey, 1990; Kydlans and Prescott, 1990; Mises, 1953; Nenties, 1988; Scheide, 1989; Wicksell, 1907, and Woolford, 1989.
3. Duch, 1985, contains a study of monetary conditions and business cycles in 33 countries over the years 1962 to 1982. Among his results were:

    - For most major Western countries, a change in the rate of monetary growth produces a change in the rate of growth of nominal income about six to nine months later. Inflation is hardly affected at all within this time frame, however.
    - The effect of prices of changed rate of monetary growth is distributed over time, but typically shows up some two years later. That is why you cannot stop inflation overnight.
    - Velocity of money tends to rise in the expansion phase of the business cycle and to fall in the contraction phase.

4. Robert E. Lucas received the Nobel Prize in 1995 for the development of this theory.

CHAPTER 16

1. There are descriptions of George Soros' life in Soros, 1987; Train, 1989; Business Week, 1993 and Slater, 1996. Slater's description is the most detailed.
2. A scientific test of the positive feed-back tendency in the capital markets was performed by Edgar Peters in 1991. Measuring the Hurst exponents and average cycle lengths in various financial markets, he reached the following results:

	Hurst exponent	Cycle length
IBM	0.72	18
Xerox	0.73	18
Apple Computer	0.75	18
Coca-Cola	0.70	42
Anheuser-Bush	0.64	48
McDonalds	0.65	42
Niagara Mohawk	0.69	72
Texas State Utilities	0.54	90
Consolidated Edison	0.68	90
S&P 500 (American stock index)	0.78	48
German stock index*	0.72	60
Japanese stock index*	0.68	48
British stock index*	0.68	30
T-bonds	0.68	60
USD/JPY	0.64	"undetermined"
USD/DEM	0.64	"6 years?"
GBP/USD	0.61	"6 years?"
USD/SGD	0.50	none

*Morgan Stanley Capital International

The result was striking: all markets but USD/SGD exhibited positive feed-back. (The Singapore dollar is pegged to the U.S. dollar through frequent central bank interventions). Source: Peters, 1991.

3. My descriptions of his investment philosophy are based on Soros, 1987, Train, 1989, and Slater, 1996. One example of the loops he described was the situation where the value of a collateral was increased simply through the act of lending on it. When a country borrowed, its economy would show enhanced growth, which would temporarily reduce debt ratios to deceptively low levels. Once this borrowing stopped, the economy would run into a recession and the debt ratio would suddenly explode. Another example was that of a devaluation of a currency. The devaluation would create inflation, which would, in retrospect, seem to justify the devaluation.
4. Damasio, 1994.
5. Soros, 1987.

CHAPTER 17

1. Watson, 1992.
2. Watson, 1992.
3. Grant, 1992.
4. Grant, 1992.
5. In *Journal of Portfolio Management*, Fall 1991, Jeremy Siegel of the University of Pennsylvania concluded about the American stock-market:

   "... there is almost always a decline in stock returns index before, or just after, the beginning of a recession. In fact, out of the forty-one recessions from 1802 through 1990, thirty-eight of them, or 93%, have been preceded (or accompanied) by declines of 8% or more (based on monthly averages) in the stock returns index".

Markets are better at forecasting revivals than recessions, however:
"The average lead time for a recovery has been 5.2 months, compared to a 6.4 month lead time for a recession, with a 4.6 standard deviation." Not that it didn't fail from time to time. Sometimes, as in 1987, it took a violent dive unrelated to economic factors. Since World War Two, this had happened 7 times in the USA:

Year of false alarm	Percentage decline
1946	–24.0
1956–57	–8.3
1962	–23.1
1966	–15.5
1978	–10.8
1984	–8.2
1987	–29.1

6. Tvede, 1990.
7. Lynch, 1989.
8. Bose, 1988.
9. Bose, 1988.
10. Watson, 1992.
11. Watson, 1992.

CHAPTER 18

1. The simulations are described in Mosekilde, Larsen, Thomsen and Sterman, 1992.
2. Watson, 1992.
3. Slater, 1996.
4. Slater, 1996.

CHAPTER 19

1. The economists were: Olivier Blanchard, Rudiger Dornbush, Stanley Fisher, Franco Modigliani, Paul Samuelson, and Robert Solow.
2. The incident was described in *The European*, 5–8 August, 1993 and *Financial Times*, 30 August 1993.

Bibliography

Some Sceptical Observations on Real Business Cycle Theory, Federal Reserve Bank of Minneapolis Quarterly Review, Fall 1986.

Abramovitz, M.: *Inventories and Business Cycles*, NBER, New York, 1950.

Adelman, I. and F. Adelman: The Dynamic Properties of the Klein-Golberger model, *Econometrica*, 4, 1959, pp. 596–625.

Adelman, I.: Long Cycles: Fact or Artifact?, American Economic Review, 55:444–63, 1965.

Aiyagari, S.R.: Economic Fluctuations Without Shocks to Fundamentals; Or, Does the Stock Market Dance to its Own Music?, *Federal Reserve Bank of Minneapolis*, Quarterly Review, Winter 1988, pp. 8–24.

Alfred Eichner (ed).: Why Economics is not a Science, Macmillan, London, 1983.

Allen, R.K.: *Opening Doors*, Transaction Publishers, USA, 1991.

The American Economic Association: *Readings in Business Cycle Theory*, George Allen and Unwin, London, 1944.

Andersen, D.F.: Foreword: Chaos in System Dynamics Models, *System Dynamics Review*, 4, Numbers 1–2, 1988.

Ashton, T.S.: *Economic Fluctuations in England 1700–1800*, Claredon Press, Oxford, 1959.

Azariadis, C.: Self-fulfilling Prophecies, Journal of Economic Theory, 25:380-96, 1981.

Babson, R.W.: *Business Barometers Used in the Accumulation of Money*, Babson Institute, Mass., 1920.

Beauregard, P.: *Notice sur la Vie et les Travaux de M. Clément Juglar*, Compte Rendu, L'Academie des Sciences Morales et Politiques, Feb. 1909.

Beckman, R.: *Crashes*, Grafton Books, London, 1990.

Bernstein, P.L.: Wall Street's View of Keynes and Keynes' View of Wall Street, Wattel, H.L., ed.: *The Political Consequences of John Maynard Keynes*, Armonk, New York, Sharpe, 1985, pp. 22–29.

Breit, W.S. and R.W. Spencer: *Life of the Laureates: Seven Nobel Economists*, MIT Press, Cambridge, Mass., 1986.

Bose, M.: *The Crash*, Bloomsbury, London, 1988.

Bolton, H.: Money and Investment Profits, Dow-Jones-Irwin, Homewood, Illinois 1967.

Brock, W.A.: Chaos and Complexity in Economic and Financial Science, *Social Systems Research Institute*, University of Wisconsin-Madison, paper no. 382, 1990, pp. 423– 450.

Brock, W.A.: Is the Business Cycle Characterized by Deterministic Chaos?, *Journal of Monetary Economics*, 22, 1988, pp. 71–90.

Brunner, K. & A.H. Meltzer, eds.: Stabilisation of the Domestic and International Economy, Carnegy-Rochester Conference on Public Policy, North-Holland, Amsterdam, 1977.
Buckle, T.H.: *History of Civilisation in England*, London, 1872.
Burkett, P. and M. Wohar: Keynes on Investment and the Business Cycle, *Review of Radical Political Economy*; 19 (4), Winter 1987, pp. 39–54.
Burns, A.F. and W.C. Mitchell: *Measuring Business Cycles*, NBER, New York, 1946.
Cantillon, R.: *Essai sur la Nature du Commerce en général*, reprint, Harvard University Press, Boston, 1892.
Chen, P.: Empirical and Theoretical Evidence of Economic Chaos, *System Dynamics Review*, 4, 1988.
Chen, P.: Mode Locking to Chaos in Delayed Feedback Systems, *Center for Studies in Statistical Mechanics*, University of Texas at Austin, 1986.
Chiarella, C.: *The Elements of Non-linear Theory of Economic Dynamics*, PhD Thesis, University of South Wales, 1986.
Chua, J.H. and Woodward, R.S.: J.M. Keynes' Investment Performance: A Note, *Journal of Finance*; 38 (1), Mar. 1983, pp. 232–35.
Collard, D.A.: Pigou on Expectations and the Cycle, *Economic Journal*; 93 (379), June 1983, pp. 411–14.
Damasion, A.R.: *Descartes' Error*, Grosset/Putnam, New York, 1994.
De Wolff, P.: Tinbergens Contribution to Business-Cycle Theory and Policy, *De Economist*, 118 (2), Mar.–Apr. 1970, pp. 112–25.
Deutscher, P.: *R.G. Hawtrey and the Development of Macroeconomics*, Macmillan, London, 1990.
Dutch, N.W.: Money, Output and Prices: An Empirical Study using Long term Cross Country Data, Working Paper, *University of Bristol*, Sep. 1985.
Eachus, P.: The Psychology of the Stock Market, *The Psychologist*, Mar. 1988.
Edgewort, F.: Mathematical Physics, Kegan Paul, 1881.
Einarsen, J.: *Reinvestment Cycles*, Review of Economic Statistics, Feb. 1938, pp. 1–10.
Ezekiel, M.: The Cobweb Theorem, *Quarterly Journal of Economics*, 1938.
Fama, E.F and K.R. French: Business Cycles and the Behaviour of Metals prices, *Journal of Finance*, 43 (5), Dec. 1988, pp. 1075–93.
Fazzari, S. & D. B. Papadimitriou (Eds.): Financial Conditions and Marcoeconomic Performance, M.E. Sharpe, Armonk, 1992.
Feder, J.: *Fractals*, Plenum Press, N.Y., 1988.
Fisher, I.: *Appreciation and Interest*. American Economic Association, New York, 1896.
Fisher, I: The Business Cycle Largely a Dance of the Dollar, *Journal of the American Statistical Association*, Dec. 1923, pp. 1024–28.
Fisher, I.: *The Stock Market Crash — and After*, Macmillan, New York, 1930.
Fisher, I.: The Debt-Deflation Theory of Great Depressions, Econometrica, October 1933.
Frish, R.: Propagation problems and Impulse Problems in Dynamic Economics, in Essays in Honor of Gustav Cassel, George Allen & Unwin, New York, 1933.
Fisher, N.: *My Father Irwin Fisher*, Comet Press, New York, 1956.
Forget, E.L.: John Stuart Mill's Business Cycle, *History of Political Economy*; 22 (4), Winter 1990, pp. 629–42.
Forrester, J.V.: Business Structure, Economic Cycles and National Policy, *Business Economics*, Jan., 1976.

Forrester, J.V.: Business Structure, Economic Cycles and National Policy, reply, *Business Economics*, May, 1976.

Frazer, W.J.: *Power and Ideas: Milton Friedman and the Big U-turn*, Gainsville, Fla.: Gulf/Atlantic, 1988.

Friedman, M. and A.J. Schwartz: *A Monetary History of the United States, 1867–1960*, Princeton University Press, 1963.

Friedman M. and A.J. Schwartz: Money and Business Cycles, *Review of Economics and Statistics*, vol. 45, Feb. 1963, pp. 32–78.

Friedman, B.M.: Money, Credit, and Interest Rates in the Business Cycle, in Gordon, R.J., ed.: *The American Business Cycle: Continuity and Change*, NBER, University of Chicago Press, 1986, pp. 395–438.

Friedman, B.M.: *Money Mischief*, Hartcourt, London, 1992.

Fukuyama, F.: *The End of History and the Last Man*, Avon Books, New York, 1992.

Galbraith, J.K.: *Economics, Peace and Laughter*, Houghton Mifflin, 1971.

Galbraith, J.K.: *The Great Crash 1929*, Houghton Mifflin, New York, 1955.

Garrison, C.B.: Friedman versus Keynes on the Theory of Employment, *Journal of Post Keynesian Economics*, 7 (1), Fall 1984, pp. 114–27.

Gary, H.: What Makes Stock Prices Move?, *Fortune*, vol. 118, Oct. 10, pp. 69–76.

Gleich, J.: *Chaos — Making a New Science*, Viking, USA, 1987.

Glück, H.: Transmission Mechanisms in the Austrian Economy, in Financial Structure and the Monetary Policy transmission Process, Bank of International Settlements, 1995.

Gordon, Robert A.: *Business Fluctuations*, Harper and Row, New York, 1952.

Grant, J.: *Money of the Mind*, Farra Straus Giroux, New York, 1992.

Haberler, G.: *Prosperity and Depression*, George Allen and Unwin, London, 1960.

Hansen, A. and R.V. Clemence: *Readings in Business Cycles and National Income*, 2. ed., George Allen and Unwin, London, 1959.

Havrilevski, T.: The Money Supply Theory of J.S. Mill, *South African Journal of Economics*, 40 (1), Mar. 1972, pp. 72–76.

Hawtrey, R.: *Good and Bad Trade: An Inquiry into the Causes of Trade Fluctuations*, Constable & Co., London, 1913.

Hawtrey, R.G.: Good and bad Trade: An Inquiry into the Causes of trade Fluctuations, Constable & Co. London, 1913.

Hayek, F.A.: *Monetary Theory and the Trade Cycle*, 1933.

Hetzel, R.L.: Henry Thornton: Seminal Monetary Theorist and Father of the Modern Central Bank, *Federal Reserve Bank of Richmond Economic Review*; 73 (4), July/August 1987 pp. 3–16.

Hickman, B.G.: Growth and Stability in the Postwar Economy, Brookings Institute, Washington D.C., 1960.

Hicks, J.R.: Automatists, Hawtreyans, and Keynesians, *Journal of Money, Credit and Banking*, 1 (3), Aug. 1969, pp. 307–17.

Holtrop, M.W.: Theories of the Velocity of Circulation of Money in Earlier Economic Literature, *The Economic Journal*, Jan. 1929.

Humphrey, Thomas M.: Ricardo versus Thorton on the Appropriate Monetary Response to Supply Shocks, *Federal Reserve Bank of Richmond Economic Review*; 76 (6) Nov.–Dec. 1990, pp. 18–24.

Hurst, H.E.: Long term Storage of Reservoirs, *Transactions of the American Society of Civil Engineers*, 116, 1951, pp. 711–808.

Hurst, H.E., R.P. Black and Y.M. Simaika: *Long Term Storage: An Experimental Study*, Constable, London, 1965.
Hymans, S.H.: The Structure and Properties of the Michigan Quarterly Model of the U.S. Economy, International Economic Review, 15, 1974.
Jevons, W.S.: Money and the mechanism of Exchange, H.S. King, London, 1875.
Jevons, W.S.: The Future of Political Economy, *Fortnightly Review*, Nov. 1876.
Jevons, W.S.: The Theory of Political Economy, Macmillan, London, 1888.
Jevons, W.S.: Investigations in Currency and Finance, Macmillan, London, 1884.
Juglar, C.: *Les Crises Commerciales et leur Retour Périodique en France, en Angleterre et aux Etats Unis*, 1862.
Kahn, R.: The Relationship of Home Investment to Unemployment, in Selected Essays on Employment and Growth, Cambridge University Press, Cambridge, 1972.
Kaldor, N.: The Irrelevance of Equlibrium Economics, *Economic Journal*, vol. 82, No. 328, Dec. 1972, pp. 1237–55.
Keynes. J.M.: *The General Theory of Employment, Interest and Money*, MacMillan, London, 1936.
Kindleberger, C.P.: *Manias, Panics, and Crashes*, Macmillan, USA, 1978.
Kindleberger, C.P. and J-P. Laffargue: *Financial Crises*, Cambridge University Press, 1982.
Kindleberger, C.P.: The World in Depression, 1929–1939, University of California Press, Berkeley, 1986.
Kindleberger, C.P.: Manias, Panics and Crashes, John Wiley & Sons, New York, 1996.
Kitchin, J.: Cycles and Trends in Economic Factors, *The Review of Economic Statistics*, Jan. 1923, pp. 10–16.
Klein, L.: Macroeconomics and the Theory of rational behaviour, Econometrica, 14, 1946.
Klein, M: *The Life and Legend of Jay Gould*, Johns Hopkins Press, Baltimore, 1986.
Klock, C.P.: *Konjunkturteori*, Master Thesis (unpublished), Copenhagen Business School, 1992.
Kondratieff, N.: *The Long Wave Cycle*, reprint, Richardson and Snyder, USA, 1984.
Kuznets, S.S.: *Secular Movements in Production and Prices*, Houghton Mifflin Company, New York, 1930.
Kydland, F & E.C. Prescott: Time to Build and Aggregate Fluctuations, Econometrica, 50:1345–70, 1982.
Kydland, F.E. and E.C. Prescott: Business Cycles: Real Facts and Monetary Myths, *the Federal Reserve Bank of Mineapolis Quarterly Review*, Fall 1990.
LeBaron, D.: Some Reflections on Market Efficiency, *Financial Analysts Journal*, May/June, 1983.
LeBaron, B.: Stock Return Nonlinearities: Comparing Tests and Finding Structure, *University of Wisconsin-Madison*, Nov. 1988.
Lefevre, E.: *Reminiscences of a Stock Operator*, reprint, American Research Council, New York, 1964.
Lorenz, E.: Predictability: Does the Flap of a Butterfly's Wings in Brazil set off a Tornado in Texas?, *American Association for the Advancement of Science*, Washington, 1979.
Lorenz, E.: Strange Attractors in a Multisector Business Cycle Model, *Journal of Economic Behaviour and Organisation*, vol. 8, 1987, pp. 397–408.
Lorenz, H.W.: *Can Keynesian Demand Policy Imply Chaos*?, Georg-August-Universitat Gottingen, 1987.
Lucas, R.E.: Expectations and the Rationality of Money, Journal of Economic Theory, 4, 1972.

Lucas, R.E.: *Studies in Business-Cycle Theory*, The MIT Press, Cambridge, Mass., 1981.

Lucas, R.E.: Econometric Policy Evaluation: A Critique, in Brunner, K. and A.H. Meltzer, ed.: *The Philips Curve and Labour Markets*, Carnegie-Rochester Conference Series on Public Policy 1, North-Holland, pp. 19–46.

Lucas, R.E. and T.J. Sargetnt (eds.): *Rational Expectations and Economic Practise*, University of Minnesota Press, Minneapolis, 1981.

Macaulay, F.R.: *The Movements of Interest Rates, Bond Yields and Stock Prices in the United States since 1856*, NBER, New York, 1938.

Mackay, C.: *Extraordinary Popular Dilusions and the Madness of Crowds*, reprint, Harmony Books, New York, 1980.

Mager, N.H.: *The Kondratieff Waves*, Praeger, New York, 1987.

Mandebrot, B.B.: Forecasts of Future Prices, Unbiased Markets, and "Martingale" Models, *Journal of Business*, 1966, pp. 242–255.

Mandelbrot, B.B. and J.R. Walls: Noah, Joseph and Operational Hydrology, *Water Resources Research,* IV, Oct. 1968, pp. 909–918.

Mandelbrot, B.B. and J.R. Wallis: Robustness of the Rescaled Range R/S in the Measurement of Noncyclic Long Run Statistical Dependence, *Water Resources Research*, 5, 1969.

Mandelbrot, B.B.: Statistical Methods for Nonperiodic Cycles: From the Covariance to R/S Analysis, *Annals of Economic and Social Measurement*, 1/3, 1972, pp. 259–290.

Mandelbrot, B.B.: The Variation of Some Other Speculative Prices, *Journal of Business*, 1966.

Mandelbrot, B.B.: When Can Price be Arbitraged Efficiently? A Limit to the Validity of the Random Walk and Martingale Models, *The Review of Economics and Statistics*, 53, Aug. 1971, pp. 225–36.

Marshall. A.: *Principles of Economics*, 8th edn., MacMillan, London, 1947.

Martellaro, J.A.: From Say's Law to Supply-side Economics, *Rivista Internazionale di Science Economiche e Commerciali*, vol. 32, Sep. 1985.

Mass, N.J. *Economic Cycles: An Analysis of Underlying Causes*, Wright-Allen Press, Cambridge, Mass., 1975.

May, R. and G.F. Oster: Bifurcations and Dynamic Complexity in Simple Ecological Models, *The American Naturalist*, 110, 1976, pp. 573–99.

May, R.: Simple Mathematical Models with very Complicated Dynamics, *Nature*, 261, 1976, pp. 459–67.

Meltzer, A.H.: Money Supply revisited: A Review Article, Journal of Political Economy, 2, 1967.

Metzler, L.A.: Factors Governing the Length of Inventory Cycles, *Review of Economic Statistics*, vol. 29, Feb. 1947, pp. 1–15.

Mezler, L.A.: The Nature and Stability of Inventory Cycles, Review of Economic Studies, 23, 1941.

Mitchell. W.C.: *Business Cycles and their Causes*, University of California Press, 1941.

Mitchell. W.C.: *Business Cycles — The Problem and its Setting*, NBER, New York, 1927.

Mitchell. W.C.: *What Happens During Business Cycles?*, NBER, New York, 1951.

Mill, J.S.: *The Principles of Political Economy with some of their Applications to Social Philosophy*, Longmans Green, London, 1920.

Millman, G.J.: *Around the World on a Trillion Dollars a Day*, Transworld Publishers Ltd., London, 1995.

Minsky, H.P.: "Can 'It' happen Again?", Armonk, New York, 1982.

Minsky, H.P.: Stabilizing an Unstable Economy, Yale University Press, New Haven, 1986.
Minsky, H.: Stabilizing an Unstable Economy, Yale University Press, New Haven, 1989.
Mises, L.W.: *Theory of Money and Credit*, Yale University Press, 1953.
Mises, M.: *Ludwig von Mises, der Mensch und sein Werk*, Philosophia Verlag, 1981.
Monticelli, C.: All the money in Europe? An investigation of the economic properties of EC-wide extended monetary aggregates (working paper No.19), Bank of International Settlements, Basle, October 1993.
Moore, G.H.: *Business Cycles, Inflation, and Forecasting*, Ballinger Publishing Company, Cambridge, Mass., 1980.
Moore, G.H.: Generating Leading Indicators from Lagging Indicators, *Western Economic Journal*, vol. 7, No. 2, Jun. 1969, pp. 137–44.
Moore, G.H. and J.P. Cullity: Little-known Facts about Stock Prices and Business Cycles, *Challenge*; 31 (2), Mar./Apr. 1988, pp. 49–50.
Mosekilde, E. and E.R. Larsen: Deterministic Chaos in the Beer Production-Distribution Model, *System Dynamics Review*, vol. 4, No. 1–2, 1988, pp. 131–47.
Mosekilde, E., E.R. Larsen, J.D. Sterman and J.S. Thomsen: Non-linear Modeinteraction in the Macroeconomy, *Annals of Operations Research*, 37, 1992.
Nenties, A.: Hayek and Keynes: A Comparative Analysis of their Monetary Views, *Journal of Economic Studies*, 15 (3–4), 1988, pp. 136–51.
Newcomb, S.: *Principles of Political Economy*, Harper & Brothers, New York, 1885.
Nordhaus, W.: The Political Business Cycle, Review of Economic Studies, 42:169–90, 1975.
Norman, St. John-Stevas: The collected works of Walther Bagehot, the economist, vol. 9.
O'Brian, D.P.: The correspondence of Lord Overstone, Cambridge University Press, 1971.
O'Connor, R.: *Goulds' Millions*, Doubleday, New York, 1962.
O'Donnel, R.M.: Keynes on Mathematics: Philosophical Foundations and Economic Applications, *Cambridge Journal of Economics*; 14 (1), Mar. 1990, pp. 29–47.
Patinkin, D.: Keynes and Econometrics: On the Interaction Between the Macroeconomic Revolutions of the Interwar Period, *Econometrica*, 44 (6), Nov. 1976, pp. 1091–1123.
Patinkin, D and J.C. Leith: *Keynes, Cambridge and the General Theory*, The MacMillan Press, London, 1977.
Patinkin, D.: *Keynes and the Multiplier*, The Manchester School, 1978, pp. 209–23.
Patterson, R.T.: *The Great Boom and Panic 1921–1929*, Henry Regnery Co., Chicago, 1956.
Peake, C.F.: Henry Thornton and the Development of Ricardo's Economic Thought, *History of Political Economy*; 10 (2), Summer 1978, pp. 193–212.
Persons, W.M. and E. Frickey: Money Rates and Security Prices, *The Review of Economic Statistics*, Jan. 1926, pp. 29–46.
Pesaran, H. and R. Smith: Keynes on Econometrics, in Lawson, T. ed.; H. Pesaran, ed.: *Keynes' Economics: Methodological Issues*, Armonk, New York: Sharpe, 1985, pp. 134–50.
Peters, E.: *Chaos and Order in the Capital Markets*, John Wiley & Sons, New York, 1991.
Pigou, A.C.: *Industrial Fluctuations*, Macmillan, London, 1927.
Pigou, A.C.: Industrial Fluctuations, Macmillan, 1929.
Pigou, A.C.: The Classical Stationary State, Economic Journal, vol. 53, 1943.
Rasmussen, D.R. and E. Mosekilde: Bifurcations and Chaos in a Generic Management Model, *North European Journal of Operational Research*, 35, 1988, pp. 80–88.

Rasmussen, S. and E. Mosekilde, and J.D. Sterman: Bifurcations and Chaos in a Simple Model of the Economic Long Wave, *System Dynamics Review*, vol. 1, Summer, 1985.
Rasmussen, S., J. Holst and E. Mosekilde: Empirical Indication of Economic Long Waves in Aggregate Production, *European Journal of Operational Research*, 42, Oct. 1989, pp. 279–93.
Robertson, D.H.: *A Study of Industrial Fluctuations*, P.S. King and Son, Westminster, 1915.
Robinson, A.: John Maynard Keynes: Economist, Author, Statesman, *The Economic Journal*, June, 1972.
Routh, G.: The Origins of Economic Ideas, Macmillan, London, 1989.
Samuelson, P.: Economics, 3rd edition, McGraw Hill, New York, 1955.
Sargent, T.J. and Neil Wallace: Rational Expectations and the Theory of Economic Policy, Journal of Monetary Economics, vol. 2, 1976.
Savitt, J.: When Random is Not Random: An Introduction to Chaos in Market Prices, *Journal of Futures Markets*, 8 (3), June 1988, pp. 271–90.
Say, J.B.: *A Treatise on Political Economy on the Production, Distribution, and Consumption of Wealth*, John Grigg, Philadelphia, 1827.
Sayers, C.L.: Chaos and the Business Cycle, *Department of Economics, University of Houston*, May 1989.
Schumpeter, J: The Theory of Economic Development, harvard University Press, 1934 (first published in 1926).
Schumpeter, J.: *Business Cycles*, McGraw-Hill, New York, 1939.
Schumpeter, J.: *The History of Economic Analysis*, Allen and Unwin, London, 1954.
Schumpeter, J.: *The Theory of Economic Development* (reprint), Harvard University Press, Mass., 1961.
Schumpeter, J.: *Ten Great Economists*, George Allen and Unwin, London, 1951.
Scheide, J.: On Real and Monetary Causes for Business Cycles in West Germany, *Schweizerische Zeitschrift fur Wolswirtscaft und Statistik*; 125 (4), Dec. 1989, pp. 583–95.
Scinasi G.J. & M. Hargraves: Boom and Bust in Asset Markets in the 1980s: Causes and Consequences, International Monetary Fund, Staff Studies for the Economic Outlook. Washingtion D.C., 1993.
Scott, W.R.: *Adam Smith as Student and Professor*, Jackson, Son & Co., Glasgow, 1937.
Shaffer, S.: Structural Shifts and the Volatility of Chaotic Markets, *Journal of Economic Behaviour and Organisation*, vol. 15, Mar. 1991, pp. 201–214.
Sharp, M.S.: *The Lore and Legends of Wall Street*, Dow Jones-Irwin, 1989.
Shefold, B.: Schumpeter as a Walrasian Austrian and Keynes as a Classical Marshallian, Waqener, H.J., ed.; Drukker, J.W., ed.: *The Economic Law of Motion of Modern Society: a Marx-Schumpeter Cennential.*, Cambridge, University Press, 1986, pp. 93–111.
Shiller, R.J.: *Market Volatility*, MIT Press, Cambridge, 1990.
Shiller, R.J.: Unltimate Sources of Aggregate Variability, American Economic Review and Proceedings, 77:78–92.
Siegel, J.J.: Does it Pay Stock Investors to Forecast the Business Cycle?, *Journal of Portfolio Management*, vol. 18, Fall 1991, pp. 27–34.
Sirkin, G.W.: Business Structure, Business Cycles and National Policy, Comment, *Business Economics*, Mar. 1976.
Slater, R.: *Portraits in Silicon*, M.I.T., Massachussets, 1987.
Slater, R.: *Soros*, Irwin, New York, 1996.

Smith, A.: *An Inquiry into the Nature and Causes of the Wealth of Nations*, Modern Library Edition, New York, 1937.
Somary, F.: *Erinnerung Aus Meinen Leben*, Manesse Verlag, 1963.
Sperling, J.G.: *The South Sea Company*, Baker Library, Boston, Mass., 1962.
Spiegel, H.W.: *The Growth of Economic Thought*, Duke University Press, Durham, North Carolina, 1983.
Spiegel, H.W. and W.J. Samuels: *Contemporary Economists in Perspective*, JAI Press Inc., Greenwich, Connecticut, 1984.
Staley, C.E.: *A History of Economic Thought: From Aristotle to Arrow*, Basil Blackwell, Cambridge, Mass., 1989.
Stigler, G.J.: The Successes and Failures of Professor Smith, *Journal of Political Economy*; Dec. 1976, pp. 1199–1213.
Sterman, J.D.: Deterministic Chaos in an Experimental Economic System, *Journal of Economic Behaviour and Organisation*, 12, 1989, pp. 1–28.
Sterman, J.D.: Modeling Managerial Behavior: Misperceptions of Feedback in Dynamic Decision Making Experiment, *Management Science*, vol. 35, No. 3, March 1989, pp. 321–39.
Sylos-Labini, P.: Keynes's General Theory and the Great Depression, Sylos-Labini, P.: *The Forces of Economic Growth and Decline*, MIT Press, 1984, pp. 227–43.
The role of asset prices in the formulation of monetary policy, Bank of International Settlements (Conference Paper No.5), Basle, March 1998.
Tobin, J.: Keynesian Models of Recession and Depression, American Economic Review, 65, 1975.
Tobin, J.: Review of Stabilizing an Unstable Economy by H.P. Minsky, Journal of Economic Literature 27, 1989.
Thomas, G. and M. Morgan-Witts: *The Day the Bubble Burst*, Hamish Hamilton, London, 1979.
Thomas, H.: *An Unfinished History of the World*, Papermac, London, 1995.
Thomsen, J.S.: *Analyse af Komplekse Ulineære Dynamiske Systemer*, Fysisk laboratorium III, Denmarks Technical University, Copenhagen, 1990.
Thomsen, J.S., E. Mosekilde and J.D. Sterman: Hyperchaotic Phenomena in Dynamic Decision Making, in Mosekilde, E., ed.: *Complexity, Chaos, and Biological Evolution*, Plenum Press, New York, 1991.
Thornton, H.: *An Enquiry into the Nature and Effects of the Paper Credits in Great Britain*, Library of Economics, London, 1939.
Train, J.: *The New Money Masters*, Harper and Row, N.Y., 1989.
Trevelyan, G.M.: *Illustrated English Social History*, Penguin Books, Middlesex, 1960.
Tufte, E.R.: The Political Control of the Economy, Princeton University Press, 1978.
Tvede, L.: *The Psychology of Finance*, Norwegian University Press, with Oxford University Press, London, 1990.
Tvede, L.: Reasons Trends may be Predictable in Financial Markets, *The Journal of International Securities Markets*, vol. 6, Spring 1992.
Van der Linden: Economic Thought in the Netherlands: The Contribution of Professor Jan Tinbergen, *Review of Social Economy*, 46 (3), Dec. 1988, pp. 270–88.
Van der Ploeg, F.: Rational Expectations, Risk and Chaos in Financial Markets, *Economic Journal*, 96, 1986, pp. 151–62.
Waldrop, M.: Complexity, Penguin, London, 1993.

Warburton, C.: Depression, Inflation and Monetary Policy, Johns Hopkins University Press, 1966.

Watson, P.: *From Manet to Manhattan*, Tandom House, New York, 1992.

Weblen, T.B.: The Theory of Business Enterprice, Scribner, New York, 1904.

Volker, P.A.: *The Rediscovery of the Business Cycle*, Free Press, New York, 1978.

Wicksell, K.: The Influence of the Rate of Interest on Prices, *Economic Journal*, vol. 17, 1907, pp. 213–20.

Willis, K.: The Role in Parliament of the Economic Ideas of Adam Smith 1776–1800, *History of Political Economy*, 11 (4), Winter 1979, pp. 505–44.

Wolf, A.S., J.B. Swift, H.L. Swinney and J.A. Vastano: Determining Lyapunov Exponents from a Time Series, *Physica, 16D*, July, 1985.

Wolfe, J.N.: Marshall and the Trade Cycle, *Oxford Economic Papers*, vol. 8, 1956, pp. 90–101.

Wolfson, M.H.: Theories of Financial Crises, in Semmler, W., ed.: *Financial Dynamics and Business Cycles*, Armonk, New York, 1989, pp. 221–227.

Woodford, M.: Finance, Instability, and Cycles, in Semmler, W., ed.: *Financial Dynamics and Business Cycles*, Armonk, New York, 1889, pp. 18–37.

Index